Yes We Can!

Improving Urban Schools Through Innovative Education Reform

edited by

Leanne L. Howell
Texas A&M University

Chance W. Lewis
University of North Carolina at Charlotte

Norvella Carter
Texas A&M University

INFORMATION AGE PUBLISHING, INC.
Charlotte, NC • www.infoagepub.com

Library of Congress Cataloging-in-Publication Data

Yes we can! : improving urban schools : through innovative education reform
/ edited by Leanne Howell, Chance W. Lewis, Norvella Carter.
    p. cm.
Includes bibliographical references.
ISBN 978-1-61735-635-3 (pbk.) – ISBN 978-1-61735-636-0 (hardcover) –
ISBN 978-1-61735-637-7 (ebook)
1. Urban schools–United States. 2. Education, Urban–United States. 3.
Educational change–United States. 4. School improvement programs–United
States. I. Howell, Leanne. II. Lewis, Chance W. (Chance Wayne), 1972- III.
Carter, Norvella.
LC5131.Y47 2011
371.009173'2–dc23

                                                                2011038818

Yes We Can!

Improving Urban Schools Through Innovative Education Reform

A volume in
Contemporary Perspectives on Access, Equity, and Achievement
Chance W. Lewis, *Series Editor*

CONTENTS

PART II

EMPOWERING URBAN STUDENTS AND TRANSFORMING THEIR SCHOOLS

Section 1: Teachers' Roles in Urban School Settings

Section 2: Culturally Responsive Pedagogies and Curriculum for Urban School Reform

Section 3: Policies, Politics, and Urban School Reform

PROLOGUE

HOPE *IS* ALIVE!

Envisioning the Future Possibilities of Urban Schools

Leanne L. Howell and Chance W. Lewis

As we settle into a new century, it seems urban schools are in more crisis than ever. Even as this book goes to print, the complicated funding outcomes that undergird the day-to-day operations of school systems across America are in political turmoil. This certainly does not bode well for any school campus or school district. However, students and educators in urban settings have the most to lose by the current political battle over budget allocations for their schools, and unfortunately, many of these same schools are not provided with financial parity from previous budget battles. Certainly teachers in these settings can succeed in educating urban youth despite these almost certain budget cuts; however, the time is imminent to take another step forward not only in recognizing challenges brought about by inequities, but in identifying the roots of these evils and then embracing solutions to bring about reform in urban education. No longer can these inequities be simply recognized and discussed; they must be acted upon

Yes We Can! Improving Urban Schools Through Innovative Educational Reform, pages ix–xii
Copyright © 2011 by Information Age Publishing
All rights of reproduction in any form reserved.

with a vigilant effort to make sustainable changes for the sake of all associated with urban education.

We, the editors, applaud the thousands of students who have been classified as "marginalized" but succeed and persevere in academic settings on a daily basis. Despite obstacles such as racial and class discrimination, poverty, outdated and/or limited curriculum resources, and less than acceptable facilities, as well as many other problems associated with inner-city life, there are many students who embody resilient spirits and refuse to be statistical failures. In as much, we choose to abandon the age-old adage of "at risk" and fervently advocate these students and all of their peers as "at promise." In this context, we believe that there *is* hope for all students who attend urban schools—hope for students to reach their full potential, both academically and in other life-long pursuits.

One primary reason for us to write a book on urban education reform is not only to proclaim that hope *is* alive, but to also produce a body of literature that examines current practices and then offers practical implications for all involved in this arduous task. We hope you find this book filled with real-world strategies to implement in your quest to inspire and bring about reform. Additionally, we hope that you garner hope from the school personnel, school campuses, and school resources used as examples within the body of this work.

We offer this book to all stakeholders who find themselves associated with urban schools: teachers, administrators, parents, and even students. Just as Kincheloe (2007) proclaims that a primary goal of urban pedagogy is to enhance human agency; we, too, believe that the primary goal for all involved in urban education is to maximize rather than minimize potential and to transform rather than undermine sustainable systems of hope and change. Consider this book a guide as you consider being a part of this transformation. We hope that it not only inspire you to adopt the "Yes We Can" spirit, but also empower you to be the beacon of light for urban students whose very future relies on people like you to keep the torch alive.

This book has been divided into two main parts. Part I examines specific environments of urban school reform, while Part II contains chapters that focus on empowerment and transformation. Still further, each of these two parts is divided into sections and chapters. Section 1 is composed of two chapters that both identify specific school districts and the transformational changes taking place within each. In Chapter 1, Robert W. Simmons and Robert D. Carpenter provide an in-depth look at two urban charter schools in Detroit receiving recognition for their emphasis in academic accomplishments and innovative service-learning. Chapter 2, by Molly S. Taylor, highlights another specific school district located in the state of Texas that has also adopted a "Yes We Can" spirit in meeting the needs of its urban learners, especially those from low socio-economic backgrounds.

Section 2 highlights urban community initiatives, support structures, and other influences that potentially affect students' academic performance. In Chapter 3, Lamont A. Flowers and Tiffany A. Flowers examine characteristics on African American students' mathematics achievement. In Chapter 4, Jamilia J. Blake, Collette Nero, and Concepcion M. Rodriguez highlight the successful inclusion of mental health services within two urban school districts—services that are essential if all students are to be considered "at promise."

Part II shifts gears to an in-depth look at empowerment and transformation. In Section 1, Chapter 5, Stephen D. Hancock and Tehia V. Starker analyze the perspectives, attitudes, and dispositions of urban teachers and discuss how all three of these elements directly influence student performance. Using Fundamental Attribution Error Theory (FAET) as a means to explore teacher perceptions, the authors challenge each of us to examine our own perceptions of others and then provide stakeholders with solid implications for practice that encourage deconstruction of FAET. In Chapter 6, DeMarquis M. Hayes examines how parent-perceived teacher support affects the achievement outcomes of African American high school adolescents. This chapter is essential for all stakeholders to understand as a means to increase parental involvement in urban schools.

Ryan M. Vernosh and Julie Landsman begin Section 2 with Chapter 7. Vernosh, as the first author, gives a compelling account of his day-to-day experiences in St. Paul, Minnesota, of teaching in a single-gender classroom of 6th grade males. This reflective chapter describes specific ways that Vernosh builds bonds between himself and his urban students, as well as between the students and each other. This powerful chapter reminds us all of what it means to hold everyone within the classroom walls accountable and embrace high expectations on a daily basis. Recently selected as the 2010 Minnesota Teacher of the Year, Mr. Vernosh provides a compelling and heart-wrenching account of what it is like to lead a group of young men down the halls of academic and life-long success using culturally relevant pedagogy. Co-authored by Julie Landsman, the nationally acclaimed co-author of the book, *White Teachers, Diverse Classrooms*, this chapter leaves us all believing single-gendered classroom environments are essential ingredients for urban school reform.

Chapter 8 within this section brings forth the idea that true educational reform must be child-centered. This chapter, written by Ginny Riga and Michelle Moody, explores the transformational nature of the Montessori curriculum used in two public, urban school settings. It highlights the benefits of students as learners, as well as the benefits of teachers as facilitators. Montessori is labeled an education for life—one that works and sustains itself on its own merits and has positive implications for learners as it instills learners with confidence, independence, and motivation. In Chapter 9, Patricia J. Larke, Jemimah L. Young, and Jamaal R. Young make a case for learning by linking emphasis on the achievement and reporting needs of African American females on NAPE test results.

Section 3 analyzes the effects of policies and politics on urban school reform. In Chapter 10, Meredith B. L. Walker and Bettie Ray Butler investigate the media influences in shaping African American males' identities and values. Implications are offered to policy makers and other stakeholders concerning strategies to subvert negative media influence among this population. In conclusion, Chapter 11, written by Augustina Lozano and Anthony Rolle, provides a summarized, fifty-year overview of educational finance, politics, and policy that have influenced urban districts, schools, and students. Perhaps by investigating lessons of the past, we can be more cognizant of good decision-making for the future.

Together, we try to provide thoughtful insight, pose deep and complicated questions, and offer specific examples and implications for practice to turn the tide in improving urban education through innovative and sustainable educational reform. Although certainly not an end to this mean, we hope that this book provides you, the reader, with the hope to transform and the courage to tackle new and challenging issues that seem to consistently erode the landscape of educating city students. Certainly teaching, leading, and even attending urban schools is layered with complexity and oftentimes more questions than answers. It is our hope that some of those answers can be found within the pages of this book. Read, comprehend, and digest each page and then embark on improving urban schools with a "Yes We Can" spirit. Hope *is* alive because educators are the heartbeat of educational reform. We hope you enjoy!

REFERENCE

Kincheloe, J. L. (2007). Why a book on urban education? In S. R. Steinberg & J. L. Kincheloe (Eds.), *19 urban questions: Teaching in the city* (pp. 1–27). New York, NY: Peter Lang.

PART I

ENVIRONMENTS OF URBAN SCHOOL REFORM

Section 1: Traditional and Charter School Settings:
Success and Sustainable Change

CHAPTER 1

YES WE CAN—
EVEN IN DETROIT

Quality Education, High Academic Achievement, and Service-Learning[1]

Robert W. Simmons III
Loyola University Maryland

Robert D. Carpenter
Eastern Michigan University

ABSTRACT

Public education in Detroit has long been derided for its abysmal outcomes—low graduation rates, inadequate facilities, dreadful drop-out rates, etcand so on. Complicated by a contentious relationship between the traditional public school system and the rise of charter schools, some would argue that innovative educational reform in Detroit is only a dream. Nonetheless, this chapter highlights two charter schools whothat have designed innovative educational experiences grounded in high academic standards and community-service learning. Having received state and national recognition, both schools represent the YES WE CAN in the city of Detroit.

Yes We Can! Improving Urban Schools Through Innovative Educational Reform, pages 3–21
Copyright © 2011 by Information Age Publishing
All rights of reproduction in any form reserved.

In a special issue of *Time* (October, 5, 2009), Detroit was described as being on life support. This description of Detroit is due to the variety of challenges that have the 11th largest city in America in a financial hole that leaves the city government $300 million short. In spite of the large portion of media attention that has focused on the challenges facing the automobile industry, the ongoing legal troubles of former mayor Kwame Kilpatrick, and a public school system that suffers from improper management, many children in Detroit are obtaining a quality education. Be it public schools, charter schools, or private schools, the educational landscape in Detroit is replete with examples of schools that embody the "yes we can" motto espoused in the title of this book. As such, it is the intention of this chapter to explore the innovative practices of two public charter schools who are not only innovative in their approach to education, but connect academic excellence and community engagement—Detroit Service Learning Academy (DSLA) and Detroit Edison Public School Academy (DEPSA).

EDUCATION IN DETROIT

Education in Detroit's public school system has been wrought with administrative incompetence, fiscal mismanagement, and corruption (Bergmann, 2008). With a graduation rate that hovered around 30%, a mere 6% of high school students passing the state exam, and 25 of the city's 245 elementary schools being accredited, a state takeover of the schools had been brewing since the late 1980s (Franklin, 2003). The state takeover of the Detroit Public schools began in 1999 and lasted until 2005. The school board was no longer elected by the residents of the city, but rather appointed by the Detroit mayor and governor, which led many city residents to associate the state control with the decades-long divide between the city and the suburbs. More succinctly, and to the point, the conversation subtly rotated on a fulcrum that vacillated between discussions about the intrusion of the state into city affairs, and the ever-enduring racial discourse in a largely African American city, surrounded by its mostly White suburban neighbors. While the state-appointed board was dissolved in 2004, the public schools of Detroit have suffered through a variety of issues since then (Stover, 2006). Considering the decline in state aid, as well as the mass exodus of a significant number of students, Stover (2006) indicates that the public confidence in the public school system in Detroit has wavered to levels similar to feelings prior to and during the state takeover of the schools.

With a lack of confidence in the public school system, many Detroiters have turned to charter schools. Originally designed to be "small, self-governing yet public institutions" (Sizer & Wood, 2008, p. 3), the role of charter schools in the education of Detroit youth has been hotly debated by educators and politicians. Both sides of the debate seem willing to acknowledge a need to improve the educational opportunities for children in Detroit, but Keith Johnson (2009), president of the Detroit Federation of Teachers offers that charter schools are a "drain upon our school district as more and more parents begin to turn to charter schools as an alternative for the education and safety of their children" (p. 2). Regardless as to the accuracy of Johnson's assertion, 30,000 school-aged children attend 49 charter schools in Detroit (Riley, 2009).

As charter schools serve as a potential innovation in the educational conversation in Detroit, additional efforts have ignited a community conversation to discover what's needed and what should be changed in the city's educational system. In a recent report published by *Excellent Schools Detroit*, a wide variety of civic leaders from across the city asserted that teachers, students, and families need more support if education in Detroit is to work for all students. Additionally, through community meetings held during November and December 2009, five significant ideas were revealed (Excellent Schools Detroit, 2010):

- More parental involvement, but schools needed to be more welcoming and proactive
- Improved safety in the schools including keeping gangs out of the schools and ensuring safety in the bathrooms
- More nonacademic services (health care, social services, etc.) in the schools that foster greater cooperation between city/community agencies and the school community
- More diverse academic offerings
- Stronger accountability and transparency

Some would believe that the ideas discovered through the previously mentioned study are dreams lost in a city that has avoided making substantial changes to its public education system. However, the Skillman Foundation's *Good Schools Guide* (2009) clearly indicates that all schools in Detroit don't situate administrative incompetence, fiscal mismanagement, and corruption as the status quo. Noting exemplary schools—public, charter, and private—the *Good Schools Guide* highlights 76 schools in Detroit whose students not only strive for excellence, but attend schools where academic excellence is the standard.

EDUCATION IN DETROIT AMIDST ECONOMIC UPHEAVAL

The education conversation in Detroit is situated amidst the ongoing, and well publicized, economic struggles of Michigan. Michigan, whose flagship university's fight song touts, "Hail! Hail! To Michigan, The leaders and best!" (Elbel, 1898), has gained the dubious distinction of leading the nation in the current economic crisis. Michigan was the harbinger of what many pundits have called the "Great Recession" (Rampell, 2009) as its economy shifted away from manufacturing without another viable business sector to absorb the displaced workers. In 2000, the state began to separate itself from the rest of the country and track an economic trend that the nation would soon follow. Unemployment began to rise as domestic automakers, the largest employers in the state, began to reduce production costs by cutting ties to their parts divisions (which lead to new companies that subsequently went bankrupt) and slashing workers through buyouts (both early retirement and severance packages) and direct layoffs. For example, over half of all Ford blue-collar workers (38,000 out of 75,000) applied for the first round of buyouts in 2006 (Hoffman, 2006). The state lost almost half of all manufacturing jobs between 2000 and 2009 (from 893,100 to 452,900), and the city of Detroit was even more devastated by industry shutter (from 144,900 to 69,667) (U.S. Bureau of Labor Statistics, 2009). To put the half-a-million lost manufacturing jobs in perspective, Ohio was second in the nation in jobs lost over the same period of time (they lost 213,000 jobs), prompting one Cleveland columnist to describe Michigan's economy as "unprecedented, Depression-level" (Mezger, 2008). As the harangued leadership of the auto industry flew their private jets over the blighted landscape of Detroit to request government assistance, which resulted in loans and bankruptcy for General Motors and Chrysler, the already reeling city below would experience a jump in their unemployment rate from 9.6% to almost 18% by the fall of 2009 (U.S. Bureau of Labor Statistics, 2009). The bankruptcies also left an additional 25 million square feet of manufacturing capacity vacant in the city (Aguilar, 2009).

The loss of manufacturing jobs and high unemployment rates strongly impacted all aspects of Michigan family life. By 2007, Wayne County (which includes Detroit) led the nation in property foreclosures (Aguilar, 2007) and the Michigan foreclosure rate continues to be amongst the highest in the nation. In 2008, there were over 145,000 new foreclosures, with new foreclosures in 2009 ranking Michigan third in the nation (Realtytrac, 2009), Unfortunately, January, 2010 data show the trend continuing, with more than 17,500 new foreclosures for the month (Realtytrac, 2010). Over this period of time, families have been leaving Michigan in droves searching for economic opportunities. The city of Detroit itself has lost over 325,000 residents between 2000 and 2008 (Frey, 2009).

"YES WE CAN" SCHOOLS IN DETROIT

Despite the challenges associated with in the city of Detroit, as well as the complex financial situation in the city and state, two public charter schools have provided light in the darkness. Recognized by the Skillman Foundation (2009, 2008) as two of the best schools in Detroit, the Detroit Service Learning Academy (DSLA) and the Detroit Edison Public School Academy (DEPSA) have not only succeeded in promoting high academic achievement, but they have also engaged students in a variety of community issues through service-learning and other community engagement. Through a series of focus groups, interviews, surveys, and school visits, we found that DSLA and DEPSA are two schools in Detroit who truly embody a "yes we can" spirit.

Detroit Service Learning Academy (DSLA)

We build the capacity of families and educators to prepare students for lifelong learning, leadership and community service. Our vision is to provide the community with proud, responsible citizens who learn, who lead, and who serve through academic excellence and positive behavior.

Originally known as the YMCA Service Learning Academy, DSLA is located in the northwest corner of Detroit, Michigan. As a public charter school, DSLA formally opened its doors in 1999 comprising kindergarten through 5th grade. In 2000, grades 6–8 were added. Originally chartered through a partnership between the YMCA and EdisonLearning, the new chartering organization is Lake Superior State University. Consequently, the YMCA Service Learning Academy became the Detroit Service Learning Academy (DSLA) in 2008.

DSLA has a student population of well over 1,100 children. Representing 20 different zip codes in the Metro Detroit area, 700 families join with the school staff to create a dynamic learning environment. While EdisonLearning is no longer involved with the school, portions of that educational model are still in existence. Emphasizing a strong curriculum and varied assessments, students at DSLA have an extended school day of core academic courses that include daily "specials" such as computers, choir, strings, and Spanish. As the EdisonLearning educational model utilizes the longer school day to support student achievement, DSLA students are consistently found to be proficient on the tested subjects on the Michigan Educational Assessment Program (MEAP)—English/language arts, reading, writing, mathematics, science, and social studies (Detroit Service Learning Academy, 2010). As such, the state of Michigan and the Skillman Foundation have recognized the staff and students at DSAL for their commitment to academic excellence.

Certainly the standardized test scores are one indication of quality education at DSLA. However, their ability to integrate service-learning, connecting the curriculum to community needs, and still maintain high academic achievement is what truly makes DSLA innovative. With service-learning projects that have focused on such issues as raising awareness about healthy eating in the Black community, the demolition of burned-out homes surrounding the school, and increasing the number of registered adult voters, DSLA has been recognized as a leader in the field of service-learning. Notably, they have received such awards as:

- Recipient of a six-year Learn and Serve grant
- 2009 winner of Learn and Serve *Innovative Programming Award*
- Grade-level team published in service-learning online journal
- Recipient of Perkins Malo Hunter Foundation gift

With over 85% of students in third through eighth grades scoring at or above a proficient level on the reading and math sections of the 2009 MEAP and the impressive development of service-learning projects, we are called to understand how this learning environment is able to produce such results. (Detroit Service Learning Academy, 2010)

Academic Excellence

As framed by staff and administrators at DSLA, academic excellence is a byproduct of numerous factors. Citing a rigorous curriculum, as well the rigorous assessment of the students, academic excellence at DSLA does not exist by mistake. Using a variety of ongoing assessment tools, students' strengths and weaknesses are determined. The role of the assessments in assuring all students are achieving academically is undeniable. However, equally as important in allowing academic excellence to be the status quo would be the self-reflective nature of the staff. Never allowed to rest on past successes, the staff at DSLA constantly asks:

- What is our purpose?
- Why are we here?
- What do these data really mean?
- What are we doing here and how are we going to do it?

Student engagement.   Teachers use a variety of instructional techniques to engage students by focusing on making school relevant to life outside of the classroom. In addition, teachers use a multitude of assessment practices, closely aligned to their instructional objectives, to continually adjust their instructional practices to meet individual student needs.

When looking at innovative instructional strategies in the classroom, several teachers utilized music.

> My best teaching strategy is incorporating music into my classroom. New concepts that I introduce to my students are learned best with a beat or song. Even literary term examples can be found in music. (Mrs. Jones, 6th grade teacher)

> My students are more interested and excited to learn when I turn on some music and teach the concept this way. I think this works because students in this day and age things are technologically and musically driven. They listen to iPods, music on computers, and watch videos all the time, so they can relate. In my opinion, relatability is sustainability. (Mr. Thomas, 4th grade teacher)

Additionally, the usage of hands-on activities, which are more related to the students' lives, captures the minds of many students at DSLA.

> One of my strategies this year is to really work hard to relate our topics to their lives as best as possible. I will ask the kids questions to get some information about them personally. Then I will take the topic and do whatever it takes to relate it to them, individually if I can. Then they all want me to put their specific situation into the equation. (Mrs. Jones, 6th grade teacher)

Finally, DSLA staff do not only look at data from assessments to improve scores; they take a more holistic approach to data analyses. Teachers move beyond the cognitive measures prevalent in other schools and make sure to collect and interpret affective "data" as well. By analyzing data from such domains as attendance, tardiness, and transportation, DSLA is prepared to offer the non-academic support that is missing from many schools.

> Our check-in/check-out program is one way we address the social needs of our children. Through this program we pair our students with an adult in the building who [sic] they check in with on a daily basis. This adult may not be their teacher, but might be the janitor, the media specialist, or someone like that. If we don't tend to their emotional needs as young people, the academic achievement won't matter. (Mr. Webster, administrator)

Parental engagement.   As a result of DSLA addressing the social needs of students, the families see that the school cares about their children and are more inclined to develop an educational partnership. It is through this partnership that the families are more willing to trust the staff with their children.

> I think the other part is that we truly work to develop a partnership with our parents. If you can get your parents to buy in and they don't just wanna do a drop-off, but you give them a reason to come into your building and get to know what you're doing, we can have everyone buying into an expectation for success. (Mrs. Good, administrator)

While many educational professionals lament the failure of parents to be involved in the schooling experience of their child, DSLA tends to focus on how it can be done as opposed to why it's not being done. At the core of their efforts is the development of a *parent university*. With 82% of the families in DSLA living in poverty, the *parent university* program is designed to provide education and information for the parents related to issues such as finding affordable health care, locating community organizations that offer free dental care, or creating a resume. Additionally, there is an attitude in the building that "we" want you here. As noted in the survey of community members in Detroit (Excellent Schools Detroit, 2010), parents want schools to be more welcoming. DSLA meets this expectation and then some.

> Free diapers, free food giveaways, whatever it takes, because we want to be the hub for our parents for information. Our parent resource rooms, where they can come in and do their transcripts, they can come in and get information; they use our social worker, they use or school nurse, they use our guidance counselor. So, we're the hub for our parents and we truly do invite them in and we do embrace them when they come. (Mrs. Good, administrator)

Leadership.   The student engagement, parental support, and exceptional efforts of the teachers to understand data do not occur without a supportive administrative team. This multiple-layered partnership is the foundation of DSLA's solid academic reputation and takes unique leadership characteristics to work. One administrator explained their role as:

> I see myself as a servant. I'm here to make sure that everybody has what they need to be successful. We listen to their voices—the teachers, the non-instructional staff, the parents. We literally have a chorus and a choir before we make ultimate decisions. This creates a greater sense of loyalty; a greater sense of ownership; a greater sense of "this is my house" from everybody who works here because they do have that voice. (Mr. Webster, administrator)

The "this is my house" mentality is not without its challenges. Citing issues of sustainability due to a reduction in state funding, administrators are concerned with how the pending cuts might impact staff morale. Additionally, considering the amount of money spent on professional development related to service-learning, what happens if staff is lost? This harsh reality leaves the administrative staff with some sleepless nights.

> It's hurtful. It has put us in some very challenging places. And when it gets down to having to talk about layoffs for good people, that's painful. It kills a little part of you, but it also says wow, how do I cover the gap of that hole that I'm about to make because I still want to program services that they were offering. (Mr. Webster, administrator)

Service-Learning at DSLA

Considering that *service-learning* is included in the name of the school, service-learning is without question a critical element of the mission of the school. Boasting projects that have attempted to reduce the number of vacant homes to projects that have collaborated with the community to refurbish two parks near the school, it is evident that DSLA has not only made their mark in the community, but has mastered the balance between academic success and service-learning achievement. Having received the *Spirit of Detroit Award*, for a 6th grade service-learning project designed to identify and tear down vacant homes, from the Detroit City Council, service-learning at DSLA is recognized by local community leaders. Certainly the sixth grade project received significant recognition but other grade level projects have also made a significant impact in the community. Some of these include:

- Seatbelt awareness campaign (3rd grade)
- Asthma awareness campaign and the development of a non-toxic cleaner (4th grade)
- Refurbishing two parks near the school (4th/5th grade & 8th grade)
- Recycling Festival (7th grade)
- Fundraising concert for homeless shelter (Performing Arts)

While the school has always had service-learning in the school name, a more intentional focus began three years ago. Through professional development and the successful application for grant funds, service-learning at DSLA has managed to enhance the connection between the school curriculum and community needs. Thus, the teaching staff has become more knowledgeable about the community, but also connected the service-learning projects to the school curriculum, which has contributed to student achievement.

> I have balanced NCLB and state testing by prioritizing and pacing myself. Since the MEAP is given at the start of the school year, I prepare them for the

test, but also get to know my students. This allows me to also discuss the type of service-learning project we will be doing. (Mrs. Jones, 6th grade teacher)

As far as impact on academic achievement, I think service-learning drives my students to master a variety of state standards without even knowing they are doing so. For example, my students are supposed to learn to write formal letters in English. When I teach it to them, and we complete tasks in the book, only some master the concept. When the student actually has a valid reason to write a formal letter (for their service learning project), they have more of an interest in the letter and master the concepts more quickly. As a result, I think it creates some intrinsic motivation that is sometimes hard to create in students who are not normally motivated. (Mrs. Jones, 6th grade teacher)

The need to succeed academically is duly noted in the school's mission. However, equal attention, as stated in the mission, is given to developing contributing citizens to our democratic society. As such, service-learning at DSLA also enhances student self-efficacy when it comes to solving social issues in the community.

They [the students] have learned that service-learning lets you have a voice in an adult-centered world. Many times students do not try certain things because they know they may not be taken seriously due to their age. My students have learned that through service-learning, students can be heard more than adults. As a result, when students identify a problem, they no longer look for adults to solve the problem primarily, but they look for a way to assist with the problem. (Mr. Howell, 6th grade teacher)

Defining DSLA for Others: Expect Nothing but the Best!

On the west side of Detroit, looking out of the DSLA windows on Seven Mile and Lasher, it becomes apparent that, as Amber Darden (sixth grade teacher and 6–8 service-learning coordinator) stated, "expect nothing but the best and the students will rise to that expectation." As the students rise to the occasion at DSLA, the staff exhibits an unflinching commitment to service-learning, high expectations, and superior academic performance. Certainly the challenges of working with a student body of over 1,000 students, in an unstable economic environment, is a daunting task. However, the staff at DSLA charges ahead everyday! It is evident by looking into classrooms on the two floors, students are learning, and engaged in critical conversations about the mandated state curriculum, but also the social conditions that frame many of their service-learning projects. The staff from DSLA offer three things that are innovative in urban education, but also foster a sense of excellence in their school culture.

- Be collaborative—it's not just collaboration from teacher to teacher, it's collaboration from teacher to administrator, parent to teacher.

- "You gotta breathe it, you gotta smell it, you gotta think about it and accept the challenge."
- Don't hire people who aren't really there for the children.

DSLA's emphasis on building a community of learners, both within and without the school walls, and tying real-world issues faced by the community to the pedagogy and curriculum that is aligned with state standards has lead to students performing very well on accountability measures (i.e., the MEAP) while truly serving as they're learning. The more holistic notion of "data", which includes student affect and parental needs, creates the opportunity for this collaborative learning community to thrive.

Detroit Edison Public School Academy (DEPSA)

Detroit Edison Public School Academy exists to prepare students entrusted to our care for a future as global citizens and successful life-long learners. Utilizing a proven researched-based curriculum, academic development is achieved in a dignified and supportive environment that incorporates family, staff, and community partnerships, in pursuit of educational excellence.

When the doors of the Detroit Edison Public School Academy (DEPSA) opened in September 1998, the Detroit Edison Public School Academy embarked on a mission to create global citizens. Authorized and chartered by Oakland University, there are nearly 1,100 students in grades pre-kindergarten through 8th grade. With families from all over Metropolitan Detroit, this school of 99.8% African American students boasts a school structure that has three academies—Primary (PreK–2), Elementary (3–5), and Junior (6–8). This school within a school structure allows for a balance between academic structure and the nurturing of student creativity. Noting the development of their strong reputation for academic excellence, students at DEPSA routinely score at or above the state average on the MEAP (Michigan Educational Assessment Program) while making significant contributions to improving the Detroit community through service-learning projects. As a result DEPSA has been recognized in numerous ways:

- *School of Success* by the National Center for Learning and Citizenship in conjunction with the Education Commission of the States (ECS)
- *Exemplary High Performing School* from the Skillman Foundation
- *The 5th Annual Spirit of Choice Award* from the Black Alliance for Educational Options

- *Exemplary Michigan Blue Ribbon Award* from the Michigan Department of Education. DEPSA was the first charter school to ever be awarded this prestigious honor since its inception in 1982.
- *National Charter School Award* winner from the Center of Educational Reform in Washington, DC
- *Charter School of Excellence Award* from the Michigan Association of Public School Academies (MAPSA)

Considering all of the accolades and success that DEPSA students have obtained, the larger question becomes—how do they do this?

Mediocrity Is Not an Option

DEPSA provides an educational framework such that mediocrity is not an option. Being ordinary sits outside the school door—being extraordinary is the only possibility allowed into the classrooms. As noted by the administrative staff at DEPSA, and also considering that many pundits have deemed the educational environment in the city of Detroit the worst in the United States, DEPSA considers themselves an oasis—not because they have to, but because the students deserve it. To create a school where being extraordinary is the status quo, one of the primary goals of the staff at DEPSA is to nurture well-rounded students.

> We are student achievement driven but ensure that our students are well rounded. Our goals are based upon a collaboration of all instructional, non-instructional and administrative staff. Because of this, our academic goals are data driven to ensure that all students receive a 21st century global learning experience that will prepare them for their future. (Mrs. Gray, administrator)

It is very noticeable that the goals for students at DEPSA revolve around a balance between academics and other real-world skills they need to navigate in society. However, their goals related to academic achievement are based on high expectations, and making data-driven decisions.

> We have high expectation for students and staff. We are data driven and make our achievement decisions based upon data reviewed during grade level meetings. Support is given to students who are falling below school expectations during and after school. (Mrs. Golden, administrator)

> Academic excellence is the expectation at our school. To insure that no one "falls through the cracks" we monitor instruction, adherence to pacing charts, review lesson plans, have curriculum nights for parents/guardians and so much more. (Mr. Smith, administrator)

Administrative Support

Maintaining high expectations, as well as the constant usage of data at DEPSA, has created an environment where academic excellence is the norm. Although the teachers work directly with the children day in and day out, the administrative staff at DEPSA offers tremendous support to the staff. Not singularly focusing on managing the staff, DEPSA administrators routinely check in with staff to determine their needs and desires. This ongoing focus of the administrative staff has fostered an environment of trusting relationships whereby the focus is always on doing what's best for the children.

> I [administrator] have a major role in ensuring that staff has the necessary tools needed to do their jobs. I am responsible for the curriculum the teachers are required to implement and the materials the students use daily. Annually, I discuss with staff their needs and desires for the upcoming year. In addition, I develop a plan in ordering and distributions of materials. (Mrs. Gray, administrator)

This administrative perspective related to supporting the teachers extends beyond the day-to-day operations but also includes the initial induction process for teachers starting during the interview.

Professional Development

At DEPSA, professional development takes place year-round, but the most intensive professional development occurs at the beginning of the school year and focuses on such issues as curriculum development and creating positive learning environments in the classroom. Given the expectation that extraordinary is the norm, teachers are held to a very high standard. As such, teachers spend approximately 100–120 hours preparing for the arrival of students at the beginning of the year. Certainly some of that preparation is allotted for professional development, but equal attention is given to teacher preparation in the classroom and contacting families prior to the beginning of the school year. As the school year progresses, the administrative staff recognizes the need for ongoing and timely professional development. They indentify foci based on experiences throughout the year and by examining research on professional development. Teachers at DEPSA are involved in ongoing professional development related to topics such as: (1) the usage of technology in the classroom, (2) media resources, (3) service-learning, and (4) project-based planning.

The development of committed teachers and exemplary academic achievement is not an accident at DEPSA. To support their endeavors, DEPSA staff and administrators have developed a daily schedule that maximizes the collaborative nature of all aspects of education in the building. Grade level teams and academy (PreK–2, 3–5, 6–8) meetings occur on a weekly basis to discuss student achievement, program design, customer satisfaction, financial management, and systems growth.

Service-Learning at DEPSA

Recognized as a School of Success by the National Center for Learning and Citizenship in conjunction with the Education Commission of the States (ECS), DEPSA incorporates service-learning, and it plays a vital role in the lives of students. As all students are required to participate in a service-learning project, yet achieve academically, DEPSA has managed to balance these competing demands.

> It is imperative that all service-learning projects be connected to the grade level state standards, benchmarks, and expectations. This provides a richer service-learning project and leads to a continuation of high MEAP scores. (Mrs. Golden, administrator)

Of particular importance to the service-learning projects at DEPSA is the role of the community, and the fact that the majority of the students are from Detroit. With a large portion of service-learning projects in urban communities involving non-urban community members (Wade, 2000; Webster, 2007), students at DEPSA offer a differing perspective from this common practice by working as stewards in their own community. Given the economic issues facing Detroit almost 20% unemployment (U.S. Bureau of Labor Statistics, 2009), DEPSA staff believe that service-learning is a powerful tool aimed at improving academic achievement but also fulfilling their stated mission of creating global citizens.

> Innovative hands-on, inquiry based activities that augment community experiences make the academic subjects more appealing to students, and active discovery has been found to promote interest in these disciplines... Many of the world's most complex and difficult problems like hunger, pollution, literacy, and prejudice can be found on most every continent. In collaboration with local community organizations, DEPSA believes that an effective way to address these problems is by empowering young people to take charge of making a difference starting in their own community. Changing one community can feed change into adjacent areas, starting a movement and, eventually, a global and cultural shift. (Ms. Smith, teacher)

Admittedly, the balance between fulfilling the state-mandated requirements in the curriculum and supporting the communities' needs through service-learning is not something that has taken place overnight. However, DEPSA believes that service-learning and having the students involved in the community increases students' critical thinking skills and metacognition.

Service-learning at DEPSA helps our students develop skills for living in a knowledge-based, technological society. Solving highly complex problems requires that students have both basic skills (reading, writing, mathematics) and foundation skills (teamwork, problem solving, research, time management, information synthesizing, using technology tools). By bringing real-life context and technology to the curriculum through projects and problems, teachers encourage students to become independent workers, critical thinkers, and lifelong learners.

Defining DEPSA for Others: Excellence Is NOT an Option

DEPSA's reputation for academic achievement is built on high expectations and the development of service-learning projects. Those who educate the youth of Detroit are given an assignment amidst one of the worst educational crisis to hit the state in many years. As a result, DEPSA has been more deliberate in their approach to apply for grants and secure additional funding for the school. Regardless of the economic conditions surrounding this school that sits amidst the historic Eastern Market on the east side of Detroit, their expectations have remain unchanged. In fact, they are more resolute than ever to provide an educational oasis for all children attending their school. DEPSA staff and administrators offer three pieces of advice for all those who work daily in urban schools:

- Excellence is NOT an option
- Have high expectations for students
- Really care about your students

DSLA AND DEPSA—THE GUIDING LIGHT IN EDUCATING THE YOUTH OF DETROIT

Education in Detroit has long been derided by some as the worst in the United States. While the metric used to determine whether it's the best or worst is arguable, the educational success of the Detroit Service Learning Academy and the Detroit Edison Public School Academy is not debatable. When one looks at how the students from both schools perform on the MEAP test, there is no doubt that this measure of academic success positions both schools as two of the best in Detroit. However, in a city that suffers from numerous social maladies and "brain drain," there is tremendous potential to create a new generation of leaders. Not just leaders, but leaders who understand the value of changing the community through not only great ideas, but through a spirit of collaboration, elbow grease, and innovation. Welcome to the new Detroit—a city led by an innovative spirit at the Detroit Service Learning Academy and the Detroit Edison Public School Academy.

Implications for Practice

The Detroit Service Learning Academy and Detroit Edison Public School Academy are remarkably successful given that they are embedded in the economic hardships of a state and community devastated by post-industrialization. Their stories provide an example of how schools can provide the physical, emotional, and cognitive space to reignite communities and serve as examples of how we can improve educational practice for all students. Although separate, both schools embody traits that appear to be instrumental to students' overall success. Consequently, both schools provide models for other urban schools to emulate.

Service-Learning Ethos

One important characteristic of both schools is that they are steeped in an overarching ethos of service-learning, which infuses an ethic of engaged care throughout the curriculum and the community. This ethic is embedded throughout the academic and non-academic experiences of students, as recommended by leading service-learning programs (King, 2002); it is also a fundamental element of how school personnel conduct business every day, which could be described as "service teaching." Teachers begin their school year weeks before students arrive to improve their pedagogical prowess, utilize multiple forms of assessment to evaluate where students are in their learning, and use the results to adjust classroom practice to meet the students' individual needs. In addition, they employ hands-on learning to personalize the material and motivate students. Administrators at both schools view their role as servants to the cause of improving student learning by supporting students, teachers, and parents in the quest for life-long learning. For example, they create family supports such as Parent University to identify resources (e.g., health care, job training, etc.) to reduce potential family stressors such as disease or unemployment.

As a result of the "starter culture" (similar to creating the right environment for dough to rise in a good bread) incubated by school personnel, students from across the city come together to deeply engage in working to improve the community around the school, whether it is making blight right, building community gardens, improving neighborhood parks, or raising awareness and money for issues such as homelessness. These active transformative experiences of changing the world around them can have significant impact on the students themselves. Previous research has found that middle school children who engage in service-learning-oriented programs are significantly more efficacious than their non-participating peers (Scales, Blyth, Berkas, & Kielsmeier, 2000). In addition, undergraduate college students have shown significantly higher social awareness, self- and community efficacy, and long-term academic benefits in a service-learning-focused class compared to their traditionally taught peers (Simons & Cleary, 2006; Strage, 2004). The mechanism through which service-learning can lead to more engaged students, improved efficacy, and increases in academic outcomes is likely the impact of "personal performance" accomplishments, derived when students see for themselves the significant impact they have in their surrounding adult community and their emotive engagement in making a difference in their world (Bandura, 1977). Recent research has shown that increased engagement in school leads to significantly better academic performance for urban youth (Perry, Liu, & Pabian, 2010).

CONCLUSION

The latest issues in Detroit have placed the former mayor in prison, the current mayor calling for control of the Detroit Public Schools, and the continued unemployment of large portions of the community. In spite of these issues, students at DSLA and DEPSA have been successful academically and in the community. Perhaps their efforts amidst the uncertain economy and educational climate in Detroit should be considered special and extraordinary. Perhaps their success should be the standard for schools in Detroit, or other urban enclaves in the United States. Regardless of how one frames their efforts and success, staff commitment to high expectations and the impact the students make on the community through service-learning is undeniable. Furthermore, as we look to improve the educational experiences of urban youth, the Detroit Service Learning Academy and the Detroit Edison Public School Academy are innovative and demonstrate a *"yes we can"* spirit.

NOTE

1. Special thanks to Eylastine Davis, Robert Davis, Rod Wallace, Amber Darden, Luvenia Perkins, and Ebony Walker (DSLA); Ralph Bland, Nancy Garvin, Kim Bland, and Paul Szymanski (DEPSA).

REFERENCES

Aguilar, L. (2007, February 13). Wayne Co. foreclosure rate leads the nation: Wayne County claims highest rate of major metro areas in Jan.; Results push Michigan into 2nd place in U.S. *The Detroit News*. Retrieved from http://detnews.

com/article/20070213/BIZ/702130339/Wayne-Co.-foreclosure-rate-leads-the-nation

Aguilar, L. (2009, June 22). Cities scramble to recycle plants. *The Detroit News*. Retrieved from http://www.detnews.com/article/20090622/AUTO01/906220310/Michigan-cities-scramble-to-recycle-auto-plants/?imw=Y.

Bandura, A. (1977). Self-efficacy: Toward a unifying theory of behavioral change. *Psychological Review, 84*(2), 191–215.

Bergmann, L. (2008). *Getting ghost: Two young lives and the struggle for the soul of an American city*. New York, NY: The New Press.

Detroit Service Learning Academy. (2010). *Full annual education report*. Retrieved from http://dl.dropbox.com/u/1657944/FullAnnualEducationReport.pdf)

Elbel, L. (1898). *The Victors*. South Bend, IN: Elbel Brothers.

Excellent Schools Detroit. (2010). *Where we stand: Community meeting survey results*. Retrieved from http://www.excellentschoolsdetroit.org/home

Franklin, B. (2003). Race, restructuring, and educational reform: The mayoral take-over of the Detroit Public Schools. In L. Miron & E. St. John (Eds.), *Reinterpreting urban school reform: Have urban schools failed or has the reform movement failed urban schools* (pp. 95–127). Albany, NY: State University of New York Press.

Frey, W.H. (2009). *The great American migration slowdown: Regional and metropolitan divisions*. Brookings Institution. Retrieved from http://www.brookings.edu/reports/2009/1209_migration_frey.aspx.

Hoffman, B. G. (2006, November 29). Half take Ford buyout. *The Detroit News*. Retrieved from http://detnews.com/article/20061129/AUTO01/611290416/HALF-TAKE-FORD-BUYOUT

Johnson, K. (2009, May). The facts on unionizing charters; school closures; and layoffs. *The Detroit Teacher, 47*(8). Retrieved from http://mi.aft.org/dft231/index.cfm?action=cat&categoryID=ddc5f008-3872-4fe5-b490-ce9f1ff0da6a

King, K. (2002). Students realize they can shape the world. *Momentum, 33*(3), 61–64.

Mezger, R. (2008, October 22). Ohio job loss second only to Michigan since 2000. Retrieved from http://blog.cleveland.com/business/2008/10/ohio_job_loss_second_only_to_m.html

Perry, J.C., Liu, X., & Pabian, Y (2010). School engagement as a mediator of academic performance among urban youth: The role of career preparation, parental career support, and teacher support. *The Counseling Psychologist, 38*(2), 269–295.

Rampell, C. (2009, March 11). "Great recession": A brief etymology. *New York Times*. Retrieved from http://economix.blogs.nytimes.com/2009/03/11/great-recession-a-brief-etymology/

Realtytrac. (2009). *U.S. foreclosure market data by state—2008*. Retrieved from http://www.realtytrac.com/contentmanagement/pressrelease.aspx?channelid=9&accnt=0&itemid=5681#statetable

Realtytrac. (2010). *Michigan foreclosures*. Retrieved from http://www.realtytrac.com/states/michigan.html

Riley, R. (2009, September 11). It's time to end the charter school fight. *Detroit Free Press*. Retrieved from http://www.freep.com/apps/pbcs.dll/article?AID=/20090911/COL10/909110389/1319/It-s-time-to-end-charter-school-fight&template=fullarticle

Scales, P.C, Blyth, D.A., Berkas, T.H., & Kielsmeier, J.C. (2000). The effects of service-learning on middle school students' social responsibility and academic success. *Journal of Early Adolescence, 20*(3), 332–358.

Simons, L., & Cleary, B. (2006). The influences of service learning on students' personal and social development. *College Teaching, 54*(4), 307–319.

Sizer, T., & Wood, G. (2008). Charter schools and the values of public education. In L. Dingerson, B. Miner, B. Peterson, & S. Walters (Eds.), *Keeping the promise: The debate over charter schools* (pp. 3–16). Milwaukee, WI: Rethinking Schools.

Stover, D. (2006). Dealing with decline: For urban districts, dramatic drops in enrollment and resources leave nothing but difficult decisions ahead. *American School Board Journal, 193*(12), 42–44.

Strage, A. (2004). Long-term academic benefits of service-learning: When and where do they manifest themselves? *College Student Journal, 38*(2), 257–261.

The Skillman Foundation. (2008). *2008 good schools guide.* Retrieved from http://www.skillman.org/publications-perspectives/

The Skillman Foundation. (2009). *2009 good schools guide.* Retrieved from http://www.skillman.org/publications-perspectives/

U.S. Bureau of Labor Statistics. (2009). *Databases, tables & calculators by subject.* Retrieved from http://www.bls.gov/data/

Wade, R. (2000). Service-learning for multicultural teaching competency: Insights from the literature for teacher educators. *Equity & Excellence in Education, 33*(3), 21–29.

Webster, N. (2007). Enriching school connection and learning in African American urban youth: The impact of a service-learning feasibility project in inner-city Philadelphia. In S. Gelmon & S. Billig (Eds.), *From passion to objectivity: International and cross-disciplinary perspectives on service learning research* (pp. 159–176). Charlotte, NC: Information Age Publishing.

CHAPTER 2

TEXARKANA INDEPENDENT SCHOOL DISTRICT

Blazing a Trail for Urban Learners

Molly S. Taylor

ABSTRACT

The purpose of this chapter is to highlight Texarkana Independent School District and provide examples of programs that have been instrumental in helping this Northeast Texas school district achieve success for all learners. Further, this chapter explores avenues of administration, curriculum, teachers, staff development, and community leadership as important components of sustained reform. The author chooses to share this chapter in a first-person narrative context.

In 1919, the Superintendent of Texarkana Independent Schools, Texas stated:

Whatever the community is to be in the next decade, the school must make it. The Texarkana of today must determine what the Texarkana of tomorrow is to be by declaring what kind of schools it will have. A broadly conceived system of education is a good investment for any community, no matter what

Yes We Can! Improving Urban Schools Through Innovative Educational Reform, pages 23–37

it costs, and for Texarkana the investment in good schools will pay a hundred-fold. (McAlphin & Cain, 1989, p. 38)

This philosophy is still echoed throughout this community as people talk about how Texarkana Independent School District (TISD) is a district where children are experiencing academic success, even at very young ages. As I walked through the schools, there is an overall sense of pride and accomplishment. The staff is proud to work here. Most of the student population is composed of students of color, and from the outside looking in, it is obvious they come from diverse backgrounds; however, the similarities are what I notice the most. These children are not only learning, but they are having fun while doing so. I can see why TISD is known throughout the nation as a district that is good at educating children (National Center for Educational Accountability, 2007); they are blazing a trail for these young learners.

Texarkana, Texas has a population of 35,682 consisting of 61.2% Caucasian, 35.4% African American, and 4.7% Hispanic (U.S. Census Bureau, n.d.). The median age for the citizens in Texarkana is 37.1, with an average per capita income of $22,326 (U.S. Census Bureau, n.d.). Texarkana, including both the Texas and Arkansas side, has six school districts within a relatively small radius. If these six districts were combined, there would be a total of 17,530 children enrolled in public school. TISD is located on the Texas side of the city and located in the middle of the other five districts, placing it at the heart of the city.

The district is comprised of 6,860 students who are being served in eleven schools across Texarkana, Nash, and Wake Village, Texas. Student demographic percentages of the district are: 48% African American, 9% Hispanic, 41% White, 1% Native American, and 1% Asian (www.tea.state.tx.us). Enrollment in recent years has been balanced between the Caucasian and African American populations. The current growth in the Hispanic population suggests that in the future, the TISD population will be balanced between these three groups. According to Texas Education Agency (TEA) 54% of the students in this district qualify for free meals and 9% of the students qualify for reduced meals. Of this diverse population, 63% are considered to be economically disadvantaged. Diversity and socioeconomic issues work together to provide complex issues that face many urban schools.

The current 2010 Texas Education Agency ratings show an increase in schools receiving an exemplary rating. As Tables 2.1 and 2.2 illustrate, the number of exemplary schools grew from three schools in 2009 to five schools in 2010.

Tables 2.3 and 2.4 give an overview of the district's TAKS performance, broken into subjects, of economically disadvantaged students. These tables

TABLE 2.1   2009 Texas Education Agency Ratings

Exemplary	Recognized	Acceptable
Highland Park Elementary	Dunbar Elementary	Texas Middle School
Morris Elementary	Wake Village Elementary	
Nash Elementary	Texas High School	
Theron Jones Early Literacy Center		
Spring Lake Park Elementary		
Westlawn Elementary		

TABLE 2.2   2010 Texas Education Agency Ratings

Exemplary	Recognized	Acceptable
Highland Park Elementary	Dunbar Elementary	Texas Middle School
Morris Elementary	Westlawn Elementary	Texas High School
Nash Elementary	Theron Jones Early Literacy Center	
Wake Village Elementary		
Spring Lake Park Elementary		

TABLE 2.3   2009 TAKS Scores/Percentages of Economically Disadvantaged Students

Reading	Math	Writing	Science	Social Studies
88% passed	76% passed	93% passed	71% passed	93% passed

TABLE 2.4   2010 TAKS Scores/Percentages of Economically Disadvantaged Students

Reading	Math	Writing	Science	Social Studies
87% passed	77% passed	92% passed	79% passed	94% passed

illustrate that these students experienced growth in all but two categories—reading and writing.

Texarkana Independent School District is one of the leading schools in the nation according to *Forbes* magazine (Settimi, 2010), but this has not always been their story. In 1919, when the superintendent of schools made his report to the Board of Education, he shared this dream for the district, but it has taken many years to reach their current status (McAlphin & Cain, 1989). Sixteen years ago, TISD was operating from a negative financial balance, many teachers were unsatisfied, and the turnover rate was high. According to former superintendent Dr. F. Larry Sullivan, these negative issues have changed and no longer plague this district.

Theron Jones Early Literacy Center and Dunbar Elementary are located in Texarkana's most economically challenged neighborhood. In the past, these two schools were known to be the most problematic in more ways than one. Both campuses experienced a high number of students who qualified as economically disadvantaged. These two schools are within walking distance of each other and had been sources of much controversy within the African American community. Both schools were rated low-performing schools two years in a row (as per TEA) and were, therefore, facing closure by the state. Discipline and procedural policies were inconsistent within each school, and staff turnover was high. According to Mrs. Jennell Ingram, principal at Theron Jones Early Literacy Center, the average daily attendance at both schools was below state and local levels. The mobility rate between the two schools was also excessive.

Historically, pupils' attendance tends to be lower in schools with high levels of socioeconomically disadvantaged students (West, 2007). Additionally, parental involvement was minimal, and many students lacked an abundance of prior knowledge, vocabulary, and language skills necessary for vocabulary development. Frequent changes in administration and school principals had also been the norm, and the staff and student morale were extremely low. Mrs. Ingram offered that community and parent confidence and participation in these schools were basically non-existent. These bleak characteristics did not necessarily mean that students' parents did not want them to be successful. Gant (2006) states that parents and grandparents of children born into poverty simply want what all loving parents want for their children. They often recognize the role education plays in their child's future. They know that the quantity and quality of a child's education will most likely determine the life options their child will have.

In 1998, this school district faced some very large issues, and was in desperate need of reform. According to Stone (2001), urban school reform requires civic capacity: "a broad base of involvement along with a shared and durable understanding of public education as a major area of community concern and a high priority for action" (p.156). Additionally, Stone calls it the "conscious creation of actors seeking to establish a content in which extraordinary problem solving can occur" (p. 156). In 1998, the Texarkana ISD Board of Trustees hired a new superintendent by the name of Dr. F. Larry Sullivan. Dr. Sullivan shared their vision of excellence and passion for the children of this community and accepted the task of reforming this urban school district.

The School Board and Dr. Sullivan made many strides in improving a very problematic district. In 2001, the board agreed to put important steps in place with teachers and staff in mind. They implemented a significant raise in teachers' salaries to a competitive level and spent a significant amount of money on teacher and staff training. As Dr. Sullivan took over the leadership of the district, about half of the administration team came to TISD from the corporate world and the district inherited a group of individuals who looked at school improvement from a corporate management model. The administrators and Board of Trustees understood the concept of return on investments; they knew that in order for students' academic achievement to improve, money was going to have to be spent on the students who needed help the most.

Dr. Sullivan spent the first two years of his tenure educating and training the school board and staff on the idea of cultural capital. This refers to the non-financial assets including educational, social, and intellectual knowledge provided to children who grow up in families who expose them to the world in a way that coincides with what they are expected to know in school (Sullivan, 2001). West (2007) offers that evidence points towards factors outside of school as being of great significance to the child's success, with the family being of fundamental importance and financial and material resources also playing key roles. This concept propelled the district to shift Title 1 funds to the aforementioned Theron Jones Early Literacy Center and Dunbar Elementary. Additionally, the district increased the salaries of teachers who worked in these schools and made efforts to hire extremely experienced teachers. Guided by the research that indicates that preschool interventions could improve lifetime outcomes in the areas of cognitive and social competences (Duncan, Ludwig, & Magnuson, 2007), they focused every effort on the youngest of students on these campuses—the three and four year olds. School board members and administration began to hold the staff accountable for student progress. The bar was set very high for every student to experience academic success, and the financial and emotional investment in the children became the focus of the district.

DISTRICT INNOVATIONS

AVID

On a broader level, Texarkana Independent School District has many initiatives to improve the education of all of the students within the district. One such program is called the Advancement via Individual Determination (AVID) program (www.avid.org). This program promotes advanced academics and challenges to disadvantaged students who may not have the family support to encourage them to take rigorous academic courses they are capable of. These students are identified by counselors, teachers, parents, or the students themselves, and they must meet certain criteria to participate in the program. The main goals of this program are to prepare students to succeed in rigorous academics, participate in mainstream school activities, enroll in a four-year college upon graduation from the local high school, and become educated and responsible participants and leaders in a democratic society.

Students in the AVID program are often the first in their family to enter college. Consequently, this program places them with other high-performing students to serve as role models and encouragers. The district implemented this program in 2004, and they had their first graduating class of AVID students in 2009. In fact, the 2009 AVID graduating class produced a Gates Millennium Scholar who received a $450,000 scholarship. Twenty-six college- or military-bound students from this graduating class also received scholarships.

Open Enrollment Policy

Each of the elementary schools in TISD has a special focus. From Nash Elementary's leadership curriculum based on the *7 Habits of Highly Effective People* by Dr. Steven Covey (1989) to Wake Village Elementary's focuses on technology to Spring Lake Park Elementary's focus on the Arts, all of these elementary schools approach learning from different aspects. TISD has an open enrollment policy, which allows families to decide *which* program and *which* school best suits the needs of their child. According to current TISD superintendent, James Henry Russell, over a thousand students from middle- to upper-income families are transferring into TISD because of its course offerings and educational opportunities. Mr. Russell shares, "The typical scene across the United States in cities with any size at all is that the middle class families are moving to the suburbs to obtain a quality PK–12 education. That is not the case in Texarkana, Texas in our district." Of the 7,000 students enrolled in the school district 1,100 of those are commonly referred to as "tigers by choice" by district officials. These students make up 16% of the district student population, and they represent mainly middle-class families that live outside of the district. Families are choosing to transfer their children to this diverse school district because of the academic and extracurricular opportunities that are not available in any other district within a 70-mile radius. While subtle, this perception helps to encourage suburban parents to actively consider transferring into the more diverse student environment. Because of this, the district realized the importance of hiring and keeping quality faculty within the school district. This focus made transferring into the district potentially even more desirable. Former TISD superintendent, Dr. Sullivan says, "The knowledge that the quality of course offerings and instructional delivery must be of a standard that it will competitively attract suburban students helps drive quality to even higher standards." The qualitative effect for the urban district is the creation of a more diverse student population that is taught by highly motivated urban teachers who believe deeply that they must exceed the expectations of both internal and external customers.

STEM

Another relatively new district initiative is the K–16 Science, Technology, Engineering and Math Program (STEM). This program is a collaborative project between Texas A&M University–Texarkana and TISD and offers a vertically aligned K–16 engineering education executed in four stages. This initiative begins with a K–5 public elementary school (Martha and Josh Morriss Mathematics & Engineering Elementary School) that provides mathematics and pre-engineering integrated curriculum. Upon leaving Morriss Elementary, students matriculate into the pre-engineering "school within a school" at Texas Middle School and then later at Texas High School. Finally, three engineering-related programs of study at Texas A&M–Texarkana are offered for students to choose from three different Bachelor of Science degrees. The overarching goal of the engineering collaborative is to increase the quantity and quality of engineering students educated in the United States (Stripling, 2008).

Increasing Minority Teachers

One issue that continues to be important to the district is the underrepresentation of minority teachers in the classroom. In 2001 TISD formed a special committee known as the Diversity Awareness Committee to address this shortage. The goal of this committee was to recruit, retain, and support qualified educators that would reflect the ethnicity of the district's diverse population. The long-term goal of this group was to increase the number and diversity of the teaching faculty to reflect the current demographics of the city of Texarkana, Texas, and ultimately the nation as a whole.

To accomplish this task, the TISD Diversity Awareness Committee sent out letters and emails to potential teaching applicants and referred qualified applicants to the district to assist in recruitment of these professionals. They also encouraged current TISD employees to assist in recruiting and identifying prospective teacher candidates. This goal is still a work in progress, as the current teaching staff consists of 75 African American teachers, 16 Hispanic teachers, 397 White teachers, and 7 teachers of various other ethnicities. In 2007, the TISD Diversity Awareness Committee adopted three new goals:

1. We are a voice and advocates for students and parents. Our schools should ensure respect and acceptance of all.
2. We should look for similarities among diverse groups while honoring differences.
3. We will ensure that our children will have appropriate role models to prepare them for the future by hiring and retaining diverse personnel.

Further, the district has shown a commitment to diversity by having one of its own administrators, Jo Ann Rice, trained and certified as a Franklin Covey Championing Diversity Facilitator.

Another initiative in attracting diverse teachers has been the instructional practices, education, and training known as the Ready, Set, Teach program at Texas High School. This program is designed for students who are interested in being teachers. The courses offered are field-based internships that provide students with background knowledge in child and adolescent development, as well as principles of effective teaching and training practices. These students have the opportunity to work under the joint direction and supervision of both a teacher with knowledge of early childhood education and exemplary educators in direct instructional roles with elementary, middle school, and high school students. According to Mark Schroeder of TISD, these students learn to plan and direct individualized instruction and group activities, prepare instructional materials, develop materials for educational environments, assist with record keeping, and complete other responsibilities of teachers. Additionally, this program shows TISD's commitment to training, educating, and keeping their own teachers by not only paying them higher wages than the state average, but also paying for some of their teachers to receive their master's degree in curriculum and instruction specialization via a collaboratively developed program with Texas A&M University–Texarkana.

Focus on Early Childhood

The school that educates TISD's youngest and most vulnerable students is Theron Jones Early Literacy Center. Theron Jones has made dramatic changes over the last ten years. One of the first action items to change was their student/teacher ratio of 16:1 from the typical distribution of 22:1. The principal, Mrs. Jennell Ingram, said, "Using an eclectic approach of relating to our students, we use the best practices of several programs and theories of thought in teaching our students." Some of those programs include: (1) Great Expectations (n.d.), (2) Boys Town, (n.d.), (3) Marva Collins' work (Collins, 2006), (4) Ron Clark's program (Clark, 2004), (5) Love and Logic (n.d.), and (6) Kids at Hope (n.d.). Mrs. Ingram further offers that from these philosophies her staff teaches, nurtures and inspires in their students a love for learning.

The Direct Instruction Reading Program is used as the main curriculum model. According to a long range study conducted by Hirsh (2005) on reading programs for disadvantaged students, programs like Direct Instruction are much more effective than programs that put less time and effort into directly teaching reading skills (Hirsh, 2005).

> Former 4th grade TISD teacher Brooke Williams Akin shared the following story: When I was teaching 4th grade Math and Writing for TISD, the TAKS writing prompt one year was "Write about an adventure you have had." These children were expected to write a two page essay on something they had never experienced before. My students were not familiar with any adventures. They were asking me "Is riding my bike to a friends house an adventure, or watching my favorite movie?" All I could say to them was "Go try your best." They truly didn't have any reference point or experience with having an adventure, not because they had never seen the word or read it before, but because their experiences outside of school were so limited.

Duncan et al. (2007) offer that three-year olds in families of low socio-economic status have half the vocabulary of their more affluent peers, which in turn could be explained by the lower quality and quantity of parental speech inside the home. The Direct Instruction Reading Program used at Theron Jones emphasizes systematic teaching of basic skills such as sounding out words and doing simple arithmetic grammar lessons. Research shows that reading ability is cumulative and is dependent on general knowledge as well as broad experience of language (Hirsh, 2005). Hirsh offers that there are things that can be done on the margins to speed up vocabulary growth in both oral and written languages. Hirsh further opines that there may be periods around the third, fourth or fifth grades when vocabulary gains begin to speed up for some students, especially those who have benefitted from having heard or read a lot of utterances. One of the main goals of this reading program is the opportunity to read out loud in a certain teacher-paced-rhythm. Another key element is comprehension. As the students read stories, teachers ask them to answer questions about what they have read. Understanding the process by which vocabulary gain occurs is critical in order to guide teachers to make better use of school time (Hirsch, 2005).

At Theron Jones, the PreK classes use the Language for Learning portion of the Direct Instruction Reading Program. The students are required by their teachers to use complete sentences and learn new vocabulary words every week. The teachers at Theron Jones set goals for their students to read at least 100 sight words before they enter the 1st grade.

The K–1 classes use the Reading Mastery portion of this curriculum. This aspect focuses heavily on phonics and is a scripted reading method. It is amazing to watch the teachers and their students actively perform these lessons. While conducting research, I had the joy of spending some time in Mrs. Bridget Ivory's first grade class at Theron Jones. Mrs. Ivory has 15 years of teaching experience, and after observing in her classroom, it was apparent that she holds very high expectations for each of her students. As I observed her teach reading, she used a rhythm in her voice that captivated the children. They were expected to have good posture and they had to listen carefully for cues as she asked them individually to sound out the new words. Once complete, the students had to answer Mrs. Ivory's questions about the content of what they had read. As I was leaving her classroom, Mrs. Ivory expressed to me that her first graders were reading on more of a second grade level. This certainly was no surprise after I witnessed her reading strategies.

Still further, Theron Jones students have the unified support of all faculty in their endeavor to become avid and capable readers. During reading instruction, the whole staff is available to support the teachers in their quest for student success. During my visit, I saw the principal, counselor, curriculum specialist, librarian, and many other paraprofessionals helping the students learn to read. I witnessed an amazing team effort in an attempt to ensure that every student learned to read well.

Teaching Towards Diversity

When asked to describe Theron Jones today, the principal said, "Theron Jones Early Literacy Center is staffed with a caring, dedicated, and committed staff who take a holistic approach to teaching students." After a rigorous application and interview process using the Gallup Urban Teacher Perceiver (2002), staff undergo training and staff development in the area of effectively teaching students of diverse socioeconomic backgrounds. These efforts are paying off, as Theron Jones Early Literacy Center is now performing at levels that exceed the state's Academically Acceptable rating. In fact, for the fifth year in a row, this campus has received Recognized status from the Texas Education Agency (2010).

Still further, Mrs. Ingram proudly shares that their Early Literacy Program has gained local attention with surrounding school districts and private schools that have toured the school and later replicated some of their programs. Mrs. Ingram stated, "We are very proud of the work and effort that has gone into turning this school around, and we continue to push our students and ourselves to higher and greater goals. Our students are happy, well adjusted, and smart universal learners." The students from Theron Jones are receiving an early education that will help lay a healthy foundation for future learning because of school reform initiated by the leaders of this district and supported by a community as a whole.

School Board Accolades

School reform involves the public, and its support is crucial for improvements to take place (Shipps, Fowlkes & Pelzman 2006). These same scholars offer that parents and community members should thoroughly debate the consequences of any change in urban school governance (Shipps et al., 2006). In Texarkana, Texas, the School Board of Trustees is so well trusted by the community that the trustee election in 2007 was cancelled due to unopposed candidates, a trend that has become common not because of apathy, but as a result of trust and proven success. As a result, the board members fully continued their roles for an additional three years, further guaranteeing a continuity of leadership.

In another effort to applaud their tireless efforts, the TISD Board of Trustees was named the Region VIII School Board of the Year in 2007. The Board was applauded for their dedication to meeting the needs of a diverse student population; the courage to be innovative in maximizing resources, and an insatiable desire to continue moving forward on improving student performance. The school board was also instrumental in gleaning other awards for the district through their active involvement as change agents. In 2007 the district won the Texas Parent Involvement Partnership Award for the parental involvement at Texas Middle School. Additionally, TISD received the highest possible rating under Texas Schools Financial Accountability Rating System for the 5th year in a row and the district was given a Superior Achievement rating in all 21 indicators, confirming its excellence in managing and reporting taxpayer dollars. Considering the fact that in 1994 the district was operating from a negative fund balance, this was quite extraordinary. *Texas Monthly* named Nash Elementary, Spring Lake Park Elementary, Wake Village Elementary and Texas High School in a list of the "Best Public Schools in Texas" (National Center for Educational Accountability, 2007). The list of achievements for the district as a whole continues to mount. All stake holders within the district- the teachers, administrators, school board, parents, and most importantly the students themselves continues to move in a positive direction.

More Than a Job

Texarkana Independent School District is doing fantastic in a plethora of areas, but the attitude throughout the district is to only reach higher in setting new goals. Complacency is not an option here. The current superintendent, James Henry Russell, believes that TISD's strength comes from the diversity within the district. He said,

> The fact that we have approximately 16% of our student body transferring in from the suburbs that includes a population of largely high-performing students from middle class families, shocks many of our peers from around the country. Our belief that we can continue this trend by working harder than our competition and offering more and better products to our customers is a philosophy that is not seen in many school districts around the country and certainly not in urban school districts.

When asked about the current state of the district Mr. Russell said, "We certainly have our faults and so many areas where we know we need to improve, but we also have a passion for sustaining the level that so many in this community have worked so hard for. This is much more than a job; it is a mission and a passion that so many in the community share."

Community Support

Texarkana Independent School District is an example of positive change because of a community who shares a passion for education. School reform is a difficult and highly controversial topic. Shipps et al. (2006) suggest that a city's civic capacity for school reform is created by a combination of governmental and nongovernmental actors who commit themselves to the pursuit of a distinct and feasible reform agenda. Leadership is required to mobilize a cross-sector coalition and develop a form of cooperation that can sustain engagement in the face of competing priorities (Shipps et al., 2006). These coalition members such as the superintendent, administration, and the school board had to draw on their own resources, knowledge, and commitment to pursue the agenda they helped to create; therefore, producing an urban school district that is doing extraordinary things for extraordinary students.

IMPLICATIONS FOR PRACTICE

How can others emulate the change that has taken place in this district? The implications of this chapter begin with the mindset of the community, inasmuch as the goal of the citizens must be to give students the chance they deserve by laying down a foundation of knowledge and putting into action every cornerstone to ensure that it is possible for every student to achieve success. Texarkana, Texas has done an amazing job of coming together as a community in an attempt to build a school system that gives every student, regardless of socioeconomic or cultural background, the opportunity for success. In this quest, it is essential that the community actively select school board members who support sustained change. Ideally, the community should encourage capable school board members to run for office.

Research and implementation of programs such as those described above that are designed for urban learners should be a major focus of those desiring change. The principals at each campus should be trained on the characteristics of diverse student populations and should have the support of the superintendent and school board for making decisions regarding their staff and students. As such, administrators should seek and offer professional development opportunities for teachers regarding best practices in reaching diverse student populations. TISD allows staff to participate in annual in-service days, offering many different topic choices and presenters. These annual in-service days are modeled after a professional development conference and allow teachers the power to choose what interests them the most and what applies to their specific jobs. Giving teachers the choice of which training to attend is also important.

Teacher salaries are also important. When teachers feel validated by their administration and feel rewarded monetarily, it changes the perception of their importance. Additionally, curriculum and supplies are very important for urban students because many may lack the exposure to books and other learning materials at home. One example of how TISD is working on this issue is a book mobile. TISD is currently exploring funding options for a mobile library so that students can have access to books in their neighborhood while school is not in session. It is also essential that the curricula of the elementary schools within a district be aligned so that students can move from one school to the next (within the district) with the hope of picking up right where he or she left off. This is referred to as horizontal alignment and is critical in all schools, but is a non-negotiable in an urban school district such as TISD where the student mobility rate is often high.

Reading programs are vital to the short- and long-term achievement of students. This focus must be evident with even the youngest students in a school system. Additionally, a low teacher-to-student ratio is also critical to ensure that every student receives the guidance and nurturing needed to develop good school habits. Lastly, collaboration between the teacher and the family is important. This is not always easily achieved, but with good teacher training there are steps that can be taken to ensure communication between these two settings occurs.

CONCLUSION

Texarkana Independent School District is paving the way for other urban school districts in their example of making and sustaining urban school reform. Every stakeholder in this district has supported significant changes over the last twelve years in an effort to provide a quality education for each and every student within the district. Texarkana ISD has created the perception to those living outside the geographic boundaries of the district that the programs and teaching are of such quality that competing to transfer into this urban district is potentially a desirable action. People are trying to get into the district rather than get out of the district—something few other urban communities can claim.

REFERENCES

Advancement Via Individual Determination (AVID). (n.d.). Retrieved from http://www.avid.org

Boys Town. (n.d.). *Saving children, healing families.* Retrieved from http://www.boystown.org/HowWeCanHelp/Pages/EducationalInstitutions.aspx.

Clark, R. (2004). *The excellent 11: Qualities teachers and parents use to motivate, inspire, and educate children.* New York, NY: Library of Congress.

Collins, M. (2006). *Marva Collin's way.* New York, NY: Penguin Putnam Inc.

Covey, S. (1989). *7 habits of highly effective people.* New York: NY: Free Press.

Duncan, G., Ludwig, J., & Magnuson, K. (2007). Reducing poverty through preschool interventions. *The Future of Children, 17*(2), 143–160.

Gallup Urban Teacher Perceiver. (2002). Retrieved from http://education.gallup.com/select/themeTeach.asp

Gant, V. (2006). The economics of school choice. *The Journal of Education, 186*(2), 1–7.

Great Expectations. (n.d.). *Great expectation tenants.* Retrieved from http://www.greatexpectationsok.org/about.php

Hirsh, E.D. (2005). Education reform and content: The long view. *Brookings Papers on Education Policy, 1*(1), 175–205.

Kids at Hope. (n.d.). *Who we are.* Retrieved from http://www.kidshope.org/whoweare.html

Love and Logic. (n.d.). *What is love and logic for teachers?* Retrieved from http://www.loveandlogic.com/what-is-for-teachers.html.

McAlphin, M., & Cain, A. (1989). *Pages from the past: A history of Texas high school.* Texarkana: Southwest Printers and Publishers.

National Center for Educational Accountability. (2007, December). Best public schools. *Texas Monthly, 35*(12), 91–121.

Settimi, C. (2010). *Forbes Magazine: The best schools for your housing buck.* Retrieved from http://www.forbes.com/2010/04/05/best-schools-for-your-housing-buck-business-beltway-greatschools_2.html

Shipps, D., Fowlkes, E., & Pelzman, A. (2006). Journalism and urban school reform: Versions of democratic decision making in two American cities. *American Journal of Education, 112*, 363–391.

Stone, C. (2001). *Building civic capacity: The policies of reforming urban schools.* Lawrence, KS: University Press of Kansas.

Stripling, R. (2008). *2008 STAR Award Application.* Unpublished manuscript, Texas A&M University-Texarkana.

Sullivan, A. (2001). Cultural capital and educational attainment. *Sociology, 35, 4*, 893–912.

Texas Education Agency. (2010). Retrieved from www.tea.state.tx.us.

U.S. Census Bureau. (n.d.). *Fact finder.* Retrieved from http://www.factfinder.census.gov/home/saff/main.html?_lang=en

West, A. (2007). Poverty and educational achievement: Why do children from low-income families tend to do less well at school, *Benefits, 15*(3), 283–297.

PART I

ENVIRONMENTS OF URBAN SCHOOL REFORM

Section 2: Urban Community Initiatives
and Support Structures

CHAPTER 3

EXAMINING INFLUENCES ON AFRICAN AMERICAN HIGH SCHOOL STUDENTS' MATHEMATICS ACHIEVEMENT

Lamont A. Flowers
Clemson University

Tiffany A. Flowers
Georgia Perimeter College

ABSTRACT

Controlling for the effects of demographic characteristics and students' experiences, data from a national sample of high school students revealed that African American students' achievement in mathematics was positively influenced by family income, parental expectations of their child's educational attainment, and hours spent doing homework.

Yes We Can! Improving Urban Schools Through Innovative Educational Reform, pages 41–52
Copyright © 2011 by Information Age Publishing
41

EXAMINING INFLUENCES ON AFRICAN AMERICAN
HIGH SCHOOL STUDENTS' MATHEMATICS ACHIEVEMENT

Technological advances and enhanced labor market requirements are increasing the importance of mathematics education in America. Moreover, jobs utilizing mathematics knowledge are projected to increase in forthcoming years (Bureau of Labor statistics, 2010). As a result, gaining competencies in mathematics is becoming more important for workplace entry and job security in the information age (National Science Board, 1999). Furthermore, as originally predicted by Johnston and Packer (1987), a considerable number of fields and occupations are expected to require increasingly higher levels of skills and competencies in mathematics.

Despite the relationship between mathematics knowledge and school and career outcomes, some African American students score at or below the basic proficiency level on standardized mathematics assessments (Bozick & Ingels, 2008; Grigg, Donahue, & Dion, 2007; Johnson & Kritsonis, 2006; National Assessment of Educational Progress, 2010, 2011). Moreover, recent data from the National Assessment of Educational Progress (NAEP) show that, in 2009, African American 4th grade students scored an average of 222 and Caucasian students scored an average of 248 on the NAEP mathematics assessment (National Assessment of Educational Progress, 2010). Additionally, data reveal that African American 8th grade students scored an average of 261 and Caucasian students scored an average of 293 on the NAEP mathematics assessment. National data also show that African American 12th graders scored lower than any other racial group in 2009 on the NAEP mathematics assessment (National Assessment of Educational Progress, 2011). Moreover, reports indicate that African American students are not taking upper level math courses in high school at the same rate as students from other racial groups (Adelman; 2006; Johnson & Kritsonis, 2006; Roper, 2008). Viewed collectively, national educational assessment data and research suggest that some African American students may have difficulty obtaining high scores on the mathematics component of college entrance examinations, which may put them at a disadvantage in terms of competing for admissions to postsecondary institutions (Johnson & Kritsonis, 2006; Thomas, 2000). This information also indicates that African American students may be left behind as they attempt to apply for jobs in industries that require mathematical knowledge (Johnson & Kritsonis, 2006; Thomas, 2000). In light of this information, more empirical studies on the factors impacting mathematics achievement for African American high school students are greatly needed (Thomas, 2000).

REVIEW OF RESEARCH ON AFRICAN AMERICAN
STUDENTS AND MATHEMATICS EDUCATION

Several studies have examined the plight of African American students with respect to their achievement in mathematics (Fordham, 2001; Hoffman & Llagas, 2003; Stiff & Harvey, 1988). While much of this research describes the achievement gap among African American and Caucasian students (Peng, Wright, & Hill, 1995; Thomas, 2000), a considerable segment of this scholarly literature considers the manner in which African American students experience mathematics education in comparison to students from other racial groups. For example, Johnson and Kritsonis (2006) identified several reasons for the underachievement of African American students, such as the lack of technology used to teach mathematics in predominantly African American classrooms.

Previous research has also explored approaches for creating and reforming effective learning environments (Johnson & Kritsonis, 2006; Ladson-Billings, 1997; Malloy, 1997; Matthews, 2005; Nasir & Cobb, 2006; Secada, Fennema, & Adajian, 1995; Strutchens, 2000; Tate, 1995). Many of the studies in this area attempt to provide a better understanding of the factors that may improve mathematics achievement for African American students. For example, Peng and Wright (1994) report that African American high school students whose parents discuss their child's school work scored higher on mathematics achievement assessments. Thomas (2000) contended that increasing the number of math courses taken, facilitating supportive home and classroom environments, and modifying students' out-of-classroom activities may improve students' mathematics achievement. In a study by Ikpa (2003) it was shown that students who attend desegregated schools performed better on a mathematics assessment than did students who attend segregated schools. In another article that has implications for mathematics education and African American students, Martin (2007) advanced the view that mathematics teachers who teach African American students should be expected to know and make use of cultural knowledge that is both historical and political. He also asserts that teaching African American students how to apply mathematics both theoretically and practically should be emphasized over current practices that seem to focus on the transmission of discrete facts. Utilizing various data sources to examine issues impacting African American students' achievement in mathematics, Flores (2007) concludes that teacher expectations, teacher quality, and school finance issues negatively impact African American students' achievement in mathematics.

It has also been suggested that teachers should utilize culturally sensitive academic materials to improve student learning (Hale-Benson, 1986; Malloy, 1997; Martin, 2007; Ladson-Billings, 1997; Tate, 1995). In this regard, Fordham (2001) examined the intersection of gender and race on the underachievement of African American females in math. Her analyses of several incidents and situations indicated that the achievement of African American females in mathematics requires a detailed analysis of home and school environments as well as an examination of the overt and covert messages students receive from school personnel regarding their ability to pursue math-related careers.

THEORETICAL FOUNDATION

While there have been several studies designed to better understand the effects of an array of educational and psychosocial variables on African American high school students' achievement in mathematics, the present study sought to provide additional information by estimating the unique effects of family-level and individual-level variables on mathematics achievement utilizing a nationally representative sample of African American high school students. Given the particular focus of this research, this study was informed by Bandura's (1986) social cognitive theory. According to Bandura, social cognitive theory is useful in providing a conceptual foundation for explaining how individuals utilize their environment for intellectual development.

Considering the tenets of social cognitive theory, researchers have examined the extent to which students' social learning environments support positive educational outcomes (Fortier, Vallerand, & Guay, 1995; Guay & Vallerand, 1997; Vallås & Søvik, 1993; Vallerand & Bissonnette, 1992). This area of research suggests that formal and informal learning takes place interactively between the learner and his or her environment through iterative processes that seek to transmit values, skills, and knowledge. Social cognitive theory also posits that individuals learn by encountering different modes of thinking and behavior, which they use to derive meaning about their own perspectives and actions. Thus, as the theory suggests, through a series of interactions and negotiations with aspects of the social environment, individuals acquire skills and knowledge (Bandura, 1997).

METHODS

Data Source

Data from the Educational Longitudinal Study of 2002 (ELS: 2002), were analyzed for this study. According to Ingels, Pratt, Rogers, Siegel, and Stutts (2005), "[o]f 17,591 eligible selected sophomores, 15,362 completed a base-year questionnaire, as did 13,488 parents, 7,135 teachers, 743 principals, and 718 librarians" (p. 13). In the first year of data collection, ELS: 2002 measured students' achievement and obtained information about their intellectual orientations, academic experiences, and social activities (Bozick & Lauff, 2007; Ingels, Pratt, Rogers, Siegel, & Stutts, 2004; Ingels et al., 2007). Because the present study sought to examine African American high school students, data from the base year were used. Accordingly, the sample for this study consisted of 2,020 African American students. Approximately 51% of the sample consisted of African American males and 49% of the sample consisted of African American females.

Variables

The dependent variable for this study consists of African American high school students' mathematics test scores (see Table 3.1). Based on an earlier study by Peng and Wright (1994), the present study incorporated a number of independent variables. The first set of independent variables consisted of demographic and family characteristics. The second set of variables described students' experiences outside of school. These independent variables have been used in other studies estimating the impact of family and student characteristics on academic achievement (e.g., Astone & McLanahan, 1991; Bui, 2007; DePlanty, Coulter-Kern, & Duchane, 2007; Singh, Chang, & Dika, 2007; Thomas, 2000; Walberg, 1984).

Data Analysis Procedures

This study employed nationally representative data to estimate the net effects of demographic characteristics and students' experiences on African American students' mathematics achievement. Data analysis occurred in a three-stage process. In the first stage of data analysis, descriptive statistics were computed for selected variables. In the second stage of data analysis, employing ordinary least squares regression, the dependent variable was regressed on the entire set of independent variables, simultaneously, while applying statistical controls for the effects of the other variables in the equation (Pedhazur, 1997). All statistical results were reported significant at $p < .01$. In the third stage of data analysis, effect sizes were computed by dividing the metric regression coefficient of each significant factor by the pooled standard deviation of the dependent variable to examine the practical significance of the statistically significant effects (Cohen, 1988; Hays, 1994).

TABLE 3.1   Operational Definitions of Variables from the ELS: 2002

Dependent Variable

Mathematics Achievement:
   A continuous variable based on a standardized assessment of mathematics achievement.

Independent Variables

Gender:
   A categorical variable was coded: 1 = female, 0 = male.

Parent's Educational Attainment:
   A categorical variable based on the highest educational level attained by either parent
   was coded: 1 = Did not finish high school, 2 = Graduated from high school or GED,
   3 = Attended 2-year school, but did not earn a degree, 4 = Graduated from 2-year
   school, 5 = Attended college, but did not earn a 4-year degree, 6 = Graduated from
   college, 7 = Completed master's degree or equivalent, 8 = Completed PhD, MD, or other
   advanced degree.

Family Income:
   A categorical variable based on the student's family income in 2001 was coded: 1 = None,
   2 = $1,000 or less, 3 = $1,001-$5,000, 4 = $5,001-$10,000, 5 = $10,001-$15,000, 6 = $15,001-
   $20,000, 7 = $20,001-$25,000, 8 = $25,001-$35,000, 9 = $35,001-$50,000, 10 = $50,001-
   $75,000, 11 = $75,001-$100,000, 12 = $100,001-$200,000, 13 = $200,001 or more.

Parent's Expectations of Child's Educational Attainment:
   A categorical variable based on the parent's self-reported assessment of how far they
   expected their child to go in school was coded: 1 = Less than high school graduation,
   2 = High school graduation or GED only, 3 = Attend or complete 2-year college/
   school, 4 = Attend college but not complete a 4-year degree, 5 = Graduate from college,
   6 = Obtain master's or equivalent, 7 = Obtain PhD, MD, or other advanced degree.

Mathematics Self-Efficacy:
   A 5-item scale measuring a student's self-efficacy in mathematics.

Hours Spent Doing Homework:
   A continuous variable based on a student's self-reported assessment of the amount of
   time they spent doing homework.

Hours Spent Watching Television or Playing Video Games:
   A categorical variable based on a student's self-reported assessment of how many hours a
   week he or she spent watching television or playing video games was coded: 0 = 0 hours,
   1 = 1 hour, 2 = 2 hours, 3 = 3 hours, 4 = 4 hours, 5 = 5 hours, 6 = 6 hours, 7 = 7 hours,
   8 = 8 or more hours.

Hours Spent Working:
   A categorical variable based on a student's self-reported number of hours he or she spent
   working per week was coded: 0 = 0 hours, 1 = 1–5 hours a week, 2 = 6–10 hours a week,
   3 = 11–15 hours a week, 4 = 16–20 hours a week, 5 = 21–25 hours a week, 6 = 26–30 hours
   a week, 7 = 31–35 hours a week, 8 = 36–40 hours a week, 9 = over 40 hours a week.

RESULTS AND DISCUSSION

The data analyses indicate that African American male students scored
higher than African American female students on a measure of mathemat-

TABLE 3.2   Regression Analysis Summary

Independent Variables	Regression Coefficient
Gender	−1.210*
Parent's Educational Level	0.292
Family Income	0.557*
Parent's Expectations Child's Educational Attainment	0.746*
Mathematics Self-Efficacy	0.130
Hours Spent Doing Homework	0.033*
Hours Spent Watching Television or Playing Video Games	−0.006
Hours Spent Working	0.112

* $p < .01$

ics achievement ($B = -1.21$, $d = -2.425$). It was also shown that family income exerted a significant and positive effect on mathematics achievement ($B = .557$, $d = .215$). The effects of parental expectations of their child's educational attainment was also positive ($B = .746$, $d = .570$). Additionally, the effects of hours spent doing homework on African American students' mathematics achievement were significant and positive ($B = .033$, $d = .002$).

This study was informed by social cognitive theory (Bandura, 1986, 1997), which hypothesizes that particular segments of an individual's knowledge base are obtained through actual or imagined experiences and interactions with others. Accordingly, the present study sought to examine the impact of critical variables on African American high school students' mathematics achievement. This study yielded three major findings. First, controlling for an important set of variables (Peng & Wright, 1994), African American high school students' mathematics achievement was positively impacted by family income. Consistent with other studies measuring the influence of socioeconomic status on academic achievement (Johnson, McGue, & Iacono, 2007), this finding highlighted the positive impact of income on mathematics achievement.

Taking into account an array of independent variables, the study found that African American high school students' mathematics achievement was positively impacted by their parents' expectations of their future educational attainment. This finding, which is supported by other scholars (Powell & D'Angelo, 2000; Prins & Toso, 2008; Rodríguez-Brown, 2009), suggests that African American high school students whose parents believe that they will pursue academic degrees beyond the high school diploma are more likely to score higher on a measure of mathematics achievement. This finding suggests that parental expectations act as socializing agents for students, which results in higher achievement in school settings (Jeynes, 2007; Kaplan, Liu, & Kaplan, 2001; Yan, 1999).

This study also found that African American high school students' mathematics achievement was positively impacted by the amount of time they spent doing homework. This finding indicates that time spent engaging in homework resulted in higher mathematics achievement scores for African American high school students, which is also consistent with previous research (Cooper, Robinson, & Patall, 2006; Peng & Wright, 1994; Trautwein, & Köller, 2003). Overall, the findings in this study are significant for researchers, counselors, teachers, and parents who seek to create meaningful and enriching educational experiences for African American high school students. Moreover, the findings suggest that African American students' mathematics achievement can be improved by enhancing their educational environments at home and in school (Thomas, 2000).

IMPLICATIONS FOR PRACTICE

The statistical analyses reported in this study support the need to examine issues and factors that impact student learning in mathematics. Also, as Thomas (2000) suggests, educational professionals who seek to improve student achievement in mathematics should design approaches that increase the likelihood that parents and teachers collaboratively encourage student interest in mathematics during and after school. It can also be inferred from this study that scholars and educational professionals should collaborate to determine the most effective approaches to help preservice and inservice teachers learn how to utilize culturally sensitive and historically appropriate instructional practices to teach mathematics (Ladson-Billings, 1995; Tate, 1995). Findings from the literature review conducted for this study also suggest that practicing teachers and teacher educators should collaborate to create, develop, and assess innovative curricula to teach African American students mathematics. To support these and related efforts, teacher education programs should offer courses to teach preservice teachers how to utilize instructional approaches that highlight African American history and contemporary issues in the African American community (Ladson-Billings, 1995). To further enhance mathematics instruction, teachers should consider utilizing pre- and post-test action research designs to obtain mathematics achievement data from students while testing the effectiveness and impact of different instructional strategies. Employing this research-based approach to teaching may help to explain why certain approaches are not effective in the classroom and how new approaches may be modified to enhance African American students' achievement in mathematics.

In light of today's multicultural student body, it is imperative that educational personnel in public and private schools prepare students for the global society they will encounter throughout their lives. To support the academic and social development of students in the 21st century, educators, researchers, and administrators may need to develop additional skills to work with an increasingly diverse student body. Moreover, researchers need to continue to develop empirically based strategies for teaching, advising, and working with students and parents from diverse and multicultural backgrounds. Finally, teacher preparation programs must offer courses and learning experiences that provide practical strategies that teachers can use to effectively encourage and motivate students who are culturally different from themselves.

REFERENCES

Adelman, C. (2006). *The toolbox revisited: Paths to degree completion from high school through college.* Washington, DC: U.S. Department of Education.

Astone, N. M., & McLanahan, S. S. (1991). Family structure, parental practices and high school completion. *American Sociological Review, 56,* 309–320.

Bandura, A. (1986). *Social foundations of thought and action: A social cognitive theory.* Englewood Cliffs, NJ: Prentice-Hall.

Bandura, A. (1997). *Self-efficacy: The exercise of control.* New York, NY: Freeman.

Bozick, R., & Ingels, S. J. (2008). *Mathematics coursetaking and achievement at the end of high school: Evidence from the Education Longitudinal Study of 2002 (ELS:2002)* (NCES 2008-319). Washington, DC: U.S. Department of Education.

Bozick, R., & Lauff, E. (2007). *Education Longitudinal Study of 2002 (ELS:2002): A first look at the initial postsecondary experiences of the sophomore class of 2002* (NCES 2008-308). Washington, DC: U.S. Department of Education.

Bui, K. (2007). Educational expectations and academic achievement among middle and high school student. *Education, 127,* 328–331.

Bureau of Labor Statistics. (2010). *Occupational outlook handbook, 2010–11.* Washington, DC: U.S. Department of Labor.

Cohen, J. (1988). *Statistical power analysis for the behavioral sciences* (2nd ed.). Hillsdale, NJ: Erlbaum.

Cooper, H., Robinson, J., & Patall, E. (2006). Does homework improve academic achievement? A synthesis of research. *Review of Educational Research, 76,* 1–62.

DePlanty, J., Coulter-Kern, R., & Duchane, K. A. (2007). Perceptions of parent involvement in academic achievement. *Journal of Educational Research, 100,* 361–368.

Flores, A. (2007). Examining disparities in mathematics education: Achievement gap or opportunity gap? *The High School Journal, 91,* 30–42.

Fordham, S. (2001). Why can't Sonya (and Kwame) fail math? In W. H. Watkins, J. H. Lewis, & V. Chou (Eds.), *Race and education: The roles of history and society in educating African American students* (pp. 140–158). Needham Heights, MA: Allyn & Bacon.

Fortier, M. S., Vallerand, R. J., & Guay, F. (1995). Academic motivation and school performance: Toward a structural model. *Contemporary Educational Psychology, 20,* 257–274.

Grigg, W., Donahue, P. L., & Dion, G. (2007). *The nation's report card: 12th-grade reading and mathematics 2005* (NCES 2007-468). Washington, DC: U.S. Department of Education.

Guay, F., & Vallerand, R. J. (1997). Social context, student's motivation, and academic achievement: Toward a process model. *Social Psychology of Education, 1*, 211–233.

Hale-Benson, J. E. (1986). *Black children: Their roots, culture, and learning styles.* Baltimore, MD: Johns Hopkins University Press.

Hays, W. L. (1994). *Statistics* (5th ed). Fort Worth, TX: Harcourt Brace College.

Hoffman, K., & Llagas, C. (2003). *Status and trends in the education of Blacks* (NCES 2003-034). Washington, DC: U.S. Department of Education.

Ikpa, V. W. (2003). The mathematics and the science gap between resegregated and desegregated schools. *Education, 124*, 223–229.

Ingels, S. J., Pratt, D. J., Rogers, J. E., Siegel, P. H., & Stutts, E. S. (2004). *Education Longitudinal Study of 2002: Base year data file user's manual* (NCES 2004-405). Washington, DC: U.S. Department of Education.

Ingels, S. J., Pratt, D. J., Rogers, J. E., Siegel, P. H., & Stutts, E. S. (2005). *Education Longitudinal Study of 2002: Base-year to first follow-up data file documentation* (NCES 2006-344). Washington, DC: U.S. Department of Education.

Ingels, S. J., Pratt, D. J., Wilson, D., Burns, L. J., Currivan, D., Rogers, J. E., & Hubbard-Bednasz, S. (2007). *Education Longitudinal Study of 2002: Base-year to second follow-up data file documentation* (NCES 2008-347). Washington, DC: U.S. Department of Education.

Jeynes, W. H. (2007). The relationship between parental involvement and urban secondary school student academic achievement. *Urban Education, 42*, 82–110.

Johnson, C., & Kritsonis, W. A. (2006). The national dilemma of African American students: Disparities in mathematics achievement and instruction. *National Forum of Applied Educational Research Journal, 20*(3), 1–8.

Johnson, W., McGue, M., & Iacono, W. G. (2007). Socioeconomic status and school grades: Placing their association in broader context in a sample of biological and adoptive families. *Intelligence, 35*, 526–541.

Johnston, W. B., & Packer, A. H. (1987). *Workforce 2000: Work and workers for the 21st century.* Indianapolis, IN: Hudson Institute.

Kaplan, D., Liu, X., & Kaplan, H. (2001). Influence of parents' self-feelings and expectations on children's academic performance. *The Journal of Educational Research, 94*, 360–370.

Ladson-Billings, G. (1995). But that's just good teaching!: The case for culturally relevant pedagogy. *Theory into Practice, 34*, 159–165.

Ladson-Billings, G. (1997). It doesn't add up: African American students' mathematics achievement. *Journal for Research in Mathematics Education, 28*, 697–708.

Malloy, C. E. (1997). Including African American students in the mathematics community. In J. Tentracosta (Ed.), *Multicultural and gender equity in the mathematics classroom: The gift of diversity* (pp. 23–33). Reston, VA: National Council of Teachers of Mathematics.

Martin, D. B. (2007). Beyond missionaries or cannibals: Who should teach mathematics to African American children? *The High School Journal, 91*, 6–28.

Matthews, L. E. (2005). Towards design of clarified equity messages in mathematics reform. *The High School Journal, 88*(4), 46–58.

Nasir, N. S., & Cobb, P. (2006). *Improving access to mathematics: Diversity and equity in the classroom.* New York, NY: Teachers College Press.

National Assessment of Educational Progress. (2010). *The nation's report card: Mathematics 2009* (NCES 2010-451). Washington, DC: U.S. Department of Education.

National Assessment of Educational Progress. (2011). *The nation's report card: Grade 12 reading and mathematics 2009 national and pilot state results* (NCES 2011-455). Washington, DC: U.S. Department of Education.

National Science Board. (1999). *Preparing our children: Math and science education in the national interest* (NSB 99-31). Washington, DC: National Science Foundation.

Pedhazur, E. J. (1997). *Multiple regression in behavioral research: Explanation and prediction* (3rd ed.). Orlando, FL: Harcourt Brace College.

Peng, S. S., & Wright, D. (1994). Explanation of academic achievement of Asian American students. *The Journal of Educational Research, 87*, 346–352.

Peng, S. S., Wright, D., & Hill, S. T. (1995). *Understanding racial-ethnic differences in secondary school science and mathematics achievement* (NCES 95-710). Washington, DC: U.S. Department of Education.

Powell, D. R., & D'Angelo, D. (2000). *Guide to improving parenting education in Even Start Family Literacy Programs.* Washington, DC: U.S. Department of Education.

Prins, E., & Toso, B. W. (2008). Defining and measuring parenting for educational success: A critical discourse analysis of the Parent Education Profile. *American Educational Research Journal, 45*, 555–596.

Rodríguez-Brown, F. V. (2009). *The home-school connection: Lessons learned in a culturally and linguistically diverse community.* New York, NY: Routledge.

Roper, C. G. (2008). *The relationship between upper level math courses in high school and college success* (CHHC Research Brief, January 2008, No. 1). Clemson, SC: Clemson University, Eugene T. Moore School of Education, Charles H. Houston Center for the Study of the Black Experience in Education.

Secada, W. G., Fennema, E., & Adajian, L. B. (Eds.). (1995). *New directions for equity in mathematics education.* Cambridge, MA: Cambridge University Press.

Singh, K., Chang, M., & Dika, S. (2007). Effects of part-time work on school achievement during high school. *Journal of Educational Research, 101*(1), 12–22.

Stiff, L. V., & Harvey, W. B. (1988). On the education of Black children in mathematics. *Journal of Black Studies, 19*, 190–203.

Strutchens, M. E. (2000). Confronting beliefs and stereotypes that impede the mathematical empowerment of African American students. In M. E. Strutchens, M. Johnson, & W. Tate (Eds.). *Changing the faces of mathematics: Perspectives on African Americans* (pp. 7–14). Reston, VA: National Council of Teachers of Mathematics.

Tate, W. F. (1995). Returning to the root: A culturally relevant approach to mathematics pedagogy. *Theory into Practice, 34*, 166–173.

Thomas, J. P. (2000). Influences on mathematics learning and attitudes among African American high school students. *Journal of Negro Education, 69*, 165–183.

Trautwein, U., & Köller, O. (2003). The relationship between homework and achievement—Still much of a mystery. *Educational Psychology Review, 15,* 115–145.

Vallås, H., & Søvik, N. (1993). Variables affecting students' intrinsic motivation for school mathematics: Two empirical studies based on Deci and Ryan's theory of motivation. *Learning and Instruction, 3,* 281–298.

Vallerand, R. J., & Bissonnette, R. (1992). Intrinsic, extrinsic, and amotivational styles as predictors of behavior: A prospective study. *Journal of Personality, 60,* 599–620.

Walberg, H. J. (1984). Improving the productivity of America's schools. *Educational Leadership, 41*(8), 19–40.

Yan, W. (1999). Successful African-American students: The role of parental involvement. *Journal of Negro Education, 68,* 5–22.

CHAPTER 4

MENTAL HEALTH DELIVERY IN URBAN SCHOOLS

It Takes a Village to Empower a Child

Jamilia Blake
Texas A&M University

Collette Nero
Omaha Public Schools

Concepcion M. Rodriguez
Dallas Independent School District

ABSTRACT

Meeting the mental health needs of school-age children is a national concern. Given the considerable amount of time that children spend in school and the effects of behavior and psychological functioning on student learning (Welsh, Parke, Widaman, & O'Neil, 2001), schools provide the most optimal setting for providing psychological services to children. The delivery of mental health services in urban schools is particularly important given the barriers many families and children from urban communities face with respect

Yes We Can! Improving Urban Schools Through Innovative Educational Reform, pages 53–74
Copyright © 2011 by Information Age Publishing
All rights of reproduction in any form reserved.

to accessing quality and affordable mental health care. The purpose of this chapter is to discuss the mental health needs of students in urban schools and to highlight two urban school districts that are successful in providing mental health services to students.

Meeting the mental health needs of school-age children is a national concern (U.S. Department of Health and Human Services, 2000). Approximately one in five children and adolescents (20%) in the United States have a diagnosable psychological disorder marked by disruptive behavior or symptoms of anxiety or depression that adversely impacts their social or academic functioning (U.S. Department of Health and Human Services, 1999). For children living in urban communities, the risk for experiencing mental health problems is far greater than for children who reside in non-urban communities due to the concentrated poverty and the declining economic and social conditions that characterize many urban neighborhoods (American Psychological Association Taskforce on Urban Psychology, 2005). Children from urban communities are more likely to experience significant life stressors (Morales & Guerra, 2006) and have greater exposure to violence (Youngstrom, Weist, & Albus, 2003), which may, in turn, increase their risk for exhibiting aggression, disruptive behavior problems, and symptoms of depression (Attar, Guerra, & Tolan, 1994; Foster, Rollefson, Doksum, Noonan, Robinson, & Teich, 2005). For example, research suggests that relative to children in rural settings, children from urban communities are not only more likely to exhibit disruptive behavior and symptoms of depression and anxiety (Weist, Myers, Danforth, McNeil, Ollendick, & Hawkins, 2000), but their emotional and behaviors problems are perceived to be more severe than children from non-urban communities.

Despite the overwhelming need for psychological services in urban communities, many children's mental health needs go unmet, particularly low-income African American and Latino children (Kataoka, Zhang, & Wells, 2002). According to Kataoka et al., 80% of children in need of mental health care services do not receive these services. When children do receive mental health services, they are more likely to receive psychological services in the schools than in community-based mental health clinics (Zahner, Pawelkiewicz, DeFrancesco, & Adnopoz, 1992). These findings imply that much of the burden for mental health delivery falls upon schools (Zahner et al., 1992; Zahner & Daskalakis, 1997).

Schools may serve as a primary setting for mental health delivery for children because schools inherit the social and structural characteristics of the communities in which they are located (Alderman & Taylor, 2003; Wilson, 1987). This is especially true for urban schools in which much of staff time and school resources are devoted to addressing disruptive and aggressive behavior of students (Foster et al., 2005). Children may also be more likely to receive mental health care in urban schools because schools reduce transportation and financial barriers that often prevent low-income, ethnically diverse children and families from accessing quality mental health care (U.S. Department of Health and Human Services, 2001). Although schools provide the most optimal setting for providing psychological services to children, given the considerable amount of time that children spend in school, debate exists as to whether schools are actually responsible for addressing the mental health needs of their students.

Research suggests that social competence and academic achievement have reciprocal effects (Welsh, Parke, Widaman, & O'Neil, 2001). Children who are socially and psychologically adjusted excel academically, and academic achievement increases social and emotional competence. Given these findings, it appears that psychological adjustment and academic achievement are intertwined (Elias & Haynes, 2008; Schwartz, Gorma, Nakamoto, & McKay, 2006). In order to promote children's academic achievement, it is imperative that urban schools adopt a holistic approach to education in which students are not only provided with quality instruction to enhance learning, but also psychological services to foster their social and emotional development. By aligning achievement goals with student support through the provision of mental health services, urban schools can move toward a more comprehensive and effective method for educating urban students. The purpose of this chapter is to identify urban school districts that have been successful in delivering school-based mental health services to students. We begin with a discussion of four delivery models for school-based mental health and provide examples of how two large urban school districts implement school-based mental health services within their schools. We conclude the chapter with recommendations for urban school districts on how to provide comprehensive psychological services to students within their schools.

MODELS FOR MENTAL HEALTH DELIVERY IN SCHOOLS

Multiple models exist for the provision of school-based mental health delivery in urban schools. These models include: (1) pupil support services (Alderman & Taylor, 2003), (2) expanded school mental health programs (Flaherty & Osher, 2003), (3) full service schools (Dryfoos, 1995), and (4) school-wide interventions (e.g., positive behavioral support and social emotional learning programs; Lassen, Steele, & Sailor, 2006; Simonsen & Sugai, 2007). Each of these models provides unique methods for offering mental health services to students in schools that can be administered independently or as part of an integrated service delivery model.

Pupil Support Services

Pupil support services is the most common mental health delivery model implemented in urban schools (Alderman & Taylor, 2005). Within this model, schools employ school-based mental health professionals such as school counselors, school psychologists, and school social workers to deliver indirect and direct psychological services to students with minor adjustment difficulties and to students who pose risk for experiencing more severe emotional or behavioral problems or psychological disorders. For example, psychological services delivered directly through the pupil support services model may include short-term counseling implemented by a school counselor for children who evidence difficulty managing their anger or who have experienced a death in their family, or a psychological evaluation conducted by a school psychologist for a student who is failing academically and exhibits disruptive behavior. Psychological services may also require school psychologists or school counselors to provide indirect mental health support (e.g., crisis intervention services; Brock, Nickerson, Reeves, Jimerson, Lieberman, & Feinberg, 2009) to students and school staff in the aftermath of a school crisis such as the suicide of a student or the death of a well-known staff member.

Although academic guidance, short-term counseling, and crisis intervention are available to students in the general education setting, the most extensive psychological services delivered through the pupil support services model are usually limited to students who meet eligibility criteria for special education services (Alderman & Taylor, 2005). One advantage of the pupil support services model is that school-based mental health professionals (e.g., school psychologists, school counselors, and school social workers) possess unique skills in addressing the mental health needs of students not observed in other mental health professionals. Given their combined knowledge of children's psychological development, understanding of the structure and nature of the schools, and recognition of the ethical limitations associated with providing psychological services in schools, school counselors, school psychologists, and school social workers may be more effective than other mental health professionals in delivering psychological services in school.

Expanded School Mental Health Programs

Expanded school mental health (ESMH) programs extend the services provided by school counselors, school psychologists, and school social workers in that all students who exhibit minor or subclinical behavior problems, as well as those with more impairing psychological symptoms, are provided with in-depth mental health care. Under the ESMH model, licensed mental health practitioners, such as a licensed psychologists, school psychologists, or licensed professional counselors, are placed in schools to provide case management and treatment services to students in general and special education. Mental health practitioners may be funded by the school district or funded through a variety of sources including federal and local grants (e.g., Safe and Drug Free Schools) or partnering community agencies. Students may be referred to mental health practitioners if short-term counseling is ineffective in relieving the student's psychological symptoms and the student requires more intensive psychological counseling (e.g., services that may last for six months or the entire school year). Thus, ESMH programs are distinct from the traditional psychological services delivered in schools in that ESMH programs have more personnel to provide long-term individual and group counseling to students and families.

Full Service Schools

Full service schools utilize a different approach to mental health delivery, marked by collaboration and the integration of community resources to better serve the needs of children and families. Professionals who provide services to students and families in full service schools are usually not employed by the school district, but rather are employed by community or social service agencies. Delivery models for full service schools vary considerably, with services provided on-site or outside of the school. Some examples include the provision of primary health care services, in which physicians and community nurses conduct health screenings and offer medical treatment on a sliding scale to low-income children, or mental health professionals from private practices or outpatient hospitals provide long-term psychological counseling for families or conduct parent trainings to assist parents with managing the behavior of their children.

School-Wide Interventions

School-wide or system-level interventions such as positive behavioral support and social emotional learning programs provide additional methods for meeting the mental health needs of students through prevention. Positive behavioral support is a continuum of proactive discipline procedures used to actively decrease problem behaviors while increasing positive interaction between students and teachers through the implementation of clearly defined standards for student behavior (Sugai, Sprague, Horner, & Walker, 2000). Positive behavioral support involves teaching students behavioral expectations in a non-punitive manner, increasing active supervision by adults, and creating a school-wide reinforcement system for the display of appropriate student behavior (Simonsen & Sugai, 2007). Positive behavioral support programs require administrators to assemble an interdisciplinary team of teachers and staff members to identify the behavioral expectations that they would like students to meet. School discipline guidelines are reviewed for clarity and adapted to be in accordance with identified behavioral expectations. A reinforcement system is established to reinforce students when they are observed to adhere to behavioral expectations. All teachers and staff are trained on student behavioral expectations and the school-wide reinforcement system.

In contrast to positive behavior support programs, which are more behaviorally oriented, social emotional learning programs assist children with developing social and emotional competencies by teaching children self-awareness, empathetic reasoning, behavior and emotional management, decision making, and problem solving skills (Collaborative Academic, Social and Emotional Learning, 2003). Social emotional learning programs are usually manualized interventions with a specified curriculum taught by teachers. Teachers are trained to implement a series of structured classroom-based activities from the social emotional learning curriculum that educate children on how to identify and manage their emotions and problem-solve solutions using adaptive coping strategies.

The advantage of school-wide intervention programs such as positive behavior supports and social emotional learning programs is that they can be implemented by teachers and supported with consultation from district-employed school psychologists and school counselors. Thus, they do not require additional funding outside of the cost of materials and initial staff training. More importantly, these programs, if implemented effectively and consistently, can reduce children's risk for behavioral and psychological maladjustment (Chi-Ming, Greenberg, & Kusche, 2004; Horner et al., 2009)

ADDRESSING THE MENTAL HEALTH NEEDS OF URBAN CHILDREN

School-based mental health programs that provide comprehensive and integrative mental health services are more effective than models with limited or fragmented services (Chittooran & Chittooran, 2010). Consistent with public health models of health care, mental health services in the schools should be accessible to all students, with emphasis placed on prevention (Weisz, Sandler, Durlak, & Anton, 2005). However, urban schools face a number of unique challenges that may impact their ability to implement system-level models of mental health delivery (Weist et al., 2000). For many administrators in urban school districts, the most pressing concern is how to effectively deliver mental health service to students with limited resources (e.g., financial resources and personnel with qualified training) while maximizing instructional time. The challenges in delivering mental health services in urban schools are well-documented (for review see Massey, Armstrong, Boroughs, & Hensen, 2005; Weist & Paternite, 2006; Wilson, Lipsey, & Derzon, 2003), yet there are some urban school districts that have been successful in delivering school-based mental health services, either independently or through university-based or community collaborations, without comprising academic endeavors in the process. Unfortunately, many of these urban schools are not recognized nationally or the service models implemented in these schools are not published in outlets with high practitioner readership. Therefore, we provide a brief description of two urban school districts that use an integrative mental health service delivery model to provide psychological services to students.

Omaha Public Schools

The Omaha Public Schools (OPS) is the largest district in the state of Nebraska and is comprised of 49,079 students, of which 67.2% are eligible for free or reduced lunch. Omaha Public Schools is ethnically and racially diverse, with 61.5% of the student population identified as an ethnic/racial minority (i.e., 26.7 % Hispanic, 30.8 % African American, 38.5% White/Caucasian, 2.6% Asian, and 1.4% Native American; Omaha Public Schools Research Department, 2010). OPS Division of Psychological Services is comprised of: (a) 28 school psychologists, (b) two school psychologist interns, (c) one educational diagnostician and (d) a coordinator. Whereas the Division of Psychological Services is primarily composed of school psychologists, additional school-based mental health professionals such as school counselors and social workers also provide psychological services to students. OPS adopts a hybrid model for school-based mental service delivery, in which the district primarily utilizes a pupil support services model. In addition, elements of the full service school model in which the school district links children and families to community-based resources are also employed.

OPS school psychologists provide consultation and assessment services to all students and assist with crisis intervention and post-crisis response. Consultation is provided mainly through the district's student assistance yeam, an interdisciplinary team of teachers, school psychologists, and school counselors that problem-solve and identify academic and behavioral support strategies to improve the educational outcomes of academically at-risk students. Assessment services include diagnostic testing (formal and informal) for educational planning purposes, comprehensive psychological evaluations for special education eligibility, and assessment of high ability learners. School psychologists also provide consultation and assessment services for the early childhood special education program (birth–5 years).

School psychologists provide direct and indirect intervention services for students. They may be responsible for implementing or modeling interventions or strategies for staff as part of the student assistance team problem-solving process. They may also provide individual or small group social skill-building activities to promote healthy peer relations, emotional regulation, self-esteem, and so on. School psychologists also provide crisis intervention for students expressing suicidal ideation as well as responsive services following a crisis (e.g., death of student or staff member) to help minimize the psychological trauma experienced after a crisis (Brock et al., 2009). They are also involved in the district threat assessment process, which evaluates the level of threat a student may possess for committing a violent act and determines the appropriate steps for treatment for students who present risk for violence. Indirect services include referral to the school counselor, social worker, community counselor, or a partnering agency for family support for students who need long-term psychological services. Within the special education department there are six school psychologists who work exclusively with special education students. They deliver individual and family therapy as identified on the student's individual educational plan (IEP). In addition, school psychologists provide wrap around case-management to assist families with accessing school and community resources. They also provide staff development/in-service training for staff.

OPS school counselors are assigned to one school in the district. School counselors provide services to all students within their school. Program components include curriculum, individual student planning, responsive services and system support. Counselors deliver the comprehensive K–12 guidance curriculum though classroom presentations on a variety of life competencies (social skills, coping skills, wellness, etc.). Individual student planning involves helping students set career goals, manage conflicts, and plan for post-secondary education opportunities. Counselors provide system support though their participation in the building school improvement team, positive behavior supports leadership team, and the student assistance team problem solving process. Responsive services include individual or small group counseling, assessment of suicidal ideation, or referral to various community resources to help family with basic needs (food, clothing and shelter). While school counselors are expected to fulfill a number of duties, there are many "other duties as assigned" in which they may engage in order to promote student success.

School social workers are the newest members of the district mental health providers and work in alternative education programs as well as high schools. They are expected to support students in general as well as in special education. They provide crisis intervention (suicidal ideation, community referrals for basic needs), individual and group counseling, and general student support to promote student success. They maintain contact with students with whom they have worked to monitor their progress and provide additional assistance as needed. They support students receiving special education services by helping parents/guardians to understand and engage in the IEP process. They are instrumental in helping students transition to adult services following completion of high school. School social workers also assist with building-level prevention and support programs including those for teen parents. A major focus of intervention activities involves increasing student attendance. As part of school attendance teams, they are expected to assess the barriers to school attendance and implement strategies or make the necessary referrals to overcome those barriers. As the newest members of the team, the role of the school social worker continues to evolve with the emphasis always on ways to promote a positive home–school connection and increase student engagement.

The OPS division of psychological services also provides psychological services to students through community collaborations. The community counselor program is a partnership with a local foundation that places licensed mental health practitioners in secondary schools. Licensed mental health practitioners are able to provide therapy services to students within the building at no cost to the family. They also have offices in various community locations so that other students and community members are able to take advantage of the service at no cost. Additionally, family support services are available through partnerships with local community agencies. Referred families meet with a family support worker to assess their needs and identify goals for psychological treatment. A plan of action is developed, and the family support worker assists the family with accessing the necessary community resources to address the identified needs. Although there is ongoing communication between the family support worker and the school, the services are home-based.

Dallas Independent School District

Dallas Independent School District (DISD) is the 12th largest school district in the nation, serving 159,000 ethnically and economically diverse students (i.e., 66.5% Hispanic, 27.7% African American, 4.6% White/Anglo, 1% Asian, and .2% Native American) that speak 70 different languages across 226 urban school campuses (Dallas Independent School District, n.d. a). To support the academic success of students, the DISD psychological and social services department offers psychological and social work services to students and their families through an integrative service delivery model that draws from pupil support, full service schools, ESMH, and school-wide intervention models.

Psychological and social services department is composed of school psychologists and social workers who provide counseling and coordinate community services for students in need. Any student in the DISD general education program experiencing an academic, social, or emotional challenge may be served by psychological and social services. Additionally, any special education student expressing intent to harm him- or herself or another is referred to DISD psychological and social services. Students and their families are provided access to mental health, social, and medical services through the provision of individual and group counseling services, crisis intervention, and prevention strategies.

At the onset of a crisis, a DISD psychological and social services crisis response team is sent. Crises may include violent assault on a campus or in the community, or the injury or death of a student or school staff member. The ultimate goal of the crisis response team is to return students to their regular routines as soon as possible and to mitigate psychological trauma associated with the crisis. The crisis response team first collects facts about the crisis event and verifies information to eliminate rumors. Then they communicate facts to students, staff, and parents through classroom discussions, school meetings, staff meetings, and letters sent home with students. Next, they assist crisis-impacted individuals in understanding their emotional reactions while providing individual counseling to students and staff who are having challenges coping with their reactions. Finally they develop a short- and long-term response plan with school administration. Post-crisis mental health counseling for students is available on an individual and as-needed basis.

Prevention of violence and promotion of safety through early detection and intervention is a goal of DISD psychological and social services department (Dallas Independent School District, n.d. b). One strategy for preventing violence is by conducting threat assessments (Cornell, 2003). The threat assessment process is initiated when a student communicates intent to harm him- or herself or others to a school staff member. School counselors administer a suicide risk assessment questionnaire or a risk of violence questionnaire to evaluate the potential risk of the student's claim. After assessing the risk level, a safety plan is developed and implemented. Students who do not have a strong social support system at home or in school (e.g., strained family relations, few friends, etc.) are deemed as having elevated risk for completing acts of violence to themselves or toward others. Therefore, psychological and social services staff provide additional support services to these students. Depending on the severity of students' symptoms, students may be referred for outpatient mental health services or hospitalization. Frequently, outpatient mental health services are provided through another collaborative agency, Youth and Family Centers, the ten health clinics located on DISD secondary campuses.

Youth and Family Centers are on-site school-based health centers that provide physical and mental health care to DISD students and their families (Jennings, Pearson, & Harris, 2000). Medical services such as immunizations, wellness visits and sick care evaluations, and physical exams are made available to students and families. In addition to providing medical services, Youth and Family Centers offer counseling and psychiatric services for DISD students and their families. Youth and Family Centers staff includes hospital medical personnel and DISD mental health employees that are psychiatrists, psychologists, and social workers.

The psychological and social services staff also provide transitioning services to students who are reentering school for a variety of reasons. For example, the psychology and social services might provide transition to students for legal reasons such as children who are homeless or have been adjudicated. Transitioning services are provided through the homeless education program and a collaborative program with the juvenile justice department. The homeless education program refers students without a permanent residence to social services in the community and provides families with access to after-school programs, school supplies, and school uniforms.

Psychological and social services staff also create transition plans with the juvenile justice department for students leaving the judicial system and returning to local schools. In collaboration with the Dallas County juvenile department, a psychological and social services staff person is assigned full-time to the department. The staff assigned meets with the student and family to conduct an informal needs assessment. The purpose of the assessment is to help the student find a school placement within the district that best meets the academic and mental health needs of the student. The student has several alternative school options; community options, such as Job Corps; and the option to return to their home school. Should the student decide to return to his or her home school, then the student support team (SST) chairperson is contacted to set up a meeting to assess what support the student will need to successfully complete his or her education. Psychological and social services staff assigned to the student's home school are also contacted to assist the student and family with any identified mental health needs disclosed in the initial needs assessment. The student's probation officer is given a copy of the transition plan the student has chosen so that the probation officer can provide support as needed. The psychological and social services assigned to the juvenile department also consults with the juvenile court regarding a student's school transition plans and assists with residential placement by providing school academic records.

DISCUSSION

Omaha Public Schools (OPS) and Dallas Independent School District (DISD) adopt differing models of mental health delivery for serving urban students. Similar to many school districts, OPS primarily utilizes pupil support services as a model for mental health delivery in which the majority of mental health services are implemented by district-employed school-based mental health professionals such as school psychologists, school counselors, and school social workers. Although the OPS draws from elements of the full service schools model, the majority of mental health services delivered to students are conducted by school psychologists, school counselors, and social workers. This hybrid mental health delivery model may be appropriate for smaller urban school districts, urban school districts that are in the initial stages of implementing school-based mental health programs, or districts that have limited access to community agencies who can deliver mental health services to students and families.

In contrast, DISD uses an integrative model for mental health service delivery, drawing from varying aspects of all four of the school-based delivery models identified: the pupil support, full service schools, ESMH, and school-wide intervention models. DISD is the 12th largest school district in the nation and has been delivering mental health services to students for over 10 years. The integrative mental health delivery model used in DISD reflects years of planning, revising, and collaboration with a number of agencies. This integrative model is appropriate for larger urban school districts with access to a large variety of community agencies that are able to provide mental health care to children's and families. Although OPS and DISD's service delivery models differ, both school districts illustrate that it is possible to meet the mental health needs of urban students.

IMPLICATIONS FOR PRACTICE

The process of planning and implementing mental health services within schools can be a daunting task for many administrators. Although many urban school districts may be eager to implement a school-based mental health program, it may be difficult to determine how to begin the process. Therefore, we offer the following recommendations:

1. Assemble a Mental Health Team

Prior to implementing school-based mental health services, school administrators should assemble an interdisciplinary school mental health team to plan and evaluate the effectiveness of school-based mental health services. The school mental health team should consist of an administrator, who has the authority to make decisions related to program adoption and resource allocation; a special education teacher with expertise in emotional and behavioral disorders (EBD, also called behavior disorders, BD, or emotional disorders, ED, in some states); a general education teacher; at least two school-based mental health professionals (e.g., school psychologist and school counselor or school social worker and school psychologist); the school nurse (in many school districts the school nurse is responsible for distributing medication; therefore, school nurses may have some insight into the number of students who receive medication for psychological disorders); a parent; and member of the community (e.g., religious or civic leader). Given the demands on staff time, it may be more efficient for school administrators to use an existing interdisciplinary team to serve the role of the mental health team. The student support team (also called the student assistance team or pre-referral team in some states) is charged with the responsibility of developing strategies to support children who are at increased risk for exhibiting behavior or emotional problems; therefore, the school administrator could expand the responsibility of this team to also include planning for and identifying the mental health needs of students. Prior to beginning program planning, the mental health team should review the current literature on best practices in school-based mental health service delivery.

2. Conduct a Needs and Resource Assessment of Student Mental Health

Once the school mental health team is composed, this team is charged with conducting a mental health needs and resource assessment. This assessment process will involve assessing the mental health needs of the student population and the personnel/staff resources available to meet students' mental health needs. More specifically, the mental health team should attempt to answer the following questions: (1) Who receives mental health services in the school? (2) Who is in need of mental health services in the school, but does not receive them in the school? (3) For those who do receive mental health services in the school, what do those services look like and what department or type of staff member delivers them (e.g., special education teacher, school counselor, school nurse, school psychologist), and how often are these services delivered? and (5) How many students receive mental health services outside of school and who or what agencies within the community provide these services?

Needs and resource assessments can take multiple forms (e.g., review of school records; administration of staff, parent, and community agency questionnaires; informal interviews with staff; administration of student surveys on current psychological functioning etc.); however, we recommend that the school mental health team begin with a review of school records and the administration of a brief staff and community agency survey. Collecting data from multiple sources, particularly from school staff and community-based mental health professionals, will assist the mental health team in better understanding the mental health needs of their students as well corroborate evidence obtained from school records. Data collected from the school records should be tabulated into three sections: number of students who are receiving long-term mental health services; number of students who receive short-term mental health services; and number of students at risk for social, emotional, or behavioral problems who do not receive services.

a. *Students in need who receive long-term mental health care at school.* The mental health team should identify the number of students who receive special education services or accommodations through Section 504 of the Rehabilitation Act of 1973 for emotional problems, behavior problems, or psychological disorders. For this group of students, the mental health team should also list the type and frequency of services these students receive and which staff member serves as the primary provider of these services (e.g., social skills training provided by a special education teacher or individual counseling provided by a school psychologist for depressive symptoms).

b. *Students who receive short-term mental health care at school.* Information on the number of students who receive support services through the student support team for emotional and behavioral concerns should be collected. Children who receive services through the student support team may be children who have been referred for special education services for emotional or behavioral problems, but did not meet eligibility criteria for special education services or children who exhibit social, emotional, or they may have behavioral problems that adversely impact their educational achievement but the behavior/emotional adjustment problems are not significant enough to warrant referral for special education services or are outside the scope of special education services. The mental health team should list the type and frequency of services these students receive through the student support team and which school staff members serve as the primary provider of these services (e.g., general education teacher places child on individual behavior management plan; school psychologist or school counselor provides social skills training or involves child in small group counseling).

c. *Students at risk for social, emotional, and behavior problems.* Research suggests that students who exhibit social and emotional problems are at increased risk for experiencing exclusionary discipline (e.g., suspension) as well as other discipline sanctions (Bowman-Perrott, Benz, Hsu, Kwok, Eisterhold & Zhang, under review). Further, physical aggression has been noted as a significant predictor of school removal and discipline referrals for all students (Clark, Petras, Kellam, Ialongo, & Poduska, 2003). Therefore, the team should identify the number and type of student discipline infractions that occurred in the current and previous academic years to determine whether aggression or other behavioral problems are areas of concern. Specifically, the reason for discipline infractions should be recorded (e.g., physical altercations, weapon possession, etc.). In addition, the number of recidivist students with a persistent history of exclusionary discipline who have received frequent discipline infractions should also be identified.

Finally, a brief questionnaire should be administered to school-based mental health professionals and special education teachers and mailed to community mental health agencies and local community and medical health professionals (e.g., local psychologists, psychiatrists, counselors, social workers and pediatricians) to assess the mental health resources currently available for students within the school and the larger community. That is, these professionals should be asked to report the type and frequency of mental health services they offer to students. Information collected from the needs and resources assessment should be used to identify the top three mental health needs of the school and the resources available to address these needs both within the school and in the larger community.

3. Develop a Plan

Next, the school mental health team should develop a plan and model for addressing the three top mental health needs of their school. First, based on available resources, the team should identify which service delivery model best suits the structure and needs of their district. The team may also wish to consult with neighboring schools/school districts that have successfully implemented school-based mental health services. It is recommended that the team develop a plan for prevention and intervention to address no more than three mental health needs. An evidenced-based prevention program, such as one of the school-wide interventions identified in this chapter, should be implemented school-wide to reduce students' risk for emotional and behavior problems. In conjunction with a prevention program, the team should identify which individual and small-group interventions school-based mental health professionals will be able to provide to students who evidence more severe psychological disorders and behavior problems. As the mental health team identifies primary prevention programs and secondary psychological interventions, it is important that the team recognize the scope of their expertise in meeting the mental health needs of their students as well as the resources available. Thus, the team should develop a plan that is limited in scope initially, focusing on no more than three mental health needs, with the intention of expanding the plan in coming years. The mental health team should also identify which mental health services are outside of school official's area of expertise (e.g., when a child exhibits psychotic symptoms) and potential gaps in the mental health services that the school wishes or is able to provide.

Community mental health agencies and mental health professionals identified as delivering psychological services to students via the community questionnaire could serve as a potential resource for addressing gaps in service delivery. However, before establishing collaborative relationships with community agencies and local mental health professionals, the team should invite these professionals to a planning meeting in order to discuss the team's overall goals in delivering school-based mental health serve as well as to gather additional information about the type of services these professionals provide. It is very important that community mental health professionals' credentials and training for providing psychological services to children are vetted by school psychologists on the team or the team member with the most psychological training before these professionals are invited to collaborate with the school. If the mental health team believes that these professionals are appropriately trained to work with children, then the team should discuss these professionals' willingness to receive referrals from the schools to provide psychological services to students, preferably at a discounted rate, or to contract for psychological services that district school-based mental health professionals are unable to provide.

Successful program implementation involves investment from key stakeholders, particularly district and school level administrators, classroom teachers, and parents. Therefore, the team should be diligent in making the planning process transparent. Key stakeholders should be invited to attend mental health team planning meetings, offer input on the proposed plan, and be informed of the justification for proposed services. The team's reliance on data-based decision making (i.e., needs-based assessment) for the implementation of specific prevention and intervention programs will increase stakeholders' confidence in the need for school-based mental health services.

4. Be Patient and Seek Support

Transitioning from planning to implementation of school-based mental health programs can be overwhelming, even with adequate preparation. We encourage the team to be cognizant that behavioral change takes time and that schools may not see immediate effects of prevention and intervention programming efforts. In fact, behavioral change may not be evident within the first or even second year of implementation. However, successful school-based mental health programs are those that are comprehensive and implemented consistently and correctly. During implementation, we recommend that the mental health team continue to meet, noting aspects of programming that are successful and those aspects of the program that might be ineffective. We also recommend that mental health teams consult with other school districts that are successfully implementing school-based mental health services or attend the Center for School Mental Health annual national conference, "Advancing School Mental Health," to obtain support and guidance on implementing these services.

5. Annually Evaluate the Program

Lastly, the school mental health team should evaluate the success of their school-based health programming efforts and strategies annually. This may take the form of a formal or informal program evaluation. Given the time and resources needed to effectively conduct a formal program evaluation, it is recommended that school districts partner with university colleges of education to have their school-based mental health programs evaluated. When university partnerships are not possible, the school mental health team should use student discipline records and school referrals for psychological services as a way to evaluate the effectiveness mental health services delivered in the schools. For example, the team should review records to assess whether there is a reduction in discipline referrals, school mental health referrals, or amount of time spent on delivering psychological services following the implementation of programs.

RECOMMENDED RESOURCES

The aforementioned recommendations serve as initial steps in developing a plan to implement school-based mental health services. For more in-depth information on school-based mental health service delivery as it relates to selecting appropriate mental health programs for schools and how to implement school-based mental health programs, the following resources are provided. However, please note that this list is not exhaustive and that there is a wealth of information online for schools on the delivery of school-based mental health services.

1. *Center for School Mental Health, University of Maryland.* The mission of the Center for School Mental Health is to strengthen policies and programs in school mental health. The Center for School Mental Health annually hosts a national conference, "Advancing School Mental Health," at which school officials can connect with other districts that implement school-based mental health programs as well as learn about recent programs, federal funding, and legislative updates pertaining to the delivery of school-based mental health services. The Center for School Mental Health website (http://csmh. umaryland.edu/) provides a variety of resources for school officials including policy briefs, mental health screening forms, and a brief summary of evidenced-based mental health programs.

2. *Collaborative for Academic, Social and Emotional Learning.* The purpose of this organization is to provide school districts with information on how social emotional learning programs can be implemented in schools and integrated with academic instruction to increase students' overall academic achievement. This website (http://www. casel.org) provides information on a variety of social emotional learning programs that schools may choose to implement as well guidance on how to implement social emotional learning programs.

3. *National Association of School Psychologists Toolkit: School-based Mental Health.* This electronic resource provides a compendium of book chapters, journal articles, and hand-outs on topics related to children's mental health and best practices for implementing prevention programs and providing psychological interventions to children in schools. http://www.nasponline.org/publications/booksproducts/mhtoolkit.aspx.

4. *United States Department of Health and Human Services Substance Abuse and Mental Health Services Administration (SAMHSA) National Registry of Evidence-based Programs.* This website (http://www.nrepp.samhsa.gov/) provides a database of evidence-based mental health and substance abuse programs for school-age children. Each program included in the database is evaluated and rated based on the level of empirical evidence to support its effectiveness.

5. *United States Department of Education Office of Special Education Programs, Positive Behavioral Interventions and Support.* This website (http://www.pbis.org/) provides schools with considerable information on PBIS, including how to choose and implement PBIS in schools as well how to evaluate its effectiveness.

6. *Handbook of school mental health: Advancing practice and research* (Weist, M.D. Evans, S. W. & Lever, N. A., Eds. New York: Kluwer Academic/ Plenum). One of the most well-cited texts on school-mental-based health, the *Handbook of School Mental Health: Advancing Practice and Research* provides school districts with a wealth of information on how to establish collaborative relationships with community agencies to address student mental health issues as well as how to design school-based mental health programs to meet the needs of specific populations (e.g., students who are immigrants, students with gang affiliations, etc.).

CONCLUSION

In sum, delivering mental health services in urban schools can present a significant challenge for urban school districts. However, in order to promote the academic achievement of urban students, educational leaders in urban schools must perceive the development of children's psychological adjustment and educational attainment as complimentary rather than competing goals. In this chapter, we review four of the most common mental health delivery models implemented in schools and provide two examples of how these models can be tailored to meet the unique needs of urban schools. The two districts featured in this chapter suggest that schools can be effective in meeting the mental health needs of urban students and that there is not "a one size fits all" approach to providing psychological support services to urban students.

REFERENCES

Alderman, H., & Taylor, L. (2003). Toward a comprehensive policy vision for mental health in schools. In M. D. Weist, S. W. Evans, & N.A. Lever (Eds.), *Handbook of school mental health: Advancing practice and research* (pp. 23–44). New York, NY: Kluwer Academic/Plenum.

Alderman, H., & Taylor, L. (2005). *Mental health in urban schools.* Tempe, AZ: National Institute for School Improvement.

American Psychological Association Taskforce on Urban Psychology. (2005). *Toward an Urban Psychology: Research, Action, and Policy.* Washington, DC: APA.

Attar, B. K., Guerra, N. G., & Tolan, P. H. (1994). Neighborhood disadvantage, stressful life events, and adjustment in urban elementary-school children. *Journal of Clinical Child Psychology, 23,* 391–400.

Bowman-Perrott, L., Benz, M. R., Hsu, H., Kwok, O., Eisterhold, L., & Zhang, D. (under review). Patterns and predictors of disciplinary exclusion over time: An analysis of the SEELS national dataset.

Brock, S.E., Nickerson, A. B., Reeves, M. A., Jimerson, S. R., Lieberman, R. A., & Feinberg, T. A. (2009). *School crisis prevention and intervention: The PREPARE model*. Bethesda, MD: NASP.

Chi-Ming, K., Greenberg, M. T., & Kusche, C. A. (2004). Sustained effects of the PATHS curriculum on the social and psychological adjustment of children in special education. *Journal of Emotional and Behavioral Disorders, 12*, 66–78.

Chittoran, M., & Chittoran, S. E. (2010, March/April). Urban students in high-poverty schools: Information and support strategies for educators. *Communiqué, 38*, 1–4.

Clark, M.D., Petras, H., Kellam, S. G., Ialongo, N., & Poduska, J. M. (2003). Who's most at risk for school removal and later juvenile delinquency? Effects of early risk factors, gender, school/community poverty, and their impact on more distal outcomes. *Women & Criminal Justice, 14*, 89–116.

Collaborative for Academic, Social and Emotional Learning. (2003). *Safe and sound: An educational leader's guide to evidenced-based social and emotional learning programs*. Chicago, IL: Collaborative for Academic, Social, and Emotional Learning.

Cornell, D. G. (2003). Guidelines for responding to student threats of violence. *Journal of Education Administration, 41*, 705–719.

Dallas Independent School District. (n.d. a). *Dallas Independent School District Scorecard 2008–2009*. Retrieved from http://www.dallasisd.org/scorecard, October 11, 2010.

Dallas Independent School District. (n.d. b). *Policy FFE local student welfare: Student assistance programs/counseling*. Retrieved from www.tasb.org/policy/pol/private/057905

Dryfoos, J. G. (1995). Full service schools: Revolution or fad? *Journal of Research on Adolescence, 5*, 147–172.

Elias, M. J., & Haynes, N. M. (2008). Social competence, social support, and academic achievement in minority, low-income, urban elementary school children. *School Psychology Quarterly, 23*, 474–495.

Flaherty, L. T., & Osher, D. (2003). History of school-based mental health services. In M. D. Weist, S. W. Evans, & N.A. Lever (Eds.), *Handbook of school mental health: Advancing practice and research* (pp. 11–22). New York, NY: Kluwer Academic/Plenum.

Foster, S., Rollefson, M., Doksum, T., Noonan, D., Robinson, G., & Teich, J. (2005). *School mental health services in the United States, 2002–2003*. Rockville, MD: Center for Mental Health Services, Substance Abuse, and Mental Health Service Administration.

Horner, R. H., Sugai, G. Smolkowski, K., Eber, L., Nakasato, J., Todd, A. W., & Esperanza, J. (2009). A randomized, wait-list controlled effectiveness trial assessing school-wide positive behavior support in elementary schools. *Journal of Positive Behavior Interventions, 11*, 133–144.

Jennings, J., Pearson, G., & Harris, M. (2000). Implementing and maintaining school-based mental health services in a large, urban school district. *Journal of School Health, 5*, 201–205.

Kataoka, S. H., Zhang, L., & Wells, K. B. (2002). Unmet need for mental health care among U.S. children: Variation by ethnicity and insurance status. *American Journal of Psychiatry, 159,* 1548–1555.

Lassen, S., Steele, M., & Sailor, W. (2006). The relationship of school-wide positive behavior support to academic achievement in an urban middle school. *Psychology in Schools, 43,* 701–712.

Massey, O.T., Armstrong, K., Boroughs, M., & Hensen, K. (2005). Mental health services in schools: A qualitative analysis of challenges to implementation, operation, and sustainability. *Psychology in the Schools, 42,* 361–372.

Morales, J. R., & Guerra, N. G. (2006). Effects of multiple context and cumulative stress on urban children's adjustment in elementary school. *Child Development, 77,* 907–923.

Netzel, D. M., & Eber, L. (2003). Shifting from reactive to proactive discipline in an urban school district: A change of focus through PBIS implementation. *Journal of Positive Behavior Interventions, 5*(2), 71–79.

Omaha Public Schools Research Department. (2010). *2009–10 Racial composition by grade by gender.* Retrieved from http://www.ops.org/District/LinkClick.aspx?fileticket=WvG6oFWMOA8%3d&tabid=284&mid=1343

Schwartz,D., Gorma, A. H., Nakamoto, J., & McKay, T. (2006). Popularity, social acceptance, and aggression in adolescent peer groups: Links with academic performance and school attendance. *Developmental Psychology, 42,* 1116–1127.

Simonsen, B. & Sugai, G. P. (2007). School-wide positive behavior support: A systems level application of behavioral principles. In S. W. Evans, Mark D. Weist, & Z. N. Serpell (Eds.), *Advances in school-based mental health interventions: Best practices and program models* (pp. 8-2–8-17).Kingston, NJ: Civic Research Institute.

Sugai, G. P., Sprague J. R., Horner, R. H., & Walker H. M. (2000). Preventing school violence: The use of office discipline referrals to assess and monitor school-wide discipline interventions. *Journal of Emotional and Behavioral Disorders, 8,* 94–101.

U.S. Department of Health and Human Services. (1999). *Mental health: A report of the surgeon children.* Rockville, MD: U.S. Department of Health and Human Services.

U.S. Department of Health and Human Services. (2000). *Healthy people 2010, Volume 1&2: With understanding and improving health and objectives for improving health.* Rockville, MD: U.S. Department of Health and Human Services. Retrieved from http: //www.healthypeople.gov

U.S. Department of Health and Human Services. (2001). *Mental health: Culture, Race, and Ethnicity—A supplement to mental health: A report of the Surgeon General.* Washington, DC: Author.

Weist, M.D. Evans, S. W. & Lever, N. A. (Eds.). (2003). *Handbook of school mental health: Advancing practice and research.* New York, NY: Kluwer Academic/Plenum.

Weist, M.D., Myers, C. P., Danforth, J., McNeil, D. W., Ollendick, T. H., & Hawkins, R. (2000). Expanded school mental health services: Assessing needs related to school level and geography. *Community Mental Health Journal,* 36, 259–273.

Weist, M.D. & Paternite, C. E. (2006). Building an interconnected policy-training-practice-research agenda to advance school mental health. *Education and Treatment of Children, 29,* 173–196.

Weisz, J.R., Sandler, I.N., Durlak, J.A., & Anton, B.S. (2005). Promoting and protecting youth mental health through evidence-based prevention and treatment. *American Psychologist, 60,* 628–648.

Welsh, M., Parke, R. D., Widaman, K., & O'Neil, R. (2001). Linkages between children's social and academic competence: A longitudinal analysis. *Journal of School Psychology, 39,* 463–481.

Wilson, W. J. (1987). *The truly disadvantaged.* Chicago, IL: University of Chicago Press.

Wilson, S.J., Lipsey, M.W., & Derzon, J. H. (2003). The effects of school-based intervention programs on aggressive behavior: A meta-analysis. *Journal of Consulting and Clinical Psychology, 71,* 136–149.

Youngstrom, E., Weist, M. D., & Albus, K. E. (2003). Exploring violence exposure, stress, protective factors, and behavioral problems among inner-city youth. *American Journal of Community Psychology, 32,* 115–129.

Zahner, G. E. P., & Daskalakis, C. (1997). Factors associated with mental health and general health and school-based service use for child psychopathology. *American Journal of Public Health, 87,* 1440–1448.

Zahner, G. E. P., Pawelkiewicz, W., DeFrancesco, J. J., & Adnopoz, J. (1992). Children's mental health services needs and utilization patterns in an urban community: An epidemiological assessment. *Journal of American Academy of Child Adolescent Psychiatry, 31,* 951–960.

PART II

EMPOWERING URBAN STUDENTS AND TRANSFORMING THEIR SCHOOLS

Section 1: Teachers' Roles in Urban School Settings

CHAPTER 5

DECONSTRUCTING TEACHER BIAS

Exploring Attributional Bias in Urban Elementary Schools

Stephen D. Hancock and Tehia V. Starker
University of North Carolina–Charlotte

ABSTRACT

In this chapter, we address deficit theory as an epistemological nexus that many teachers employ when working with urban students. We also explore three dimensions of attributional bias. Next, we investigate how the socio-emotional and academic development of racially diverse students are impacted by the Pygmalion effect. Critical reflection is examined as a means to deconstruct deficit thinking and attributional bias. We conclude with a consideration of the relationship between deficit theory, the attributional biases, and the Pygmalion effect.

According to the Council of the Great City Schools, urban school districts in the United States serve "40 percent of the nation's minority students and 30 percent of the economically disadvantaged students" (n.d.). Unfor-

Yes We Can! Improving Urban Schools Through Innovative Educational Reform, pages 77–90
Copyright © 2011 by Information Age Publishing
All rights of reproduction in any form reserved.

tunately, many of these students are irresponsibly warehoused and tagged with a deficit label that has been, in many cases, capriciously bestowed. The source of the duplicitous branding of many students rests in the thinking processes and the lack of diverse experiences of many urban teachers. Teacher's thinking processes and experiences with urban students seriously impacts their ability to effectively and positively teach (Tsigilis, Tsioumis, & Gregoriadis, 2006). Byrnes, Kiger, and Manning (1997) contended that teachers with inadequate experience with culturally diverse students will likely form negative dispositions and have biased academic expectations (as cited in Tsigilis et al., 2006). Given that teachers are highly influential entities in the lives of young children, there must be a concerted effort to address teacher bias as it relates to academic relationships and achievement. In fact, the power teachers wield in a student's life, especially those students in urban communities, has immense implications for future academic success or failure.

In this chapter, we first address deficit theory as a negative way of thinking about urban students. Secondly, we explore three dimensions of attributional bias that we believe employ deficit thinking and frame many teachers' perspectives in diverse classrooms. Next, we investigate how the socioemotional and academic development of diverse students are impacted by a plausible connection between deficit thinking and attributional bias that often results in the Pygmalion effect. We then investigate critical reflective practice as a means to deconstruct deficit thinking and attributional bias. We conclude with a consideration of the relationship between deficit theory, attributional biases, and the Pygmalion effect. We argue that while each of these theories hails from different disciplines, they have a common epistemological foundation.

TEACHER ORIENTATION: DEFICIT THINKING

It was 2005 and school systems all over the United States were in the midst of a vast educational experiment called No Child Left Behind (NCLB). He was a second-grade African American student, from a single-parent home. He was in a group of students who were part of the redesigned school zone plan. The plan responded to NCLB as an extended effort to diversify schools and send students from "failing" to "successful" schools. So, he was transferred from his "failing" school to a recently integrated school in an all white urban neighborhood. All of the teachers were white and female. His teacher believed that she had high expectations for all students but supposed that he would have difficulty keeping up because of his personal background. He was an early and excellent reader and an honor student at his previous school. While the teacher was impressed with his reading ability, she . . .

The initial description of the student in this narrative often conjures certain thoughts, perceptions, and beliefs. Unfortunately, these thoughts and perceptions cause one to view the student as poor, low performing, and unmotivated to learn. This type of deficit thinking is so pervasive in urban classrooms that it requires critical reflection to even recognize that the negative image of certain students is based on frail experiences with their culture, a plethora of stereotypical ideas, biased tests, and a faulty framework of poverty (Lewis, James, Hancock, & Hill-Jackson, 2008; Siwatu & Starker, 2010), none of which remotely describes the true nature or intelligence of the student. However, many teachers have allowed themselves to believe their own ignorance, to dwell in their own fears, and to segregate themselves in their own worldview of "rightness." We contend that a "worldview of rightness" from many teachers is based on a narrowly conscribed idea of others. This worldview is often fueled by a fierce attachment to the status quo. Thus, when teachers encounter students that live outside of their personal worldview of rightness, the student, rather than the worldview, is interpreted as problematic. As a result, teachers develop unfavorable thinking as it relates to people different from *their* lived norm. Hauser-Cran, Sirin, and Stipek (2003) stated that "teachers rated children as less competent academically and had lower expectations of their future academic success when they believed that the education-related values of the children's parents differed from their own" (as cited in Georgiou, 2008, p. 121). In addition, teachers' lack of cultural awareness and experience produce misconceived notions concerning the race, gender, and socioeconomic status of diverse students. For many teachers the naïve and uninformed use of race, gender and socioeconomic status compels them to draw on deficit thinking when working with urban students. Thus, supporting a negative master narrative that is prevalent among many teachers is detrimental to the success of diverse students. Ladson-Billings (2008) refers to the paucity of experience with diverse others that teachers bring into the classroom as the poverty of culture. It is apparent for many urban teachers that deficit perceptions are an outcome of their lack of experience with diverse cultures.

Milner (2006) describes deficit thinking as the perception that "students of color do not already possess the necessary skills, knowledge, and attitudes to succeed and learn" (p. 81). Ford (2007) argues that deficit thinking "exists when educators interpret differences as deficits, dysfunctions, and disadvantages" (p. 404). The fact that the student is African American, from a single parent home, and is a transfer from a low performing school equals dysfunction and disadvantage for many teachers. Unfortunately, the lack of familiarity with diverse realities jaded the teacher's perspective and dismantled any attempt to humanize and positively judge the student's disposition. Storti (1989) defined this type of deficit thinking as a product of segregation, dehumanization and hypocritical judgment (as cited in Ford,

2007). We contend that deficit thinking can only exist in classrooms where teachers inhabit fear, ignorance and prejudice toward diverse others. As stated previously, fear, ignorance and prejudice are a product of a segregated worldview of rightness. We paraphrase Storti (1989):

> The more teachers retreat from the culture of the students, the less is learned about the student. The less teachers know about students, the more uncomfortable teachers feel among students. The more uncomfortable teachers feel, the more they will withdraw. The more teachers withdraw, the more faults they find in the students. Regrettably, in the end, teachers begin to believe the lies they've created to console their conscience and demean the student.

Without personal and professional experience and knowledge of other cultures, teachers are left to their learned stereotypes and prejudice as they navigate diverse others. Making positive connections with urban students requires teachers to navigate issues of racism, elitism, and cultural illiteracy (Hancock, 2006). It is imperative that teachers embark on a journey to develop positive academic relationships to combat negative thinking and foster positive expectations. Unfortunately, deficit thinking cripples the capacity to hold positive beliefs and expectations about the ability of diverse others and halts any attempt to form prosperous thinking. Deficit thinking negatively impacts teachers' perspectives and directly influences their beliefs and expectations towards students.

TEACHER PERCEPTIONS: ATTRIBUTIONAL BIAS

> ... did not believe or expect him to test into the advanced reading program with gifted students. The testing day came and despite his reading confidence, he completed the test with much anxiety. He scored three points below the cut-off for the advanced reading program. She contributed his failure to a lack of content knowledge, comprehension, and critical thinking. The teacher didn't feel that he had tried hard enough. She felt that she'd provided him with the same instruction that the other average reading students received and prepared him thoroughly for the test. In the end, she believed it wasn't her teaching or the test but was a result of him being from a single parent, low income home. She also believed that her decision to keep him in average reading was common among other teachers. She was proud of her ability to diagnose...

It is evident that the belief and expectations teachers have about a student has important consequences for student success (Rosenthal, 2002). Unfortunately, the teacher is not aware that her poor expectations of his success are key to his performance on the test. In fact, she contributes his failure solely to the student's disposition while heralding her work as a teacher. Schunk, Pintrich, and Meece (2008) refer to this behavior as attributional bias. Attributions are the *perceived* causes of outcomes (Schunk et al., 2008), not necessarily the actual cause and are heavily influenced by our existing conceptions, beliefs, stereotypes, and experiences. Thus, beliefs and experiences are scaffolded to create an organized and meaningful view of the world in which we live. Georgiou (2008) defines attribution theory to be found "on the premise that people are not content simply to observe events as they occur, but strive to understand their causes" (p. 120). Unfortunately, when teachers' knowledge and beliefs are steeped in biased epistemologies the outcome for students is often damaging.

Attribution theory states that teachers interpret experiences in three different dimensions. Schunk, Pintrich, and Meece (2008) describes the dimensions as: (1) a locus dimension, or whether the cause of the belief, behavior or action is internal or external to the individual; (2) stability dimension, which reflects how consistent or inconsistent the cause will remain overtime; and (3) controllability dimension, which are causes an individual believes he/she can influence or change. When the three varying dimensions are not understood as one evaluates an event or individual, it is easy to see how interpretations can be distorted.

Teachers must use multiple and varied sources of data to make an inference about the locus of a cause or outcome. However, the teacher in the narrative used weak assumptions about the student's personal background to evaluate the suppose cause of his lack of "success" on the test. As the teacher evaluated the student, she assessed him based on criteria external to his intellect, as she supposed that he lacked "content knowledge, comprehension, and critical thinking" based on a test. Peterson and Barger (1984) showed that teachers are most likely to attribute causes for a students' behavior that are consistent with prior beliefs about the individual student (as cited in Schunk et al., 2008). If teachers' beliefs or expectations of students are biased or deficit-oriented, the attributes teachers form will be laced with social inequities (van den Berg, Denessen, Hornstra, Voeten, & Holland, 2010). While it is plausible that the student was not focused and did not have the aptitude to successfully acquire the three points necessary, it is highly unlikely that he would be successful in the class with a teacher who views him as academically deficient. The teacher evaluated the student with unstable criteria and believed that she couldn't influence his comprehension with quality instruction. Her cause to educate the student was not based on an internal and stable, long term and controllable effort to foster achievement rather, it was supported by teacher bias which is external to the student and a controllable and stable factor in the teacher's life. As cited in Schunk et al. (2008), Figure 5.1 displays a clear matrix of common attributes as categorized by the dimensions of locus, stability, and controllability.

Stability	Locus of Control			
	Internal		External	
	Controllable	**Uncontrollable**	**Controllable**	**Uncontrollable**
Stable	Long-term effort	Aptitude	Instructor bias/favoritism	Ease/difficulty or school or course requirements
Unstable	Skills/knowledge Temporary or situational effort for exam	Health on day of exam Mood	Help from friends/teacher	Chance Luck

Figure 5.1 Locus, stability, and controllable dimensions. *Note:* Achievement attributions classified by locus, stability and controllability dimensions From *An Attributional Theory of Motivation and Emotion,* by B. Weiner, 1986, New York: Springer-Verlag. Copyright © 1986 by Springer-Verlag New York, Inc. Adapted by permission.

Schunk et al. (2008) describe five forms of attributional bias that are often found in the classroom. Attributional bias contends that the conceptualizations and perspectives of teachers are often erroneous and can lead to confirmed stereotypes or biases. In an effort to capture biased perspectives, the continuous narrative was constructed to demonstrate three of the five forms of attributional bias: (a) actor-observer perspective, which causes (in this case) the teacher to identify her behavior as relevant and right for the situation (a result of external factors) but views the student's behavior or outcomes as personal (result of internal factors); (b) self-serving bias, which contends that the teacher will accept responsibility for success and shift ownership of failure to the student; and (c) false consensus effect, which causes the teacher to foster a hegemonic view of her beliefs and behavior. Table 5.1 is an adaptation of the Common Attributional Biases table developed by Schunk et al. (2008, p. 89). The table provides further examples and explanations of the three aforementioned attributions.

Actor-Observer

The narrative reveals that the teacher's personal schemes about African-American children caused her to assume that the student's disposition would be a detrimental factor toward his success. Consequently, when the student 'failed' to amass the required points the teacher attributed the failure to his disposition, while supporting and defending her work as an effective instructor. Schunk et al. (2008) submit that "the propensity for

TABLE 5.1 Common Attributional Biases—Teacher Perspective

Attributions	Teacher Perspective
Actor-observer perspective Attribute others behavior to disposition, but own behavior to situation	Teacher perceives his behavior as a function or classroom, but attributes students behavior to disposition
Self-serving bias Accept personal responsibility for success, deny responsibility for failure	Teacher perceives her success as due to her behavior, but attributes her failure to other factors
False consensus effect Assume that your beliefs and behavior are typical of most people	Teacher assumes that her beliefs or behaviors are representative of most other teachers

individuals to make different attributions depends on their perspective as an actor in the situation or as an observer" (p. 90). In a classic case of bias, the teacher's observer perspective of the situation attributed the student's failure to his personal background and her actor behavior as a function of teacher integrity. Rather than collect more sources to validate the student's intellectual disposition, the teacher relied on her observer perspective to make a decision that negatively altered his academic progression. Since observers are not often privy to the beliefs, motives, thoughts, and feelings of others, it is instinctive to attribute behavior to a disposition as opposed to the situation (Schunk et al., 2008).

Self-Serving Bias

Self-serving bias refers to teachers' tendency to take credit for success and avoid blame for failure. In order to maintain self-preservation, the teacher denied any personal responsibility for the student's failure to progress into the advanced reading program. She evaluated her instruction and celebrated her ability to teach and was not able or willing to perceive whether her instructional methods hindered the needs of her new student. Schunk et al. (2008) contend that self-serving bias is an attempt to build fragile egos and low self-worth. In this era of accountability, it is common for teachers to avoid consequences of poor instruction by attributing failure to students' background, socioeconomic status, or learning styles. As a result of self-serving bias, teachers are likely to form flawed interpretations of students' abilities that will impact teacher behavior to act disapprovingly (Dobbs & Arnold, 2009). For example, the teacher in the narrative believed that the student was incapable of progressing to an advanced reading program. Thus, she attributed his three-point deficit as an indictment on his intellect. Had the teacher ascribed his anxiety, unfamiliarity with the instructional style, and social environment and then coupled this knowledge with his prior reading record, she might have treated the three-point deficit as a margin of error for a new student. Instead the teacher sought to preserve the self-perpetuated idea that she was an excellent teacher and the student had academic deficiencies.

False Consensus Effect

While any bias is detrimental to student and teacher success, the effect of false consensus, in our opinion is one of the most problematic. False consensus effect refers to an assumption that teachers engage in common behaviors based on similar circumstances (Schunk et al., 2008). When teachers confer with others who also have a deficit orientation, then the consensus of that group of teachers will be biased. Fiske and Taylor (1991) argue that teachers have a tendency to gravitate to like-minded individuals; they have a proclivity toward personal opinions and a disdain for divergent views, a penchant for linking new situations to previous beliefs and biases, and a psychological need to view personal beliefs as good, right, and common (as cited in Schunk et al., 2008). Therefore, it is important to include within teacher networks individuals with multiple and diverse perspectives. In an effort to modify attributions and challenge false consensus effects, meaningful experiences with diverse and contrary perspectives must occur so that teachers might gain multiple epistemologies about diverse others. Hopefully, these diverse perspectives will combat the idea that there are common behaviors for *all* teachers in certain situations.

TEACHER IMPACT: STUDENT VERVE

... students' ability to succeed. He was devastated and lost interest in reading. His grades slipped to below average in reading and other subjects. While he was normally a mild-mannered student he became increasingly agitated and withdrawn. He was sent to the office on numerous discipline violations ranging from not cooperating and completing his work to stubbornness and disrespect. Learning was no longer interesting for him. He had become what his teacher believed and expected him to be... a low achieving student. At the parent-teacher conference she explained to his father that she'd noticed a declined interest in reading, thus the drop in reading grades. The father was perplexed because at home his son was reading constantly. The father then encouraged her to move his son to the higher reading group. She agreed but only for a trial period of two weeks. With encouragement from home he began to show interest in school work and enjoyed the advanced books immensely. After two weeks ...

Low beliefs and expectations describe the teacher's perspective of the student in the narrative. Her lack of experience with his culture and a disregard for his learning style coupled with a deficit perspective prompted her to teach him from a biased lens. The results of her deficit thinking which informed her attributional biases were manifested in the student's behavior and grades. In fact, the narrative reveals that the teacher's deficit thinking produced low expectation and beliefs which, in turn, impacted the student and caused 'much anxiety.' Too often teachers unwittingly employ deficit thinking that perpetuate gender, race and socioeconomic bias (Hallinger, Bickman, & Davis, 1996; Kennedy, 1995; Leithwood, Begley, & Cousins, 1990; McLoyd, 1998; in Georgiou, 2008). Banks and Woolfson (2008) report studies that have supported the causal relationship between student attributions and academic performance. They further suggest that negative attributions from teachers are detrimental to a student's positive attributional development. Unfortunately, deficit-informed biases are often attributed solely to the student's disposition (Siwatu & Starker, 2010). In the narrative, the student's verve was negatively influenced as a result of deficit expectations and beliefs about his capacity to learn, thus his reaction mirrored the expectation and produced a negative manifestation. The concept and practical manifestation of 'what we expect is what we receive' has roots in ancient Greek mythology.

Ancient Greek mythology tells the story of a Cypriot sculptor who falls in love with his masterpiece, an ivory statue of the ideal woman. Pygmalion loved the statue so much that he believed and expected that it (she) would love him equally as much. So, he asked the gods to grant the statue life. The gods did and the statue (woman) did indeed love Pygmalion just as much as he loved her. In 1913 George Shaw pinned a play entitled Pygmalion where the expectations of the heroine paralleled her treatment. The idea that what we expect from others will be what we receive was the moral of these stories.

Rosenthal and Jacobson (1968) were the first to bring the Pygmalion effect into the classroom with their seminal study on elementary students and their teachers. The study used placebo methods concerning the intelligence of students. The placebo test was used to deceive teachers into believing that a randomly chosen group of children were intellectually progressive. The results showed that the randomly chosen students scored significantly more in reading than the control group. While the validity of the Pygmalion effect continues to be disputed, it has highlighted the importance of teacher expectations and beliefs about student ability (Feldman, 2007). Terms akin to teacher expectancy effect, self-fulfilling prophecy (Rosenthal, 2002), and expectation bias (Boer, Bosker, & Werf, 2010) also describe the phenomenon of low teacher expectations.

In the opening story, the teacher expects and believes that the student will not test into an advanced reading program, which, according to the Pygmalion effect (Boer et al., 2010; Rosenthal, 2002; Rosenthal & Jacobson, 1968), is a contributing factor in the student's test anxiety and results, loss of interest in reading, poor grades, and behavior. Teachers' impact on students' socioemotional and academic development is crucial for school success (Davis, 2001). Graham (1990) contended that when teachers "make attributions about a student's performance based on stereotypes their reactions can communicate these attributions to the student either directly or indirectly through emotional and behavioral cues" (as cited in Georgiou, 2008, p. 120). As a result, students are able to decipher teacher expectations and often internalize teacher beliefs and expectations as a reflection of their abilities or inabilities (Georgiou, 2008). Rosenthal (2002) describes this phenomenon as the Pygmalion effect where teacher beliefs of failure become internalized in students. Banks and Woolfson (2008) suggest that the progressive relationship of deficit thinking, attributional bias, and academic performance is most damaging when students internalize failure.

The narrative depicts a student who was confident in his academic ability until his negative experience in second grade. While he was not overtly labeled as learning disabled, he was clearly marginalized by the teacher. Children who are overtly or covertly labeled are less likely to experience a high degree of academic achievement due to deficit thinking and negative attributions (Banks & Woolfson, 2008). The story depicts a student who lost interest in reading and was viewed as a problem. His academic progression was directly linked to the classroom environment and teacher disposition. Though he continued to read at home (possibly because of expectations and beliefs about his intellect), his behavior and academics in school were opposite. Thus, his behavior and academic failure can be attributed to the expectation and belief of the teacher. If deficit thinking informs attributional biases, then the Pygmalion effect is not only the manifestation of these deficit biases but it also cages these perspectives on a perpetual merry-go-round.

TEACHER AWARENESS: CRITICAL REFLECTION

. . . she pondered why the African American student was doing better than the other gifted students, why her teaching didn't reveal his true cognitive ability, and why she so quickly dismissed her initial impression of his reading prowess. She reflected on a host of reasons. After deep reflection she concluded that many reasons for his success were contributed to his intelligence; reasons for the three-point deficit could be contributed to instructional practices, his anxiety, and newness to the school environment; and

reasons for her dismissal of his reading ability were contributed to her biased perspective of the ideal student.

In the final portion of the narrative, the teacher is forced to face the reality that her attributions about the student were faulty and detrimental. While research reports that all teachers participate in some sort of reflection (Zeichner, 1996, as cited in Hancock 2003), it is apparent that the teacher in the narrative underwent critical self-analysis. As a result of critical reflection, it is evident that the teacher grappled with deep personal beliefs, assumptions, and biases toward particular students. Schon (1983) contended that critical reflective practice acts to demand divergent competencies as well as deconstruct traditional perspectives of the ideal student (as cited in Hancock, 2003). In an effort to combat deficit thinking that fuels attributional bias and manifests as the Pygmalion effect, it is imperative that teachers participate in critical reflective practice.

Gay and Kirkland (2003) and Howard (2003) explain that it is important for teachers to know who they are as teachers and to develop the same awareness for the students they teach. Questioning personal assumptions and dismantling biases are imperative for teachers in all educational settings, especially urban classrooms. While it is believed that being self-reflective is a quality of a good teacher, teachers of diverse students especially must employ critical reflection methods. We have come to a time in education when teachers must critically reflect and purposefully act on what it means to be a multicultural educator. Critical reflective practice empowers teachers to combat personal beliefs, to reverse discrimination, to expose color-blind mentality, and counter status quo rationales. Hancock (2003) provides clear descriptions of critical reflective practice as he quotes:

- "Reflective teachers think deeply about what they are doing; reflective teachers are thoughtful, analytical, self-critical, and informed decision makers" (Hunt, Touzel, & Wiseman, 1999, p.6).
- Woolfolk (1998) suggested that "reflective teachers think back over situations to improve learning for their students" (p. 8).
- Schon (1983) concludes that reflective teaching is reflection-in-action which is an active process where teachers reflect on personal knowledge in an effort to discover limits and pursue growth (p. 82).

Critical reflection requires teachers to develop an affirming and fair knowledge base towards students of color in an effort to understand that students of color can be successful. As a result of critical reflection teachers should employ methods, dispositions and perceptions to successfully teach diverse students.

CONCLUSION

In an increasingly competitive and shrinking world, the American educational system can no longer tolerate the detrimental and demeaning biases that impact student achievement. While it is evident that numerous variables contribute to student success and failure, we believe that teacher bias is at the epicenter of student achievement. As such, it is imperative that deficit thinking, attributional bias, and the Pygmalion effect are addressed in an effort to advance discourse and awareness concerning teacher bias.

Any true and meaningful effort to address the detrimental beliefs and behaviors of teachers must start with critical reflective practice. We contend that unless teachers critical analyze personal assumptions and uninformed ideals, deficit thinking will become the prevailing perspective toward diverse others. Here we framed deficit thinking as the nexus of the dysfunctional relationship between the student and teacher in the narrative. Deficit thinking then fuels attributional biases by supporting and providing a capacity for actor-observer perspectives, self-serving bias and false consensus effect. The result of attributional biases form teacher expectations and beliefs concerning student success, which in turn impacts student behavior. In Figure 5.2, Deficit, Attributions, and the Pygmalion Effect, we show the successive nature of our claim.

Any genuine commitment to combatting the successive nature of teacher bias must start with critical reflective analysis. If teachers are to move beyond good intentions and pet curriculum, a concerted effort and engagement in deconstructing personal beliefs is necessary. Unless teachers address bias, there is little hope in the development of healthy academic relationships. Academic relationships are imperative to success; thus, these interactions can either improve outcomes or become a source of conflict and dysfunction. We contend that until teachers attend to deficit thinking, attributional biases, and the Pygmalion effect, there will likely be little progress on closing the achievement gap, developing healthy academic relationships and returning the American educational system to a place of high esteem and measured success.

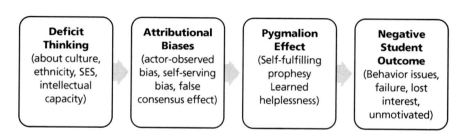

Figure 5.2 Deficit thinking, attributional bias, and Pygmalion effect.

REFERENCES

Banks, M., & Woolfson, L. (2008). Why do students think they fail? The relationship between attributions and academic self-perceptions. *British Journal of Special Education, 35*(1), 49–56.

Boer, H., Bosker, R. J., & Werf, M. P. C. (2010). Sustainability of teacher expectation bias effects on long-term student performance. *Journal of Educational Psychology, 102*(1), 168–179.

Byrnes, D., Kiger, G., & Manning, L. (1997). Teachers' attitudes about language diversity. *Teaching and Teacher Education, 13*(6), 637–644.

The Council of the Great City Schools. (n.d.). New study reveals how urban school districts boost student achievement, reduce racial disparities. Retrieved from http://www.cgcs.org/newsroom/press_release22.aspx

Davis, H. (2001). The quality and impact of relationships between elementary school students and teachers. *Contemporary Educational Psychology, 26*, 431–453.

Dobbs, J. & Arnold, D. (2009). Relationship between preschool teachers' reports of children's behavior and their behavior toward those children. *School Psychology Quarterly, 24*(2), 95–105.

Feldman, R. S. (2007). *Child development* (4th ed.). Upper Saddle River, NJ: Pearson.

Ford, D. (2007). Recruiting and retaining gifted students from diverse ethnic, cultural and language groups. In J. Banks & C. Banks (Eds.), *Multicultural education: Issues and perspectives* (6th ed., pp. 401–421). Hoboken, NJ: Wiley.

Gay, G., & Kirkland, K. (2003). Developing cultural critical consciousness and self reflection in preservice teacher education. *Theory into Practice, 42*(3), 181–187.

Georgiou, S. N. (2008). Beliefs of experienced and novice teachers about achievement. *Educational Psychology, 28*(2), 119–131.

Hancock, S. D. (2003). Balancing act: A reflective practice. In A. Green & L. Scott (Eds.), *Journey to the PhD: How to navigate the process as African Americans* (pp. 74–88). Sterling, VA: Stylus.

Hancock, S. D. (2006). White women's work: On the front lines of urban education. In J. Landsman & C. Lewis (Eds.), *White teachers/Diverse classrooms: A guide to building inclusive schools, promoting high expectations, and eliminating racism* (pp. 93–109). Sterling, VA: Stylus.

Howard, T.C. (2003). Culturally relevant pedagogy: Ingredients for critical teacher reflection. *Theory into Practice, 42*(3), 196–202.

Ladson-Billings, G. (2008). It's not the culture of poverty, it's the poverty of culture: The problem with teacher education. *Anthropology and Education Quarterly, 37*(2), 104–109.

Lewis, C.W., James, M., Hancock, S., & Hill-Jackson, V. (2008). Framing African American students' success and failure in urban settings. *Urban Education, 43*(2), 127–153.

Milner, H. R. (2006). But good intentions are not enough: Theoretical and philosophical relevance in teaching students of color. In J. Landsman & C. Lewis (Eds.), *White teachers/Diverse classrooms: A guide to building inclusive schools, promoting high expectations, and eliminating racism* (pp. 79–90). Sterling, VA: Stylus.

Rosenthal, R. (2002). The Pygmalion effect and its mediating mechanisms. In J. Aronson (Ed.), *Improving academic achievement: Impact of psychological factors on education.* San Diego, CA: Academic Press.

Rosenthal, R., & Jacobson, L. (1968). *Pygmalion in the classroom: Teacher expectation and pupils' intellectual development.* New York, NY: Holt, Rinehart, & Winston.

Schunk, D.H., Pintrich, P.R., Meece, J.L. (2008). *Motivation in education: Theory, research and applications.* Upper Saddle River, NJ: Pearson Education.

Siwatu, K.O., & Starker, T.V. (2010). Predicting preservice teachers' self-efficacy to resolve a cultural conflict involving an African American student. *Multicultural Perspectives. 12*(1), 10–17.

Storti, C. (1989). *The art of crossing cultures* (2nd ed.). Yarmouth, ME: Intercultural Press.

Tsigilis, N., Tsioumis, K., & Gregoriadis, A. (2006). Prospective early childhood educators' attitudes toward teaching multicultural classes: A planned behavior theory perspective. *Journal of Early Childhood Teacher Education, 27,* 265–273.

Van den Bergh, Denessen, Hornstra, Voeten, & Holland (2010). The implicit prejudice attitudes of teachers: Relations to teacher expectations and the ethnic achievement gap. *American Educational Research Journal, 47*(2), 497–527.

CHAPTER 6

GOING BEYOND PARENTAL INVOLVEMENT

Parent Perceptions of Teacher Support and Its Influence on the Achievement Outcomes of Urban African American High School Adolescents

DeMarquis Hayes
University of North Texas

ABSTRACT

Parental perceptions of home-based (HB) involvement, defined as parent–adolescent communication about school and learning, and teacher support (TS) were examined to determine if they were predictive of achievement outcomes (self-reported grades, school attendance, & discipline referrals received) in urban African American high school adolescents. The goals of the study were to determine if: (1) perceived TS significantly added to African American adolescents' achievement outcomes beyond the influence of HB involvement and (2) the interaction between HB involvement and TS better explained achievement outcomes. Results indicated that TS significantly

Yes We Can! Improving Urban Schools Through Innovative Educational Reform, pages 91–107
Copyright © 2011 by Information Age Publishing
91

added to the variance accounted for with all three achievement outcomes while none of the interaction effects were statistically significant. Implications of these findings and suggestions for future research are presented.

Despite academic gains over the last three decades, the achievement gap between low socioeconomic and ethnic/minority students and their White counterparts remains a persistent problem that warrants increased attention from parents, educators, and policymakers (National Center for Education Statistics, 2000a, 2000b; Perez-Johnson & Maynard, 2007). According to Lewis, James, Hancock, and Hill-Jackson (2008), nearly 90% of African American students attending urban schools in the 11 urban districts in the National Assessment of Educational Progress (NAEP) database were not meeting proficiency rates in reading and math. One way to address this persistent achievement gap has been to focus on increased parent involvement (Hill & Tyson, 2009) through initiatives such as the No Child Left Behind Act (NCLB, 2002). Parental involvement is conceptualized as the means by which parents support their children's education and development to ultimately provide a positive influence on their academic achievement and school adjustment (Hill et al., 2004; Suizzo & Stapleton, 2007). In a meta-analysis that examined the influence of parental involvement on the educational outcomes of urban secondary students, Jeynes (2007) found the positive effects of parental involvement held true for both White and minority students and concluded that parental involvement may reduce the achievement gap between White and some racial minority groups.

Another means to address this persistent achievement gap is to focus on characteristics of the school—particularly, the role teachers have in increasing the academic achievement of urban African American adolescents. According to Becker and Luthar (2002), students' perceptions of teacher support have been consistently linked with increased academic success and achievement motivation. They suggest that connections with teachers provide students with a sense of community that is needed to maximize student learning, motivation, and engagement. School connections have been found to be especially important for urban African American high school adolescents because school success depended on positive interactions with teachers despite many adolescents viewing these relationships to be nonexistent (Rosenbloom & Way, 2004).

A major issue when conceptualizing how parental involvement can help improve the achievement gap in urban African American adolescents deals with the multidimensionality of this construct (Epstein & Sanders, 2002). Parental involvement includes not only direct involvement in schools, such as volunteering in classrooms and attending school parent-teacher conferences, but also more home-based involvement, such as discussing school and family issues and conveying educational expectations (Epstein & Sanders, 2002; McWayne, Hampton, Fantuzzo, Cohen, & Sekino, 2004). It is important for parents and educators to focus on which specific aspects of parental involvement are most useful with urban African American high school adolescents. It is likely that certain forms of direct involvement (i.e., visiting teachers or helping with homework) decreases for high school adolescents as they seek to gain independence from their parents (Hill & Tyson, 2009).

HOME-BASED INVOLVEMENT

Some researchers have suggested that involvement at home, especially parents discussing school activities, has the strongest impact on academic achievement (Sui-Chu & Williams, 1996; VanVoorhis, 2003). If home-based involvement is a better predictor of achievement for urban African American adolescents, more research in this area is needed because many teachers often assume minority (African American and Hispanic) and low SES parents do not care about children's schooling if they do not engage in direct forms of school-based involvement (Auerbach, 2007). McNeal (1999) suggests that parent–child discussions (the extent to which parents and children regularly discussed education issues) had the greatest impact on the educational outcomes of African American and Caucasian adolescents. Even if direct parent involvement behaviors decrease over time, it is important to encourage African American parents to continue to engage in behaviors such as discussions about school with their adolescents in order to help them succeed. Although these behaviors are not visible by school personnel, they can still play a major role in the academic success of adolescents.

Shumow and Miller (2001) support this notion of parents engaging in behaviors that are not necessarily seen by teachers. Their results, although not focused entirely on African American adolescents, indicated that parents of struggling adolescents provided more help at home than did parents of successful students. This at-home help was described as parent–child contact that focused on the child's schooling. Although the decision to not become more directly engaged with the school environment may appear to be counterintuitive, DePlanty, Coulter-Kern, and Duchane (2007) suggested that even when parents wanted to become more involved at school they were not encouraged or felt that they did not have the support from the school to do so. In fact, in a sample of junior high teachers in a predominantly White community, teachers indicated that parents' presence at school was not important as long as parents emphasized the importance of education at home (DePlanty et al., 2007). Teachers in the DePlanty study reported that involvement at home was significantly more important than school or community involvement in affecting the academic achievement of adolescents.

TEACHER SUPPORT

Teacher support has generally been defined as the degree to which teachers listen to, encourage, and respect students (Brewster & Bowen, 2004). Stanton-Salazar (1997) suggests that support from teachers and other school personnel becomes even more important for ethnic minority students because of the perceived notion that such support is harder to obtain for minority students. Stanton-Salazar explained that difficulty in obtaining support from teachers was due to minority children not having the necessary training for effectively "decoding" the school culture on their own, thus creating barriers for opportunities to have long-term school success. Consequently, research has suggested that African American students are less likely to have positive relationships with their teachers than their Caucasian peers (Kesner, 2000; Saft & Pianta, 2001). As African American students perceive a continuous lack of support from teachers, they can become disengaged in school, which ultimately places them at greater risk for school failure.

The majority of studies examining the role of teachers in contributing to students' school success have focused primarily on elementary and early adolescents because of the perception that teacher–student relationships have the greatest impact during the early grades due to the declining importance of teachers as students get older (Furrer & Skinner, 2003; Hughes, Gleason, & Zhang, 2005). However, Tucker et al. (2002) found teacher involvement, defined as teachers caring for and taking an interest in students, was a significant predictor of academic engagement for low-income African American students across both the elementary and secondary grade levels. According to Davis and Dupper (2004), teachers underestimate the powerful impact their attitudes and beliefs have on student success. This is especially troublesome when teachers have expectations that economically disadvantaged and ethnic minority youth will perform more poorly academically when compared to their White counterparts (McKown & Weinstein, 2008). Teachers must recognize the important roles they play in the ultimate school success of minority and at-risk high school students in order to prevent school disengagement and potential school dropout.

THEORETICAL ORIENTATION

This study is grounded in an ecological theoretical perspective that views adolescents' development as influenced by factors within the child, such as gender and age, and by factors in their distal and proximal environments (Bronfenbrenner, 1979). Trotman (2001) offers that families, and in particular, parents, have the most direct environmental influence over children's and adolescents' educational process because they are the first and primary educators of their children. However, as students progress through school and seek to gain independence from their parents, teachers and school personnel have significantly increasing importance over the school success of high school adolescents (Slaughter-Defoe & Rubin, 2001). The first aim of the study examined if perceived teacher support significantly added to the achievement outcomes of urban African American high school adolescents beyond the influence of home-based involvement. It was hypothesized that perceived teacher support would impact the achievement outcomes of urban African American high school adolescents above that of parent-reported home-based involvement. Second, the study examined the interactive effects between home-based involvement and teacher support to determine if they better explained achievement outcomes in urban African American high school adolescents. It was also hypothesized that interaction effects between home-based involvement and teacher support would better predict achievement outcomes.

METHOD

Participants

Participants of this study consisted of 132 parents/guardians of urban African American high school adolescents from two large urban southwestern and southern cities in the United States. Seventy-four percent of the African American parents who participated in the study were mothers, and the remaining caregivers consisted of fathers (15%), grandmothers (8%), and other female relatives (i.e., aunts and great-grandmother, 3%). The adolescents ranged from 14 to 18 years of age and consisted of 75 boys (57%) and 57 girls (43%). Data from the southwestern city were comprised of 67 parents (75% mothers) from a large urban school district during summer school registration at a large mostly low-income to working class minority community. Parents who enrolled their students during summer school registration were used because approval for the current study was granted with one week remaining in the school year, which resulted in only 13 completed questionnaires. Therefore, summer school registration provided an opportunity to examine involvement from parents who had adolescents with potentially lower achievement outcomes than what would have otherwise been provided during the regular school year. Data from the southern city were composed of 65 parents (72% mothers) who attended a large, predominantly African American church with a congregation consisting of low-income to upper middle class members. At both sites, the researcher informed all of the parents about the study and allowed for all interested parties to withdraw from the study if they so desired. The rationale for allowing all parents at both sites the opportunity to participate in the study was to (1) increase the number of participants and (2) get a range of participants from various socioeconomic and educational backgrounds. Also, obtaining participants in two different cities allowed for a more heterogeneous sample of African American parents. The current study obtained parents from various backgrounds, as illustrated in Table 6.1. Over-

TABLE 6.1 Descriptive Statistics for African American Parents and their Adolescents

Variable	Southwestern City (67)	Southern City (65)	Total (132)
Parent Demographic Information			
Parent Education Mean (SD)	2.99 (1.14)	3.58 (.92)	3.28 (1.07)
Less than high school	6%	2%	4%
High school diploma	31%	6%	19%
Some College	36%	43%	39%
College degree	12%	31%	21%
Graduate/Professional degree	15%	18%	17%
Family Structure Mean (SD)	0.39 (.49)	0.55 (.50)	0.47 (.50)
Not married	61%	45%	53%
Married	39%	55%	47%
Family Income Mean (SD)	1.94 (.86)	2.14 (.81)	2.04 (.81)
Low ($0–$30K)	34%	26%	30%
Medium ($30K–$50K)	37%	34%	36%
High (> $50K)	29%	40%	34%
Reporting Parent Mean (SD)	1.41 (.77)	1.39 (.76)	1.43 (.79)
Mother	75%	72%	74%
Father	15%	16%	15%
Grandmother	7%	9%	8%
Other female relative	3%	3%	3%
Youth Demographic Information			
Grade Mean (SD)	2.25 (1.05)	2.43 (1.12)	2.34 (1.08)
9th	24%	25%	24%
10th	48%	32%	40%
11th	7%	18%	13%
12th	21%	25%	23%
Gender Mean (SD)	0.37 (.49)	0.49 (.50)	0.43 (.50)
Male	63%	51%	57%
Female	37%	49%	43%

all, 38% of the sample received a professional or college degree while only 23% completed high school or less. These scores differed significantly for the southwestern city (27% & 37%) and southern city (49% & 8%), respectively. In addition, more than half of the sample was not married (53%), and family income was almost evenly distributed between low, middle, and high incomes (30%, 36%, & 34%, respectively).

Procedure

The researcher obtained IRB approval from a participating university and permission from the school district, principal of the high school, and pastor of the church to work with parents for the current study. Once informed of the study, parents who agreed to participate completed a survey that not only provided family demographic information, but also assessed their level of involvement in their adolescents' lives and assessed their perceptions of their adolescents' school achievement. Two forms of recruitment were conducted to obtain a socially and economically diverse sample of ethnic minority parents. Parents from the southwestern city received information regarding the study during summer school registration. The researcher provided each parent with a brief handout that explained the study as they came into the school to register their child for summer school. Parents who agreed to participate completed the survey while they waited to finalize summer school enrollment for their adolescent. Parents from the southern city were recruited through a local church. The congregation was informed about the study at the beginning of service, and interested parties were asked to meet after the service to complete the survey.

Measures

Achievement Outcomes

Adolescent achievement outcomes were measured using parent perceptions of three variables: (1) grades, (2) days missed from school, and (3) behavioral problems at school. Grades were assessed by parental reports of the type of grades their adolescents received during the school year. This measure was based on an 8-point rating scale ranging from (1) student's grades were below D to (8) student's grades were mostly A. School attendance was assessed by parental reports of how many days of school their adolescents missed during the school year. This measure was based on a 6-point rating scale from (0) zero days absent from school to (5) 21 or more days absent from school. Finally, behavioral problems were assessed by parental reports of the number of school discipline referrals their adolescents received during the school year. This measure was based on a 6-point rating scale ranging from (0) zero discipline referrals to (5) 10 or more discipline referrals.

Parent-Reported Home-Based Involvement

Parents responded to six items assessing parental perceptions of parent-adolescent communication about school and learning. The parent reported home-based involvement measure was adapted from Trusty's (1999) measure of parent report and student report of home-based involvement. Results from principal components extraction and varimax rotation indicated that the items comprising Trusty's parent-reported home-based involvement had factor loadings ranging from .68 to .85, while items comprising the student-reported home-based involvement had factor loadings ranging from .65 to .76. For the current study, items from Trusty's parent-reported and student-reported home-based involvement were reworded to allow parents to report the frequency in which they engaged in all forms of home-based involvement activities based on a 5-point Likert scale ranging from: (1) never to (5) very often. Sample items include, "Talk to your child about school experiences" and "Know how your child is doing in school." The current study yielded a Cronbach's alpha coefficient of 0.84 for parent-reported home-based involvement.

Parent-Perceived Teacher Support

Parents were asked to respond to three items assessing teacher support. The perceived teacher support subscale assessed the degree to which parents perceived their adolescents' teachers as caring about their child's academic achievement. This measure was originally developed by Hayes and Cunningham (2003) to assess adolescents' perceptions of the level of support provided by teachers. Reliability analysis from the Hayes and Cunningham study yielded a Cronbach's alpha coefficient of 0.65 for perceived teacher support. For the current study, items were reworded to allow parents to report their perceptions of teacher support for their adolescents on a 5-point Likert scale ranging from: (1) strongly disagree to (5) strongly agree. Sample item includes, "My child's teacher really cares about him/her." The current study yielded a Cronbach's alpha coefficient of 0.63 for parent perceived teacher support.

Demographic Variables

Demographic information about parents and students were also collected. Parents reported on their child's grade (9th–12th grade), gender, and on their family structure (e.g., married vs. unmarried) and income.

Data Analysis

The relation between parent-perceived home-based involvement, teacher support, and achievement outcomes were measured using a series of hierarchical linear regressions (Cohen & Cohen, 1983). Three hierarchical regression analyses examined the relation between parent reported home-based involvement, parent perceived teacher support, and adolescents' achievement outcomes. Although part of the initial hypothesis, analysis showing the interaction between parent perceived home-based involvement and teacher support were not included in the analysis due to a lack of significance in predicting the achievement outcomes of adolescents.

RESULTS

Preliminary and exploratory analyses determined that the two groups that comprised the overall sample had equal variance on all but two of the examined variables. Specifically, results from Levene's Test for Equality of Variance indicated that parents from southern city reported statistically significant higher levels of education than the parents from the southwestern city ($F(1, 130) = 4.31$, $p < .05$). Further, parents from the southwestern city were more likely to have adolescent boys than did the parents from the southern city ($F(1, 130) = 4.36$, $p < .05$). However, the two groups were combined because there were no significant differences found in adolescents' achievement outcomes, parent-reported home-based involvement, or perceived teacher support.

Descriptive Information on Study Variables

Bivariate correlations for the examined variables are displayed in Table 6.2. As expected, a statistically significant correlation between parent reported home-based involvement and adolescents' grades ($r = .28$, $p \leq .001$), school attendance ($r = -.30$, $p \leq .001$), and discipline problems ($r = -.18$, $p \leq .05$) were found. In addition, a statistically significant correlation between perceived teacher support and adolescents' grades ($r = .41$, $p \leq .001$), school attendance ($r = -.26$, $p \leq .01$), and discipline problems ($r = -.32$, $p \leq .001$) were also found. These results suggest that as parents' home-based involvement and perceived teacher support increased, adolescents' school achievement also improved. Also, the only demographic variable that had a statistically significant relation with parent-reported home-based involvement, perceived teacher support, and adolescent outcomes was the grade level of adolescents. As students progressed through high school, parents reported lower levels of home-based involvement ($r = -.19$, $p \leq .05$), increased levels of teacher support ($r = .22$, $p \leq .05$), and increased grades ($r = .18$, $p \leq .05$).

TABLE 6.2 Correlation Coefficients, Means, and Standard Deviations of Examined Variables (*N* = 132)

Variables	Mean	SD	1	2	3	4	5	6	7	8	9
1. Grade level	2.34	1.08	—	.19	−.07	−.09	−.19ᵃ	.22ᵇ	.18ᵃ	−.01	−.04
2. Adolescent gender	.43	.50		—	−.18ᵃ	−.08	.04	.02	.12	−.03	−.05
3. Family structure	.47	.50			—	.39ᶜ	−.02	−.01	−.03	−.11	.14
4. Family income	2.04	.81				—	.04	.07	.10	−.16	.14
5. Home-based inv	4.37	.58					—	.32ᶜ	.28ᶜ	−.30ᶜ	−.18ᵃ
6. Teacher support	3.59	.84						—	.41ᶜ	−.26ᵇ	−.32ᶜ
7. Grades	5.13	1.48							—	−.32ᶜ	−.15
8. School attendance	1.02	.60								—	.27ᵇ
9. Discipline problems	.65	.72									—

ᵃ = $p \le .05$; ᵇ = $p \le .01$; ᶜ = $p \le .001$

Regression Analyses Predicting Achievement Outcomes

Three regression analyses were examined to determine the most important predictors of grades, school attendance, and discipline referrals within a sample of urban African American high school adolescents. Table 6.3 presents the results of each regression analysis and contains the variables entered at each step, the percentage of variance accounted for at each step, the amount of change in R^2 at each step, and the standardized weights for the predictor variables based on the final step of the regression equation.

For grades, the overall model was significant $(F [6, 125] = 6.21, p \le .001)$. In the first step of the regression equation, none of the demographic variables made a significant contribution in predicting adolescents' grades and only accounted for 6% of the variance. When home-based involvement was added in the second step of the regression equation, the amount of variance accounted for significantly increased to 16%. Finally, when teacher support was added in the third step of the regression equation, it also resulted in a significant increase in the percentage of variance accounted for in the model (23%). Results from the final regression equation indicate that African American parents who perceived higher teacher support for their adolescents and reported engaging in greater communication with their adolescents about school and learning were more likely to report their adolescents had higher levels of academic achievement.

The overall model predicting school attendance among urban African American high school adolescents was significant $(F[6, 125] = 3.60, p \le .01)$. In the first step of the regression equation, none of the demographic variables made a significant contribution in predicting adolescents' school attendance and only accounted for 3% of the variance. When home-based

TABLE 6.3 Hierarchical Linear Regression Predicting Achievement Outcomes (N = 132)

Variable	Grades				School Attendance				Discipline Referrals			
	R² (ΔR²)	B	SE B	β*	R² (ΔR²)	B	SE B	β*	R² (ΔR²)	B	SE B	β*
Step 1	.06				.03				.03			
Grade		.20	.12	.14		-.02	.05	-.03		.02	.06	.03
Gender		.24	.24	.08		-.05	.10	-.04		-.02	.13	-.02
Family Structure		-.11	.26	-.04		-.10	.11	-.08		.12	.13	.08
Family Income		.19	.16	.10		-.08	.07	-.11		.12	.08	.14
Step 2	.16 (.10)				.12 (.09)				.07 (.04)			
Home-Based Inv		.53	.22	.21ᵃ		-.26	.10	-.25ᵇ		-.10	.12	-.08
Step 3	.23 (.07)				.15 (.03)				.14 (.07)			
Teacher Support		.53	.15	.30ᶜ		-.12	.07	-.17		-.26	.08	-.31ᶜ
Entire Model	$F(6, 125) = 6.21^c$				$F(6, 125) = 3.60^b$				$F(6, 125) = 3.41^b$			

* Standardized regression weights for the final equation after all predictors were entered.

ᵃ = $p \leq .05$; ᵇ = $p \leq .01$; ᶜ = $p \leq .001$

involvement was added in the second step of the regression equation the amount of variance accounted for significantly increased to 12%. Finally, when teacher support was added in the third step of the regression equation the amount of variance accounted for in the model did not significantly increase (15%). Results from the final regression equation indicate that African American parents who reported engaging in greater communication with their adolescents about school and learning were more likely to report their adolescents missed fewer days of school.

Finally, the overall model predicting school discipline referrals received among urban African American high school adolescents was significant $(F[6, 125] = 3.41, p \leq .01)$. In the first step of the regression equation, none of the demographic variables made a significant contribution in predicting adolescents' discipline referrals and only accounted for 3% of the variance. When home-based involvement was added in the second step of the regression equation the amount of variance accounted for significantly increased to 7%, but did not appear to be a significant predictor of adolescents' discipline referrals. Finally, when teacher support was added in the third step of the regression equation, it resulted in a statistically significant increase in the percentage of variance accounted for in the model and was a significant predictor of discipline referrals (14%). Results from the final regression equation indicate that African American parents who perceived higher teacher support for their adolescents were more likely to report that their adolescents had fewer behavioral problems at school requiring discipline referrals.

DISCUSSION

The results of the current study provide support for the central hypothesis that perceived teacher support significantly added to the amount of variance accounted for when predicting the achievement outcomes of urban African American high school adolescents even after considering the impact of home-based involvement. However, the hypothesis of significant interactions between home-based involvement and perceived teacher support was not supported. According to Slaughter-Defoe and Rubin (2001), parents are not solely responsible for children and adolescents' early achievements and later educational goal setting. They suggest that by adolescence, parents have less influence over students' actual expectations for educational attainment than do teachers. However, parents and the home environment continue to play a significant role in the academic lives of adolescents by serving as educational role models. The findings in the current study appear to support this research because African American parents' perceived levels of teacher support significantly predicted adolescents' grades and school discipline referrals. With respect to school attendance, parent-reported home-based involvement was the only significant predictor. Overall, these findings indicate that urban African American parents perceive teachers as taking bigger roles in achievement areas most related to the school context. However, parents maintain a belief that their efforts are important in ensuring that their adolescents attend school in order to benefit from their teachers.

Results of the current study also suggest that even if parents do not perceive teachers as supportive, parents perceive that they can continue to help their adolescents achieve during the high school years when they engage in frequent parent–adolescent communications about school and learning. The importance of frequent communication between parents and adolescents about school is consistent with the work of other researchers who have reported greater benefits from parents engaging in meaningful discussion about school with adolescents as opposed to utilizing other school-directed parental involvement behaviors (Jeynes, 2005; Trusty, 1999). Therefore, parental involvement that takes place in the home and focuses on parent–student communication regarding school and education appear to better help urban African American high school adolescents succeed in school even as students attempt to gain greater independence from their parents and teachers become increasingly more necessary for direct school performance.

As for discipline referrals, it is not surprising that home-based involvement was not a significant predictor of this achievement outcome. Discipline referrals are often the result of a one-on-one interaction between students and teachers. According to Brewster and Bowen (2004), teacher support was more important in the prediction of problem behavior in middle and high school adolescents than was parental support. The current findings offer greater support for their research because parents also perceived the greater importance of teacher support in predicting behavioral problems at school.

LIMITATIONS AND SUGGESTIONS FOR FUTURE RESEARCH

There are several limitations of this research. First, this study relied solely on parent perceptions of home-based involvement, teacher support, and adolescents' achievement outcomes. Parents may not fully be able to accurately decipher how much support teachers provided their high school adolescents. In addition, reports of student outcomes may not be as accurate as objective records. Second, the small sample size leads to questions of how the current results can be generalized to a more diverse subsection of African American families. Third, parents who chose to participate in the current study inherently may have engaged in greater parent–adolescent conversations or responded to questions in a more socially desirable manner. Finally, the current study relied on cross-sectional data at only one time point, which inherently poses limitations on the predictability of variables of interest.

Future studies need to gather information concerning parental involvement and teacher support from multiple sources (parents, students, and teachers) to get a better sense of whether different perceptions from various individuals exist. Second, larger longitudinal studies that collect actual student outcome data can better examine how perceptions of home-based involvement and teacher support relate to the achievement outcomes high school adolescents over time. This will also allow for a more diverse group of parents who are randomly selected to help eliminate the possibility that only parents with inherently high levels of involvement are the only participants in the study.

IMPLICATIONS FOR IMPROVING URBAN SCHOOLS

Parents' perceptions of the importance of teacher support on the school success of urban African American high school adolescents highlights the need for schools and families to improve their communication and engage in better collaboration to improve the overall achievement of urban African American adolescents. Too often, the home and school environments place blame on the other for the failures of urban African American adolescents. However, the current study suggests that parents and schools share a common responsibility in helping urban adolescents achieve at school. High school teachers need to realize that parents value their contribution and perceive them as playing a significant role in the school success of their adolescents. However, a positive collaborative relationship cannot begin if schools value only direct forms of involvement (i.e., parents participating in school events, meetings, or organizations). It is more likely that during the high school years, parents will engage primarily in involvement that may not be present at school (i.e., engaging in meaningful conversations with their adolescents about school) but can still significantly contributes to the success of their adolescents. African American parents must recognize that they continue to positively impact the achievement outcomes of their adolescents when they engage in parent–adolescent communication about school and learning. Overall, both parents and teachers ultimately want adolescents to succeed even if they view success as developing from different behaviors or have different views on how to accomplish this goal. Greater communication between parents, adolescents, and teachers can help improve student outcomes and increase collaboration between home and school. It is acknowledged that engaging in greater home–school communication at the high school level can be more difficult due to the multiple teachers each student has and the large number of students each teacher is responsible for throughout a school day. However, both parents and teachers must be willing to make changes in their normal routines if ensuring the success of African American adolescents is of the utmost importance. Specific suggestions include:

- Parents, help prevent teachers from having lowered expectations for African American adolescents by engaging in positive dialogue with teachers early in the school year about your own expectations for your child
- Parents, encourage your child to seek assistance from teachers to improve their academic outcomes
- Parents, engage in daily conversations with your adolescents about school and what they are learning
- Teachers, make it easier to engage in more frequent and positive communication with African American parents about your expectations and how you can help their adolescents succeed
- Teachers, express these same expectations to African American students and provide them with opportunities to seek additional assistance if needed
- Teachers, make sure African American students feel supported and respected in your classroom
- African American adolescents should be informed about the frequent communication between their parents and teachers regarding their academic progress so they are aware of the collaborative effort to ensure their success

REFERENCES

Auerbach, S. (2007). From moral supporters to struggling advocates: Reconceptualizing parent roles in education through the experience of working-class families of color. *Urban Education , 42*, 250–283.

Becker, B. E., & Luthar, S. S. (2002). Social-emotional factors affecting achievement outcomes among disadvantaged students: Closing the achievement gap. *Educational Psychologist, 37*, 197–214.

Brewster, A. B., & Bowen, G. L. (2004). Teacher support and the school engagement of Latino middle and high school students at risk of school failure. *Child and Adolescent Social Work Journal, 21*, 47–67.

Bronfenbrenner, U. (1979). *The ecology of human development.* Cambridge, MA: Harvard University press.

Cohen, J., & Cohen, P. (1983). *Applied multiple regression/correlation analysis for the behavioral sciences* (2nd Ed). Hillsdale, NJ: Erlbaum.

Davis, K. S., & Dupper, D. R. (2004). Student–teacher relationships: An overlooked factor in school dropout. *Journal of Human Behavior in the Social Environment, 9*, 179–193.

DePlanty, J., Coulter-Kern, R., & Duchane, K. A. (2007). Perceptions of parent involvement in academic achievement. *The Journal of Educational Research, 100,* 361–368.

Epstein, J. L., & Sanders, M. G. (2002). Family, school, community partnerships. In M. H. Bornstein (Ed.), *Handbook of parenting, Vol. 5: Practical issues in parenting* (pp. 407–437). Mahwah, NJ: Erlbaum.

Furrer, C., & Skinner, E. (2003). Sense of relatedness as a factor in children's academic engagement and performance. *Journal of Educational Psychology, 95,* 148–162.

Hayes, D., & Cunningham, M. (2003). Family and school environments working together to impact academic achievement in African American adolescents. In C. C. Yeakey & R. Henderson (Eds.), *Surmounting all odds: Education, opportunity, and society in the new millennium* (pp. 107–123). Greenwich, CT: Information Age Publishing.

Hill, N. E., Castelliono, D. R., Lansford, J. E., Nowlin, P., Dodge, K. A., Bates, J. E., & Petit, G. S. (2004). Parental academic involvement as related to school behavior, achievement, and aspirations. Demographic variations across adolescence. *Child Development, 75,* 1491–1509.

Hill, N. E., & Tyson, D. F. (2009). Parental involvement in middle school: A meta-analytic assessment of the strategies that promote achievement. *Developmental Psychology, 45,* 740–763.

Hughes, J. N., Gleason, K. A., & Zhang, D. (2005). Relationship influences on teachers' perceptions of academic competence in academically at-risk minority and majority first grade students. *Journal of School Psychology, 43,* 303–320.

Jeynes, W. H. (2005). Effects of parental involvement and family structure on the academic achievement of adolescents. *Marriage and Family Review, 37,* 99–116.

Jeynes, W. H. (2007). The relationship between parental involvement and urban secondary school student academic achievement: A meta-analysis. *Urban Education, 42,* 82–110.

Kesner, J. E. (2000). Teacher characteristics and the quality of child–teacher relationships. *Journal of School Psychology, 38,* 133–149.

Lewis, C. W., James, M., Hancock, S., & Hill-Jackson, V. (2008). Framing African American students' success and failures in urban settings: A typology for change. *Urban Education, 43,* 127–153.

McKown, C., & Weinstein, R. S. (2008). Teacher expectations, classroom context, and the achievement gap. *Journal of School Psychology, 46,* 235–261.

McNeal, R. B. (1999). Parental involvement as social capital: Differential effectiveness on science achievement, truancy, and dropping out. *Social Forces, 78,* 117–144.

McWayne, C., Hampton, V., Fantuzzo, J., Cohen, H., & Sekino, Y. (2004). A multivariate examination of parent involvement and the social and academic competencies of urban kindergarten children. *Psychology in the Schools, 41,* 363–377.

National Center for Education Statistics. (2000a). *The condition of education.* Washington, DC: Office of Educational Research and Improvement, U.S. Department of Education.

National Center for Education Statistics. (2000b). *National Assessment Educational Process (NAEP), 1999 long term trend assessment.* Washington, DC: Office of Educational Research and Improvement, U.S. Department of Education.

No Child Left Behind Act of 2001, Pub. L. No. 107-110, 114 Stat. 1425 (2002). Retrieved from http://www.ed.gov/ploicy/elsec/leg/esea02/107-110.pdf

Perez-Johnson, I., & Maynard, R. (2007). The case for early, targeted interventions to prevent academic failure. *Peabody Journal of Education, 82,* 587–616.

Rosenbloom, S. R., & Way, N. (2004). Experiences of discrimination among African American, Asian American, and Latino adolescents in an urban high school. *Youth and Society, 35,* 420–451.

Saft, E. W., & Pianta, R. C. (2001). Teachers' perceptions of their relationships with students: Effects of child age, gender, and ethnicity of teachers and children. *School Psychology Quarterly, 16,* 125–141.

Shumow, L., & Miller, J. D. (2001). Parents' at-home and at-school academic involvement with young adolescents. *Journal of Early Adolescence, 21,* 68–91.

Slaughter-Defoe, D. T., & Rubin, H. H. (2001). A longitudinal case study of Head Start eligible children: Implications for urban education. *Educational Psychologist, 36,* 31–44.

Stanton-Salazar, R. D. (1997). A social capital framework for understanding the socialization of racial minority children and youths. *Harvard Educational Review, 67,* 1–40.

Sui-Chu, E. S., & Williams, J. D. (1996). Effects of parent involvement on eighth-grade achievement. *Sociology of Education, 69,* 126–141.

Suizzo, M. A., & Stapleton, L. M. (2007). Home-based parental involvement in young children's education: Examining the effects of maternal education across U.S. ethnic groups. *Educational Psychology, 27,* 533–556.

Trotman, M. F. (2001). Involving the African American parent: Recommendations to increase the level of parent involvement in African American families. *Journal of Negro Education, 70,* 275–285.

Trusty, J. (1999). Effects of eighth-grade parental involvement on late adolescents' educational expectations. *Journal of Research and Development in Education, 32,* 224–233.

Tucker, C. M., Zayco, R. A., Herman, K. C., Reinke, W. M., Trujillo, M., Carraway, K., & Ivery, P. D. (2002). Teacher and child variables as predictors of academic engagement among low-income African American children. *Psychology in the Schools, 39,* 477–488.

VanVoorhis, F. L. (2003). Interactive homework in middle school: Effect on family involvement and students' science achievement. *The Journal of Educational Research, 96,* 323–339.

PART II

EMPOWERING URBAN STUDENTS AND
TRANSFORMING THEIR SCHOOLS

Section 2: Culturally Responsive Pedagogies and
Curriculum for Urban School Reform

CHAPTER 7

BEYOND LIP SERVICE

Engaging Young African American Men in a Single-Gender Urban School

Ryan Vernosh and Julie Landsman

We constantly hear about high expectations. We hear about relationships with students at every training session where we fervently seek ways to make schools places of equity and possibility. Ryan Vernosh, a teacher at Maxfield School in St. Paul, Minnesota, has been struggling with these abstract concepts in concrete and meaningful ways—ways that connect to the culture and the real lives of his students. The following chapter is Ryan's understanding of what it means to be a culturally competent educator. He is a White male teaching in a single-gendered class comprised of male students of color. His self-reflections and observations are real, although students mentioned in the narrative are only identified by pseudonyms. Here is Ryan's story.

"...But you turned your back on me!"

"No, I walked away to help someone else. Our conversation was over, so I went to someone else."

Yes We Can! Improving Urban Schools Through Innovative Educational Reform, pages 111–125

"...But you still turned your back on me!"

"Kevin, I did not turn my back on you."

As educators, we are engaged in continual dialogue with our students. Of all these conversations, this was one of the most difficult of the year. It also had the greatest impact on me and ultimately Kevin's school year, as well. Here is how it unfolded:

Earlier that day Kevin and I had a conversation about the behavior choices he had made and how these resulted in his inability to complete his school work. Kevin consistently chose to act out with other students and engage in bullying behavior, neglecting the academic tasks at hand. During our conversation, Kevin didn't have much to say. He chose not to respond to my questions or my expressed concern for him. I asked if he had anything he wanted to share with me. I waited for a few minutes, but still he was silent. I assumed this silence signaled the end of our conversation, so I turned to work with another group of students. When I did this, Kevin became very upset, as indicated in the excerpt above. He ultimately spent most of the afternoon outside of our classroom community and in the office of Ms. Pierce, our cultural competence counselor.

After school, I met with Kevin, his mother, and Ms. Pierce to process the day's events. I had not expected it to be such a difficult conversation for me. Given that I pride myself on building relationships and recognizing the importance of cultural relevancy in my daily actions and dialogue with my students, I walked into the conference assuming we would focus on what *Kevin* needed to do to make positive choices in class. Although our counselor had encouraged me to stop and really listen, it was even harder to articulate how Kevin's words made me feel. The most difficult part of the conference was when Ms. Pierce asked me to step inside Kevin's shoes. Here was a young Black man whose father lived in another state and a White teacher who had turned his back on him in class. Ms. Pierce asked me to ponder what that might represent. Additionally, here was a young man who felt he let his mother down through his inappropriate classroom behavior. He was also a boy, a young child in some ways, who simply missed his father's presence in his life. This was challenging to me. It was an instance that I was oblivious to how my White skin color might come across to Kevin and how the most subtle body language can cause a rift in relationships.

Also, because I reflect daily about whiteness and how it impacts my teaching, it felt especially hard to realize that I let White privilege essentially blind me in my own classroom conversation with Kevin. When I realized this, it allowed all of us to proceed more productively in our discussion, and Kevin felt as though he finally had a voice. As difficult as this conversation was for both of us, it served as a springboard for the rest of a very successful year together.

BACKGROUND

I am in a unique position in our school. I teach a class of 6th graders who are all male students of color. I am the only White person in the classroom everyday. For me, reflecting and continually learning about whiteness and its effects on my teaching and communication with my students is essential to my growth as an educator.

The single-gender classroom concept came about at our school through the students' own initiative. During the 2004–05 school year, a year before I began teaching at Maxfield, the sixth graders engaged in a feature article genre study for Reader's and Writer's Workshop. Several students researched and then wrote an article about single-gendered classrooms. The students became intrigued with the idea of separating girls and boys into different classroom environments. They argued that it might help some of the challenges facing the unique adolescent stages that sixth graders were entering into. With encouragement from a teacher, these students discussed this possibility with the principal, Zelma Wiley. After considering the students' voice, Ms. Wiley not only considered the idea, she decided to research the concept in more depth. Later, she brought the idea to the Site Council, who, in turn, approved the concept for that campus. The following year, Maxfield began this single-gendered classroom experiment. It continues to this day.

A LOOK INTO THE LITERATURE

The main purported advantage of single-sex classrooms is an increase in academic achievement, as evidenced by an increase in test scores (Cable & Spradlin, 2008). This advantage was a reality at Thurgood Marshal Elementary in Seattle, Washington. An investigation of academic performance of this school revealed that the overall campus standardized test scores were some of the lowest in all of the state. After the principal implemented single-gendered classrooms, the test scores of males on the state standardized reading assessment increased from the 10th percentile to the 66th percentile. The females made similar progress. In the year prior to single-gendered classrooms, the passing rate for females on the same assessment in math was 0%. After moving to single-gendered classrooms, 53% of females passed this exam (Sax, 2005).

AVENUES OF LEARNING

A portion of the academic successes found in single-gendered classrooms are attributed to a difference in learning styles between males and females

(Gurian & Stevens, 2005). There is a perceived notion that males tend to be more kinesthetic learners. Many males are often on the move, tapping a pencil or foot while reading, or simply moving around in search of avenues to release energy to better focus on instruction. The logic appears to be that instruction in an all-male classroom can be set up in a manner where males can be more active without being a distraction to the girls, allowing both genders increased opportunity to focus on the lessons being taught. The traditional image of students sitting still in a classroom with their hands politely folded on their desks is not a bad image per se, but it creates dissonance with the way that many males' minds work (Gurian & Stevens, 2005).

CURRICULAR RESOURCES

Proponents of single-gendered education opportunities also offer curricular resources and materials as a potential reason for increased academic achievement. Data indicate that males tend to perform lower than their female counterparts in reading comprehension (Chudowsky & Chudowsky, 2010). The reason for this disparity in performance might be linked to feelings of alienation from traditional literary experiences, rather than lack of sheer ability. Male-oriented reading curriculum that is centered around males being the main characters and includes issues that are important and more relevant to their gender might be a major component to closing this gender gap (Tatum, 2005). In addition, nonfiction story lines that challenge male learners to learn something new are critical components of any gender-specific curriculum. Lastly, texts should support males' life experiences and include examples of how boys view themselves to increase literacy engagement and improve their desire to read (Tatum, 2005). These gender-specific characteristics in curriculum can also hold true for females.

SCHOOL BEHAVIOR

Another advantage of same-sex education is an increase in appropriate school behavior. Schools who use this model claim dramatic decreases in office referrals, especially in the intermediate grades. Proponents offer that this is due to an increased focus of gender-specific curriculum as well as a reduction in social anxiety issues that often accompany puberty (Holleran, 2007).

CRITICAL OPINIONS

There are also opponents of single-sex education who claim that single-gen-dered classrooms offer no statistically relevant improvement in academic achievement (Cable & Spradlin, 2008). A study conducted by the United States Department of Education (2005) comparing single gender and coed-ucational schooling revealed that there appear to be no drastic differences in the academic achievement (i.e., test scores) between single-gender and coeducational classrooms.

Even further, critics of single-gender education question the movement's legality. The American Civil Liberties Union opposes all single-sex public education on the basis of Title IX (Weil, 2008). In 2002, the federal gov-ernment began revising aspects of Title IX to make it easier for schools to adopt single-sex policies (Okoye-Johnson, 2008). Additionally, opponents also cite Brown vs. Board of Education of Topeka, Kansas (1954) in their claim that racially segregated schools are inherently unequal. The logic is that if separation based on race provides an unequal educational setting, the same must be said for the separation of students based on gender.

DEFINING SUCCESS IN URBAN EDUCATION

It is my belief that many of the aspects of single-gendered classrooms are absent from the literature. As a result, I offer a glimpse into my own classroom to allow readers to conclude for themselves the benefits of this classroom arrangement. I focus on issues relevant to urban education—male role models and the need to work with young men and women to establish their academic and social identities. It is my deep personal belief that an effective teacher will reach students no matter what the context. However, being a teacher in a single-gender classroom offers me unique opportunities every day to create curriculum experiences and facilitate conversations that are uniquely geared towards creating young men who are successful both in and out of the confines of school. This experience allows me to create an environment of cultural competence, provide a safe place where my students can share their life experiences, deconstruct their gender identity, and examine their predisposed beliefs of male roles in the 21st century. In addition, this environment allows adolescent males to examine their beliefs about expressing emotion and role-play examples of how to respect the opposite gender.

Creating an Environment Through Cultural Competence

I strive to create a classroom of brotherhood. It is my belief that for a learning community to thrive, the teacher and the students must all feel interconnected and willing to support and challenge each other. In order to foster this, I set the stage by referring to each of the young men in my classroom as "brother"—Brother Marquees or Brother Tou. If, during a lesson, there are side conversations occurring, I redirect by saying, "Brother Tou has the floor right now and we need to honor him by listening." Eventually students begin calling down their peers who are disrespectfully talking by proclaiming, "Kevin, let Brother Kaveon talk!"

I've actually been challenged by my students of color for using this term so freely. Some students were concerned with a White teacher referring to Black students as their brother. This concern led to a great conversation about digging deeper into the multiple meanings of brother and brotherhood. As a result, the tipping point in the dialogue came when one student connected our sense of brotherhood to Adam and Eve, saying that were all brothers in God's eyes. This theological perspective convinced those uncomfortable with the term that it was, indeed, acceptable.

One of my favorite comments pertaining to the brotherhood in my class came from a student who enjoyed challenging authority. He shared openly that our class was like a fraternity, and related it to the one his uncle shares with his college colleagues. In turn, he announced, "That's what this class is like. If it's cool for my uncle, then it's cool for me." Our classroom brotherhood goes much deeper than referring to each other as brothers. The community that we have built is based on brotherly trust and respect.

Sharing Life Experiences

To create and sustain our community trust, we begin each day with a morning meeting. As a guide for our meetings, I use the approach from the Responsive Classroom (Kreite, 2002). This meeting represents ritual and routine. It gives consistency to our day and creates a sense of order. During these meetings, I often plan group activities to create a community of learners. These activities often center around building skills of self-control, empathy, responsibility, and honesty. Additionally, we practice team-building skills that will aid these students to be successful team members not only in our classroom community, but in the real world as well.

The most meaningful component of our morning meetings is that of sharing. Although I have modified it from the curriculum offered by Responsive Classroom, my approach has been wildly successful. During this time, I invite every student to share. Much of their sharing is mundane—the purchase of a new video game or their opinions about the most recently released movie. However, the power of real sharing becomes evident when students are comfortable enough to share not only their triumphs, but their heartaches as well. It is during these times of sharing that we discover many things about families being split, students losing their homes due to eviction, and loved ones' incarceration due to breaking the law. These are challenges that often wreak havoc on students' ability to learn. Surprisingly, the potential educational upheaval is relieved when students feel safe enough to share these things within our classroom walls. It is during this time that students look to each other for support and guidance and share simply to get things off their chest. It is during this time that all of us can allow our defenses to dwindle and reveal true and honest emotions about the events of our lives. I find this sharing experience especially essential because in many cultures from which my students come, true emotion is often taught and expected to be bottled up and never shared, especially in front of females.

Deconstructing Gender Identity

In my first year of teaching, one of my first-grade students witnessed me accidentally hitting my head on a cupboard door. After my eyes filled with tears due to the unexpected pain, this student said, "Ah, suck it up Mr. Vernosh. Be a man!" That experience and comment has forever been ingrained in my mind. "Be a man." What exactly did that mean? What does it mean to be a man with male privilege? What does it mean to be a White man teaching students of color? What does it mean to be a Black man in an institutionally racist school society? These are questions that many educators shy away from. As a result, they perpetuate the cycle of racism and sexism. Rather than retreat from these complex questions, I use these as the basis for ongoing conversation and curriculum development about manhood in a variety of contexts.

We are surrounded by media images of what it means to be a man. These images emphasize that men should always be physically tough. Sometimes these images even imply or directly portray that it is acceptable to be disrespectful to women. Consequently, young men learn from this media influence that men must develop and maintain a stance of being stoic and unemotional. These are the most powerful male stereotypes that come in the door with my students. They have been exposed to them day and night.

Redefining Male Stereotypes and Examining Machismo

Many of my students portray a sense of machismo, consistently proving their self-worth by trying to show how tough or aggressive they can be. This is evident by the numbers of fights and arguments that break out during the first month of the school year. Rather than dismiss these fights, I choose to dissect them and get to the real root of the causes. One of the boys involved usually wants to prove that he is not a punk, that he is a man, and that he will not be disrespected without retaliating.

I feel this is an excellent opportunity to examine the meaning of code-switching with my students. Through the dissection of this term, I am able to establish the difference between school behavior and street behavior. There are different sets of rules for my students, rules of survival that differ on the street than in school. If street rules are used in school, students fail to thrive. The opposite is also true. There are ways students have to learn to live and walk in their neighborhoods without losing respect in the streets. Classroom discussions on code-switching allow us to talk about how this might be possible. They have to survive in both places and we all recognize that. Several of my students have been confronted by gangs and urged to join. We discuss how to say no to gangs, but still save face. None of my students wants to be labeled as a punk, but I believe that none of my students want to be violent either. I feel that as teachers, we cannot deny our students' realities outside of school. To do so would set them up for failure, or even violence, in all aspects of their lives.

Respecting the Opposite Sex

How to treat females is a topic of continued conversation in my classroom. Some of my students often refer to young women using slang terms such as "bitches" or "hos." They emulate what is portrayed in *some* styles of rap and hip-hop. Seeing this level of blatant disrespect and sexism is truly hard for me to witness. Again, as in the issue of aggressive behavior, incidents of disrespect towards females offer numerous teachable moments in the classroom. Rather than focus on the negative comments, I am consistently modeling and sharing how I treat my wife, my daughters, my sister, my mother—all females in my life. We refrain from talking about this in generalities, but rather talk about specific things we can do to show we care about girlfriends, moms, aunties, grandmothers, and anyone else of the opposite sex.

Throughout the year, my young men help me choose flowers to send to my wife. I incorporate this into several different academic tasks. We compare and contrast the different flower packages online. Each student writes what he thinks should go on the card, and then we debate each card's merit. We also discuss the mathematics of buying flowers by analyzing my budget and comparing it how much each package costs. We actively debate how much I should spend on purchasing the flowers. Activities like this incorporate meaningful curricular relevance into a broader discussion of how to treat females with the respect and dignity they deserve.

Two years ago the male and female sixth-grade communities went on a field trip to tour the campus of a local university. The weather was cold and a lot of walking was involved. On the tour, many of the students were bundled up trying to stay warm. In the nasty conditions, one of my students saw a young female student who was not wearing a coat. He went over, took off his coat, and draped it around her shoulders. That act of kindness reinforced to me the importance of our daily conversations about what it means to be a man. He had, indeed, applied our conversation to a real-world experience.

Expressing Emotion as a Man

Some of my male students will try to build an exterior of complete apathy or indifference, even coldness. They will work hard not to show any emotion. This is where my emotionality is a huge benefit for my classroom of young men. I wear my emotions on my sleeve. My students see when I my eyes fill with tears when I get so angry I could spit nails, but more importantly they also see my eyes fill with tears when I see them accomplish their goals or outwardly acknowledge their own brilliance. Rather than try to hide my emotions, I openly discuss them. That is who I am and I am not ashamed of it.

I get what I call "teacher goose bumps" on a daily basis when our community is really running smoothly. I point this out to the boys. At times, they will compete to see who can give me teacher goose bumps by doing quality work. At one point, after receiving his first A on a math test, a former student exclaimed, "Mr. Vernosh, I game myself student goose bumps!"

Creating Cultural Relevancy

Cultural relevancy is the cornerstone of my classroom. It all has to do with culture, community, and going to where the students live, think, breathe, and feel. To highlight the importance of a culturally relevant curriculum for our students who have been continually disenfranchised from our educational system, I will share a few experiences of one of my students whose name is Rashawn. In this particular case, I want to show how he responded to the curricular choices I have made for our learning community.

RASHAWN'S STORY

Rashawn is a bright young man who has had a reputation for not showing appropriate school behaviors, as defined by several of his previous teachers. Rashawn can be described as a Black American male who is fluent in English and Black English and comes from a working-class family. Yet, many see him differently. Some people who have worked with Rashawn have implied that he is not capable of performing up to standards in various academic subjects and have, therefore, tried to refer him for special education. One person even commented that he portrays himself as a "thug" who is lazy. Others have commented in ways that are blatantly racist. Unfortunately, this has resulted in appallingly lowered expectations for Rashawn.

For Rashawn, as well as a number of other students who have previously not felt welcomed in school, using a multicultural perspective has helped him embrace success. One example of the pedagogical choices that has helped him includes our discussion of social and racial identities and their impacts. Our class does not shy away from racial discourse. We speak candidly about me being the only White person in our classroom and follow up with analyzing the students' feelings about it. I strive to provide and nurture an environment where students are comfortable enough to explore their feelings about racism, while brainstorming ways to be positive agents for change—a term we use regularly. I believe conversations such as these have been building blocks for Rashawn. He is letting his guard down in our classroom community and has become a more positive and hopeful young man as a result of this dialogue.

Curriculum Hooks

Reading is the cornerstone of academic success. Using bridge-texts (smaller or modified parts of a larger text or narrative) and choosing relevant and engaging books help to capture my young men's imagination. It also helps to create a desire to read. For example, our district sixth-grade curriculum recommends Gary Paulson and Katherine Patterson for author studies. We do introduce our students to these authors and their works; however, we choose to delve much deeper into author studies from other authors such as Sharon G. Flake.

Several of the books we choose to analyze by this remarkable author are *Bang!* (Flake, 2005), *The Skin I'm In* (Flake, 1998), and *Begging for Change*

(Flake, 2003). The majority of my students, Rashawn included, comment on how "real" these books are. These books address challenges of racism, absent fathers, self-confidence, death, joy, and the triumph of overcoming obstacles in one's life. My young men love these books because they do not sugar coat many of the issues that face our youth. For example, in *Bang!*, one of the characters asks, "How a woman gonna teach a man how to raise a boy?" (Flake, 2005, p. 101). This elicits many powerful reflections from my young male students. Rashawn was one student who took great offense to this by offering that his mom is teaching him all about being a good man and future father. It is critical reflection about relevant texts like this that not only empowers our most disenfranchised students, but also helps to foster a love of reading. Love of reading, in turn, ultimately improves their academic achievement.

As an endnote to this section, I should add that after reading an excerpt from a book on Malcolm X, Rashawn exclaimed that he wanted to read more about Malcolm and asked if he could d a book and biographical report about him. Rashawn later told me that this was the first time in his life he could remember being excited about reading.

Analyzing Family Situations: Life Without Fathers

A single-gendered classroom allows gender to be a focal point of our environment. We dissect the many experiences of preteen males, especially in the context of gender roles and expectations as they exist in the African American community. At one of our lunch talks, Rashawn admitted that it is hard for him to focus on school because he is a major caretaker for his younger siblings. His mother works two jobs and relies on him to be more of a parent than most 12-year-olds have to be. When reflecting on his responsibilities, he confided that he hates his father for running out on his family. He feels like his mother would be less stressed and he could do more things if his dad were still around as a real parent. Rashawn has even expressed how he is not going to be like that when he becomes a father. He offered the following to illustrate his strong emotions regarding his future role as a father: "I'm going to be there for my kids, that's a man. A man takes care of his business. My kids aren't going to raise themselves...hell no! Sorry, Mr. Vernosh, I mean heck no!"

Language and Flocabulary: Authentic Connection to Students' Authentic Lives

We emphasize the power of language in our classroom. We talk about the need to harness that power if we are going to be agents of change. Part of our reading instruction is vocabulary. I have opted not to follow the district-recommended programs for vocabulary because they are not engaging, and my students were not adding these words to their daily classroom dialogue. Last spring, I discovered a program called the Word Up Project (Flocabulary, 2009). This is a vocabulary program that uses authentic hip-hop to teach vocabulary. The program boasts substantial gains in state achievement tests for schools and districts that have adopted it (Flocabulary, 2009). I started using it in my classroom right away and found fantastic results. My students now beg for us to do vocabulary everyday. By engaging in vocabulary studies, we are able to discuss how these hip-hop songs can help us learn the words we need in order to capture the power of language.

One example where this point can be illustrated is on a day where one of our vocabulary words was *boisterous*. A few weeks after studying that word, Rashawn spoke it in a context that showed me he knew exactly what the word boisterous meant. During a rather loud work time in math, he shouted above all of the voices, "Can y'all shut up? I can't think with y'all being so boisterous up in here!" Sometimes my young male students will use a word just to show they know how to say it but the context is way off. Rashawn used the vocabulary in a proper context without any thought and went right back to work.

Adapting Requirements to Real Lives

I have adapted my curriculum, and especially my homework requirements, for Rashawn. Family situations from which my students come don't lend themselves to completing homework, as they often involve poverty and homelessness. However, I do not lower my standards for homework projects. I must make sure that students who are busy helping raise multiple siblings after school are able to be successful in meeting these requirements. Sometimes that means extending these deadlines; sometimes it means providing materials like scissors, glue, or protractors to use at home. It also means that I need to provide other spaces and times for students to do their work. Students can come in early to class if they need help or a space to complete assignments. For students like Rashawn, these acts ensure that homework is complete while standards still remain high. I know so because he has thanked me for this on several occasions.

Rashawn, like any other student, thrives when educators think through and apply multicultural frameworks in their classrooms. This pedagogy should not have to be revolutionary; it is what teaching can naturally be. As teachers, we must teach with regard to how our students are, creating relationships with them, while at the same time, holding them to the highest possible standards. This evolution is occurring with Rashawn. Other teachers have approached me in astonishment at the positive changes they see in him. My response is simple: He is still the same young man they once knew—smart and capable. Those qualities have always been inside of him. He simply needs someone to believe in him, to trust him, and to hold him to high standards. When he feels that, he will then trust others to see his true brilliance.

BUILDING A CLASSROOM OF COMMUNITY OUTSIDE OF SCHOOL WALLS

The power of the relationships once built in our classroom community extends beyond the physical boundaries of our school. Students stop by my home, sometimes to simply say hello, and other times to help with home improvement repairs. Regardless, it is a relationship that has developed from a teacher and student dichotomy to that of a mentor/advocate and student.

I am a staunch believer that continuing the partnership outside of school pays direct dividends toward achievement inside of school. Every student has my home phone number and is encouraged to use it if needed. Students call me beyond their tenure in my class for continued assistance with homework, to ask for family transportation, or simply to keep in touch.

One of my favorite moments outside of school occurred on the night of November 4, 2008. It was approaching 10:00 p.m. when my phone rang. It was one of my students, Durien. Before he even greeted me, he blurted out, "Is he going to do it, Mr. Vernosh? They are just about to go to California. California has all those electoral votes we talked about. You really think it's gonna happen?" I could not participate in the conversation because Durien was so excited, he hardly took time to breathe. Just as I was about to say something, there was a huge uproar in the background. California had just been declared as a state that Barack Obama had won, therefore giving him enough votes to become our nation's president-elect. Durien was beside himself yelling along with the rest of his family, proclaiming, "We did it! We did it! We did it! Mr. Vernosh, we won!" His mother was even yelling over the phone about this political victory, shouting, "Do you believe it, Mr. Vernosh? I never thought. . . ." During the whole conversation with Durien, I was able to speak maybe five words, but I felt incredibly honored that in this historic moment, he and his family thought to call me and share their excitement.

I feel privileged to share important experiences in my families' lives outside of school. Most of these experiences occur because of joy or happiness. However, there are times my students' worlds fall apart. It is essential that I not just be available to my students and their families during these happy times. I must be there for the tough times as well. Sometimes my students make poor choices with consequences that involve criminal charges, time in court, and stays in juvenile detention facilities. Visiting my young men in these types of situations is tough, but it is a part of life that I feel is important that we confront as a team. It is my belief that our youth deserve to have consistent adults in their lives who believe in them, even when they make a mess out of a situation.

One such unfortunate example occurred when I was sitting in the waiting room with a mother waiting for her son's judicial hearing to begin. Through tears she asked me if I still believed in her son. She expressed very simply, "I just need to know that somebody else believes in my boy." I certainly reassured her that I did still believe in him. I did, however, express my disappointment in his choices, but I wanted her to know that did not change my support for him. This mother was so appreciative in my belief in her son that she called me over a year later (even after her son had left my class) to express her gratitude.

IMPLICATIONS FOR PRACTICE

Teaching is not just a job, it is a life choice. I believe that to be successful with my students, I must be an advocate, father, mentor, teacher, nurse, chauffer, disciplinarian, nurturer, and supporter of every kind. The depths of these relationships lead to transformative educational experiences for many of my students- many who have fallen through the cracks of our school and even society.

To this end, I offer the following recommendations for educators. Some of the recommendations are specific to single-gendered classrooms, while others are more general. Either way, urban school students will have more opportunity to thrive if these recommendations are taken into consideration.

1. Tune into your students' culture, community, and neighborhood. Ask yourself, "What are their lives like at home? What baggage are they bringing to the classroom when they arrive each morning?" Start from here. Use all of your senses to observe, hear, see and attempt to understand. Ground your academic task in what they need. Make attempts to involve their parents and/or guardians to continually ask for their assistance and feedback on how students are doing.
2. Create clear guidelines for behavior. Use constant reminders about behaviors in terms students can understand. Fill these guidelines with examples and make them from the students' own cultural reference.
3. Listen to students—really listen. Find a way to connect to them before and after school. Create times to share that allow students to express what is happening in their lives away from school.

4. Have frank and open discussions on topics that pertain to gender identity. Use opportunities in single-gendered classrooms to explore issues pertaining to gender.

5. Search for ways to teach subject matter that is relevant to your students' lives. This doesn't mean your standards have to be lowered or that your curriculum needs to be less rigorous or less demanding. It can simply create a bridge between what you want a student to learn and the environment from which they come.

REFERENCES

Brown v. Board of Education of Topeka, 347 U.S. 483, 74 S.Ct. 686, 98 L.Ed. 873 (1954).

Cable, K., & Spradlin, T. (2008) *Single-sex education in the 21st century* (Policy Brief No. 06.9). Center for Evaluation & Education Policy. Retrieved from http:/www.ceep.indiana.edu/pub.shtml#ed

Chudowsky, N. and Chudowsky, V. (2010) *State test score trends through 2007–08, part 5: Are there differences in acheivement between boys and girls?* Center on Education Policy. Retrieved from http://www.cep-dc.org/index.cfm?fuseaction=document_ext.showDocumentByID&nodeID=1&DocumentID=304

Flake, S. (2005). *Bang!* New York, NY: Jump at the Sun/Hyperion Paper Backs for Children.

Flake, S. (2003). *Begging for change.* New York, NY: Hyperion Books for Children.

Flake, S. (1998). *The skin I'm in.* New York, NY: Jump at the Sun/Hyperion Books for Children.

Flocabulary: Hip-Hop in the Classroom. (2009). Flocabulary is proven to raise scores on state reading tests. Retrieved from www.flocabulary.com/results.html

Gurian, M., & Stevens, K. (2005). *The minds of boys: Saving our sons from falling behind in school and life.* San Francisco, CA: Jossey-Bass.

Holleran, K. (2007, November 7). Educators report benefits from gender segregated teaching. *Charleston Daily Mail.* Retrieved from www.dailymail.com/news/2007

Kreite, R. (2002). *The morning meeting book.* Turners Falls, MA: Northeast Foundation for Children, Inc.

Okoye-Johnson, O. (2008, March 7). *Single sex education: A solution for low achieving inner-city public schools?* [power-point slides]. Retrieved from csun.edu/csns/events/virtual-presentation-fair-2008

Sax, L. (2005, March 2). The promise and peril of single-sex public education: Mr. Chips meets Snoop Dogg. *Education Week,* pp 34–35.

Tatum, A. (2005). *Teaching reading to black adolescent males: Closing the achievement gap.* Portland, ME: Stenhouse Publishers.

U.S. Department of Education. (2005). *Single-sex versus coeducational schooling: A systematic review* (Doc # 2005-01). Washington, DC: Author.

Weil, E. (2008, March 2). Teaching boys and girls separately. *The New York Times.* Retrieved from http://www.nytimes.com/2008/03/02/magazine/02sex3-t.html?pagewanted=all

CHAPTER 8

MONTESSORI

Education for Life

Michelle J. Moody and Ginny Riga

ABSTRACT

True educational reform must be child centered, teacher centered and family centered. Montessori education focuses on children's individuality and develops independent, confident students with the tools and motivation to chart their path in life. Implementing a public school Montessori program requires the ability to combine and protect the major tenets of Montessori while adhering to state and district initiatives and mandates. The transformational nature of Montessori is beneficial to all children regardless of their setting and fosters the development of teachers as facilitators of learning. Montessori allows all stakeholders to be involved in educating our future, the children. It is an education reform that works and sustains itself on its own merits—an education for life.

Urban and rural schools in areas with high levels of poverty need systemic changes to meet the needs of the students, families, and communities they serve. Many students in urban communities languish or fail in school (Henig, Hula, Orr, & Pedescleaux, 1999). Outcries about the "achieve-

Yes We Can! Improving Urban Schools Through Innovative Educational Reform, pages 127–143
Copyright © 2011 by Information Age Publishing

ment gap" and how to close that gap are a major focus of research, professional conferences, and educational discussion (Ferguson, Hackman, Hanna, & Ballantine, 2008). Economics plays a part in this dilemma, but many schools with high levels of poverty have transformed their classroom environments to become success-oriented with the buy-in/ownership and support of parents, teachers, administration, and the community. The students develop ownership of systemic reform once they are immersed in a learning environment that is challenging, respectful, personalized, and meaningful, making learning the joyful experience it was meant to be. Such is the experience of the students in a Montessori learning environment.

Success in school empowers students with the confidence, sense of personal responsibility, and motivation to chart their own path in life. While changing a child's home or economic reality is out of the reach of schools, changing what happens in classrooms is a moral imperative. Education should no longer be mostly imparting of knowledge, but must take a new path, seeking the release of human potentialities (Montessori, 1946). In their study on the relationship between family capital and student achievement, Parcel and Dufur (2001) concluded that family (social capital) affects student achievement. Children of poverty, whether the setting is urban or rural, more often than their middle-class counterparts, start school with significant learning disadvantages and are unlikely to catch up to their middle-class peers (Borsuk, 2007). It does not take too many years of knowing you are not measuring up to develop a poor concept of yourself as a learner. Attitude about learning is shaped during the early years of formal schooling, usually ages 4–7 (Carlton, 2003). School failure at even the tender age of four or five years affects a student for life and is an underlying cause of many of the societal ills that plague our nation from grade retention to high drop-out rates (The Annie E. Casey Foundation, 2010).

OVERVIEW OF THE MONTESSORI METHOD

Longitudinal studies of the effects of quality early childhood education show that it does have a positive impact and lasting effect on overall school performance and quality of life (Reynolds, Temple & Suh-Ruu, 2003). Over a hundred years ago, Dr. Maria Montessori worked with children in the poorest slums of Rome, Italy, with a culturally responsive pedagogy and curriculum known as the Montessori Method—Education for Life. The pedagogy, based on universal principles of child development and stages of learning, is responsive to cultures worldwide. The curriculum, while structured and carefully sequenced, also allows for students to explore areas of particular interest and social relevance. The Montessori Method works in classrooms and schools in urban and rural educational settings with children from all socioeconomic levels, heterogeneous abilities, and races. This chapter concentrates on the positive outcomes of two schools in Chicago and a district in South Carolina who use the Montessori approach as their curricular guidepost.

The Montessori curriculum is a rigorous program of academic study with great emphasis on the affective domain of learning (Seldin & Epstein, 2003). Montessori emphasizes respect for the environment and others, grace and courtesy in all interactions, peace education, and the interconnectedness of a global society. These various aspects of the Montessori classroom produce an environment for learning that creates a well-rounded individual. Further, the Montessori program works to develop strong character, build high self-esteem, and develop culturally literate children who are interested in their work and enthusiastic about learning. The focus is to educate the whole child and provide an education for life (Seldin & Epstein, 2003).

Public school Montessori programs are not in competition with those in the private sector, but rather build upon their decades of proven success in this country and around the world. Montessori programs share the same philosophy, method and materials but can vary in program structure. Some public programs operate as "total" schools, in which all students are in Montessori classes. Other programs exist in the form of the "school-within-a-school" model where several classrooms in a traditional school offer the Montessori program. Programs most often begin at the primary level, where children ages 3–5 work and learn together. This is followed by lower elementary (grades 1–3), upper elementary (grades 4–6), and middle school (grades 7–8), depending on the highest grade level served at the school.

MAJOR PHILOSOPHICAL TENETS

The Montessori philosophy and methodology turns the tenets and ways of traditional education upside down. Through many years of observation and research, Dr. Montessori came to the conclusion that children are not empty vessels or blank slates waiting to be filled by what education offers (Lillard, 2005). Instead, Montessori believed that children are born with what they need to develop and grow, and it is the job of education to provide the necessary learning environment for them to interact with for this to naturally unfold (Montessori, 1946). Major tenets of the Montessori philosophy are: (1) multi-age classrooms, (2) the prepared environment, (3) freedom within boundaries, (4) properly trained teachers who serve as facilitators and guide learning, and (5) teaching the whole child.

Multi-Age Classrooms

A foundational feature of the Montessori system is the three-year multi-age classroom structure. The multi-age groupings extend the possibility for learning by imitation or modeling of older children (Lillard, 2005). This format frees individual students from the expectation that they must reach the same levels of social and academic achievement as everyone else in their classroom simply because they share the same age. The three-year age span preserves the institutional memory of classroom traditions, norms and rituals among students who return for their second or third year, and frees the teacher from the arduous task of re-establishing expectations each fall. Each child gets a chance to be the "younger, middle and older" child as he/she moves through the three years of each level. The different ages of the children offer natural opportunities for helping other children and developing leadership skills. Students are taught to assist in running their classroom community, from its physical order to community meetings. As a consequence, independence and leadership skills emerge.

Prepared Environment

Secondly, a prepared environment should be equipped with developmentally appropriate, hands-on materials, to which Montessori devoted years of experimentation to develop and refine. Materials in the Montessori classroom are carefully sequenced (in each subject area) and many are self-correcting, which allows students to recognize errors in completing their work without teacher intervention. When students recognize their errors they can begin again, a process that encourages students to become responsible for their own learning. Much of the instruction in a Montessori classroom is given individually or in small group settings of two to five students. Once the teacher presents a lesson to students, they are allowed to practice and repeat the activities until mastery is achieved. This allows students to move at an individual pace, advancing their learning in certain areas while slowing the pace in others. Children are afforded the gift of time as they master skills and concepts at their own pace. If a child is ready to move on, he or she can, without having to wait for others. Hence the cap on the curriculum level is lifted, freeing students to soar academically.

Freedom within Boundaries

The third tenet is freedom within boundaries. The children are not "free to do as they like"; instead they are free to work or to engage in sustained and productive activity while simultaneously learning how to be-have in a community (Lillard & Jessen, 2003). Freedom for children to choose lessons each day helps them develop responsibility for their own work. Sometimes this freedom is mistakenly interpreted to mean the child is running the classroom. Not so—the freedom is in a structured environment in which children learn procedures and rules that allow the classroom to operate smoothly. The Montessori curriculum provides the freedom for students to pursue areas of interest, independently and/or collaboratively, in the areas of: history, science, geography and social studies, which are referred to as the "cultural" areas of study.

Larry Page and Sergey Brin, former Montessori students and founders of Google.com explained to Barbara Walters in a 2004 interview that the ability to learn to think for themselves and the freedom to pursue their own interests in the Montessori classroom helped them to achieve their business success. In Montessori school, "we learned to be self-directed and self-start-ers." In fact, they credited their Montessori education more than anything (including Stanford University) for their accomplishments (Walters, 2004).

The Montessori Teacher as a Guide

Montessori education requires a prepared teacher who understands how children develop and is experienced in establishing a structured environment that meets their needs at each successive age (Lillard & Jessen, 2003). The Montessori teacher is a facilitator or guide who allows for discovery, keenly observes students movement through the curriculum, and continuously prepares the environment to meet the developmental needs of the students. Teachers are trained to know when and when not to intervene in a child's work. The teacher closely observes and assesses students' progress. These observations provide data for planning the next sequential lesson for individual children.

"Highly qualified" teachers are a mandate of NCLB. Teachers in the Montessori programs in Chicago and South Carolina must hold two certifications: a state teaching certificate in which they have been deemed highly qualified and a Montessori certificate. Montessori certification is received after participation in a two-year training program. While Montessori training is rigorous and the method requires extra time to manage an individualized learning model, teachers report great satisfaction and freedom from the constraints of teaching a single grade level of standards by following a pacing guide dictated by the calendar instead of student needs. They also express great benefits from teaching children for three years and really getting to know the student and his family. Montessori teachers work hard, but they remain committed and say they cannot see themselves teaching any other way.

Teaching the Whole Child

Montessori education provides the framework for academic success as well as the growth of behavioral, social, and emotional skills. These affective skills are often downplayed and overshadowed by the pressure of standards and testing. Relegating the affective domain to soft skills that are nice to have but not really what schools should be in the business of teaching is a mistake. Socialization for young children is an important ingredient to successful learning (Hainstock, 1997). Cognitive growth and affective growth are intertwined; one does not need to be sacrificed for the other.

The seeds of personal empowerment needed to chart one's course in life—confidence, personal responsibility, motivation, independence and the ability to get along with others—permeate the Montessori class. Confidence in one's ability to learn begins to grow as a child continually completes challenging tasks on his own. The word challenging is important because it implies that the student has to solve problems and make associations in order to complete the task. The student is operating in Vygotsky's Zone of Proximal Development or Learning Zone, where he or she experiences feelings of uncertainty and questioning, and is in a state of challenge and growth or disequilibrium (Vygotsky, 1978). Often referred to as discovery learning or constructivism, these experiences preserve the joy of learning that children innately bring to school. In the constructivist model of learning, the learner actively constructs his or her own understanding of reality through interaction with the environment and subsequent reflection. (Joyce, Weil, & Calhoun, 2004).

BEGINNINGS OF MONTESSORI IN PUBLIC SCHOOLS

Montessori education in the public sector is expanding across the country in urban and rural communities. The first public Montessori school, Sandhills Elementary, opened in 1975 in Cincinnati, Ohio. During the same decade public programs began in Arlington, Virginia; Philadelphia; and Reading, Ohio. Currently (in 2009) over 250 public Montessori programs are operating nationwide in urban areas that include: Milwaukee, Cincinnati, Indianapolis, Houston, and even Honolulu, Juno, and Anchorage. Webster defines *urban* as "(comprising) a city or town of at least 50,000 inhabitants." Montessori programs in Chicago and South Carolina are a study in contrasts. Chicago is the third largest city in the nation. Although South

Carolina has cities that meet Webster's definition above, the majority of the 85 school districts in the state serve rural communities. Although separate, socioeconomic status (SES) ties them together.

The Tie that Binds

South Carolina has a general population of 4,500,000 citizens and serves approximately 710,000 students in public schools in K–12 (South Carolina Department of Education, 2010). The state has two large cities: Columbia, the state capital, and Charleston, each with a population between 111,000 and 130,000 (U.S. Census Bureau, 2008). The overall poverty level of South Carolina is 16%, three points above the national poverty level. Data obtained from the Annie E. Casey Foundation (2008) indicate that the poverty level for children (0–18 yrs.) in South Carolina is 22%. This exceeds the national poverty level of 18% for this same age group. The poverty level in nearly half (20) of the 46 counties in South Carolina is 20% or higher. So it is clear that not only do urban school districts like Chicago face the challenges of educating children of poverty, but the majority of districts in South Carolina do as well.

Chicago Public Schools, the third largest school district in the United States, served 409,279 students during the 2009–2010 school year. The student population is 9% Caucasian and 91% students of color. Eighty-five percent of students come from low income homes and 12.2% of students are limited English proficient (Chicago Public Schools, 2009). The first Montessori program in Chicago began in 1986 at a neighborhood school on the southwest side of the city. The program began as a school-within-a-school model. Between 2004–2007, three magnet Montessori programs were established. The information in this chapter relates to the three magnet school programs.

The Montessori program in Chicago was developed to attract students to underutilized facilities and/or to stabilize enrollment. When the Montessori program was introduced during the 2004–2005 school year (at the first magnet school) the mobility rate of students was 25%, higher than the district average of 24%. Four years later (2008–09), the mobility rate at the magnet school had dramatically dropped from 25% to just 2%—a decrease of 23%. During this same four-year period, the district's mobility rate dropped slightly (by 5%) while the mobility of the three magnet schools ranged from 2% to 5%, well below the district average (research.cps.k12. il.us /resweb/PageServlet?page=schoolprofile, 2010). The Montessori program has assisted both districts in creating schools that have a high demand from parents while improving academic achievement.

Celebrations and Challenges of Montessori in Public Schools

The biggest celebration in Montessori public school is increased access to families of all income levels. During the 2010–2011 school year, over 4,400 students were enrolled in Montessori classes in 42 public schools across 17 districts in South Carolina. The majority of programs in these districts are school-within-a-school programs; four are stand-alone Montessori schools. In the 38 sites in which traditional classes exist along side Montessori classes, the number of Montessori classes per site ranges from 1 to 17.

Among the 42 programs in South Carolina, over half are in schools designated as Title I (schools with high poverty levels) (South Carolina Department of Education, 2010). Like South Carolina, Chicago's magnet programs are designed to attract students from different socioeconomic backgrounds. Montessori magnets reflect this diversity goal. Across the three magnet Montessori schools, the population of low income students averages 52% (a range of 45% to 60%). In addition, the minority population averages 75%, and the number of limited English proficient students ranges from 3% to 7%. The students work, learn, and play together throughout the school year and develop an understanding and respect for each other, a benefit that extends to all members of the school family (research.cps.k12.il.us /resweb/PageServlet?page =schoolprofile, 2010).

Academic Outcomes

In the era of No Child Left Behind (NCLB) and closing achievement gaps, questions frequently arise about whether data exist showing higher student achievement in Montessori versus non-Montessori programs. While standardized test information is available, meaningful analysis of test data is often thwarted by the small size of a program and/or few years of test data available. While most Montessori students enter public programs at 3 or 4 years of age, standardized data on state report cards normally begins in third grade. However, studies on test data beginning at the third-grade level are showing positive results for Montessori students, with the greatest differences evident in the middle level grades. A meta-analysis of research studies on the Montessori method conducted from 2000–2005 showed favorable outcomes in achievement, self-image and intrinsic motivation (Jones, 2005).

Laurens School District 55

Laurens School District 55 is a rural district in South Carolina with 65% of its 6,000 students on free/reduced lunch. The Montessori program began in 1996 with two primary classes in two schools, and within 15 years it has grown to 40 Montessori classes. Every elementary and the two middle schools have a Montessori program. Laurens is a model of a district with successful school-within-a-school programs that continue to thrive and remain a popular choice for families. The breadth and longevity of the program, as well as its expansion to grade 8 in 2005, provides the opportunity to examine student test scores over time. Table 8.1 provides a summary of Palmetto Achievement Challenge Test (PACT) scores for students (most of whom began Montessori at age 3 or 4) in grades 3–8 during 2002–2006. The numbers in Table 8.1 represent the percentage of students in Montessori who scored at or above grade level standards on PACT. Data from the district on numbers of students in these grades indicated that approximately 13% of the district's students were enrolled in Montessori classes.

When these data were compared to (the) non-Montessori students at each grade level, the percentages for Montessori students were higher than their non-Montessori peers in every year and at every grade level. Differences in scores ranged from 1 to 38 percentage points higher for Montessori students. The differences were larger in the middle school grades. For example, in Language Arts, scores differed by an average of 12 percentage points in grade 3 to 28 in grade 8. The largest differences were in Science, where the difference in grade 3 (15 percentage points) jumped to a difference of 38 percentage points in grade 8.

Grade level groups of students who had test data for four to five years were examined (e.g., students in grade 3 in 2002 to grade 7 in 2006). The groups cannot be defined as cohorts since student attrition occurred and individual scores were not available for matching. Analysis of PACT test scores showed that the percentages for Montessori groups improved as much as 20–30 points over five years of testing, while those of non-Montessori students increased at a much lower rate and in some cases showed a decline over the same length of time (Laurens School District 55, 2007).

Chicago Public Schools

Students in the Chicago Montessori programs are not exempt from the statewide testing program, the Illinois Standards Achievement Test (ISAT). Table 8.2 provides ISAT data from the oldest Montessori magnet program in the Chicago Public Schools. The data indicate the percent of students who met/exceeded state standards in reading and math. Over a period of seven years, this school transitioned into a total Montessori magnet school. As each 8th grade class graduated, new three-year-olds (3K students) began the school in Montessori classes. The 2005 through 2007 test scores are those of students attending the school but not enrolled in the Montessori program. The 2008 and 2009 scores that are bolded and asterisked represent scores for students who began the Montessori program as kindergar-

TABLE 8.1 Percentage of Montessori Students Meeting/Exceeding Standards (Laurens District 55)

	Grade 3				Grade 4				Grade 5				Grade 6				Grade 7				Grade 8			
	LA	M	SC	SS	LA	M	SC	SS	LA	M	SC	SS	LA	M	SC	SS	LA	M	SC	SS	LA	M	SC	SS
2002	90	78			89	79			82	80														
2003	91	93	73	73	90	94	55	55	90	85	67	68	92	94	75	75								
2004	98	100	89	96	93	96	83	89	98	86	70	74	84	95	81	77	96	100	85	74				
2005	96	96	82	91	98	95	88	84	97	94	83	80	93	98	73	67	93	90	85	75	100	95	90	81
2006	98	90	74	90	98	98	83	79	90	81	72	64	95	97	74	90	95	86	75	71	97	91	91	79

Note: LA = Language Arts; M = Math; SC = Science; SS = Social Studies
Source: Office of Research Laurens School District 55 (2007). Montessori Data

**TABLE 8.2   Percentage of Students Meeting/Exceeding Standards
(Oldest Montessori Magnet school)**

Grade	Reading						Mathematics					
	3	4	5	6	7	8	3	4	5	6	7	8
2005	29.4		31.8			59.3	47.1		54.5			14.8
2006	40.0	81.8	56.3	75.0	70.0	86.4	90.0	81.8	50.0	70.8	70.0	72.7
2007	76.5	81.8	70.0	63.2	80.0	84.2	94.1	90.9	70.0	66.7	90.0	84.2
2008	75.0*	76.0	83.3	93.3	72.2	90.0	70.0*	88.0	66.7	73.3	66.7	80.0
2009	90.9*	94.7*	76.0	75.0	92.9	76.2	95.9*	100.0*	60.0	66.7	85.7	85.7

* Scores for students in Montessori program http://research.cps.k12.il.us/cps/accountweb/
reports

teners and took their first ISAT in grade three, after being in Montessori classes for four years.

Prior to implementation of the Montessori program, about one quarter of third graders met or exceeded state standards in reading, and less than half met or exceeded state standards in mathematics. After implementation of the Montessori program, students meeting/exceeding state standards increased. For students who began the Montessori program in kindergarten, the test scores in 2008 and 2009 show a marked improvement.

In addition to the improvement in scores of the students in Montessori, the school's principal, Mr. Neidlinger, commented that test scores in 2005, 2006, and 2007 demonstrated that the implementation of the Montessori program impacted test scores for students who were not enrolled in the Montessori program. Mr. Neidlinger noted, "While the program began at the early childhood level (ages 3–6), the entire school was involved in understanding Montessori and its methodology. From the informational sessions conducted, teaching strategies changed throughout the school. I think all our scores increased for this reason" (M. Neidlinger, personal communication, January 28, 2010). The impact of highly trained teachers and quality instruction cannot be understated.

Challenges

Innovation and change does not come without challenges, and the transition to the Montessori model of education is no different. The challenges faced by public Montessori programs are not insurmountable. If these challenges are dealt with in a manner consistent with the Montessori philosophy and basic tenets already described, the program can still be authentic. Effective implementation of any program requires fidelity to the philosophy and methodology. Challenges include: (1) veering from prescribed multi-age groupings, (2) using letter or numeric grading systems, (3) accepting only academically gifted or special needs students into the program, and (4) having untrained teachers or an incomplete set of Montessori equipment. Any one of these chips away at the philosophy and structure of the program and diminishes its authenticity.

Supply of open Montessori seats in a program versus demand presents a challenge to most of these programs. The overwhelming majority of parents are thrilled with the Montessori option in a public school setting. Like teachers, very few students leave the program. Waiting lists are a common occurrence. For the 2009–2010 school year, South Carolina programs averaged two applications for each opening. Applications for the magnet Montessori programs in Chicago have increased from approximately 200 applications at each school during their first year of operation to nearly 2,500 applications across the three schools for the 2009–2010 school year (S. Ryan, personal communication, June 30, 2009). In an article printed in the Chicago *Tribune,* Stephanie Banchero (2008) noted that it was more difficult to get into Drummond Montessori than Harvard University. According to Banchero (2008), Harvard had a 9% acceptance rate for its applicants last year while Drummond accepted only 4% of its applicants. About 995 kids applied for 36 openings at Drummond (Banchero, 2008). The Montessori program offers parents a quality education without the expense incurred at a non-public school.

Standardized testing, a common process or tool used to measure academic achievement in a public school setting, presents challenges to Montessori programs. The Montessori programs in public schools must participate in all testing programs required by the district and state. Schools must ensure that students are adequately prepared for testing while not focusing too heavily on test preparation. The process of aligning Montessori lessons or "works" with state standards supports this preparation. Teachers align lessons with the standards and create lessons for standards not covered by the Montessori curriculum. The process assists personnel in developing a deeper understanding of the standards, the Montessori curriculum, and skill development. In addition, the process allows the Montessori programs to assure parents and district personnel that students are meeting the academic standards of the state.

Overcoming the myths surrounding Montessori education and practices is a critical and ongoing effort. Informing parents and the larger school community about what the Montessori method is, and is not, is also important. Montessori personnel must share with the school community the Montessori philosophy, the instructional strategies used in the classroom as well as information regarding the major tenets of the Montessori program. Schools offer parent information sessions that extend over several weeks and include topics such as the Montessori philosophy, curriculum areas, and the home/school connection. Montessori promotes parents' involvement in the education of their children. For example, in South Carolina parents are requested to observe their child's class, have two or more parent/teacher conferences per year, and incorporate the Montessori philosophy at home. The Montessori program is designed to link the home and school in the learning process of the child (Gordon, 2001; Hainstock, 1997).

For many parents, the Montessori classroom is quite different from their educational experience. Montessori emphasizes the use of hands-on learning materials rather than worksheets and textbooks. The hands-on nature of the program also impacts the type of homework students receive. In a Montessori program, learning is extended to the home as students practice what they have learned at school. At young ages, pouring, cleaning, buttoning, and recognition of words within literature are modeled from their work at school. For elementary students, homework takes the form of monthly projects that are presented to the class, fostering growth in public speaking skills at a young age. Other common examples of elementary homework include: (1) hands-on book summaries, (2) reading logs, (3) journal writing, (4) outdoor measurement activities, (5) leaf identification (botany), and (6) conducting interviews.

Another challenge facing public Montessori programs is informing parents across all segments of a diverse community that Montessori is offered in their district as a viable educational option they may choose for their child. Magnet schools in Chicago use a variety of methods to inform parents across the district about school choice options. Schools conduct open houses and tours during the day, so parents can see the program in session. A Magnet School Fair is held, and radio and print ads are also used to communicate with families. In the urban areas of Columbia and Charleston, South Carolina, informational meetings are advertised through churches and held in community parks. Principals meet individually with parents who are unable to make meetings. School social workers deliver flyers at home visits. It is essential to have diversity among the youngest children in the program. Otherwise, since openings are limited thereafter, diversity is difficult to achieve in later years.

A final challenge is adequate training of Montessori administrators. Administrators of Montessori programs are not required to have Montessori training. Leaders of Montessori programs must understand and be able to explain the philosophy of the program. As instructional leaders, they must have knowledge about the curriculum, specialized equipment, classroom structure, and role of the teacher, which enables them to give appropriate feedback to teachers after classroom observations. Montessori principals must be flexible in making necessary accommodations for Montessori classes with respect to tangible rewards—for example, excusing participation in school wide reward programs such as Accelerated Reader stickers and prizes, and award assemblies for honor roll and perfect attendance. Instead of extrinsic rewards, the Montessori method is built upon intrinsic rewards for learning. Young children are eager and excited to learn. Research outlined by Lillard (2005) suggests that this love of learning is best sustained when extrinsic rewards are not part of the framework. In the Montessori method extrinsic rewards are viewed as disruptive to the child's concentration. Intense periods of concentration are central to Montessori education (Lillard, 2005). Academic program flexibility is also needed when a school with Montessori classes adopts a broad initiative (e.g., Reading First) with features that may clash with the Montessori philosophy and method.

IMPLICATIONS FOR PRACTITIONERS

Montessori is based on eight principles that have been thoroughly researched and found to be essential elements of an optimal learning environment (Lillard, 2005). Schools that do not offer Montessori programs can and do include many of these elements in their curriculum and pedagogy to ensure a more success-oriented environment for learners with diverse needs.

- Class configuration: Multi-age classes and multi-year teaching can stand on their own merits outside of the Montessori context. If two-year (vs. three-year) age blends are preferred, some commonly used are: K–1st; 2nd–3rd and 4th–5th. In the multi-age classroom, children practice cooperation, teamwork, and conflict resolution on a daily basis. Classes of more than a single age also offer an alternative to grade retention by allowing a child to spend an extra year in the multi-age configuration if needed without experiencing the stigma of being noticeably overage for a class. Multi-year teaching eliminates the need at the start of every school year to spend weeks or months identifying students' strengths and weaknesses. Both models allow teachers to be familiar with at least half or more of the students (and their families) when school resumes each fall.
- Individualized instruction: Teachers can begin to shift their focus from whole group teaching to more individual and small group instruction. They can plan for differentiated instruction based on (1) the developmental stages of the students within their classrooms and (2) the "sensitive periods" for learning. Schools can purchase a variety of materials that allow students to progress through the curriculum at different paces based on their learning needs.
- Motivation: Schools must ensure that classrooms are welcoming environments for students with materials that hold their interest while allowing them to learn. The use of self-correcting materials

will support students becoming more involved in and responsible for their learning. Providing students with choices for some of their instructional tasks (within appropriate boundaries) is inherently motivational and fosters development of personal ownership of work. Students must be taught to make good choices, but this can only be done if classrooms provide a safe environment for students to make mistakes and independent decisions. Teachers can implement student choice with respect to lessons and instructional equipment. Inquiry-based science may be a good starting point for this.

- Leadership skills: Educators can also provide opportunities within the classroom structure to allow older students to develop leadership skills by collaborating with the younger students, such as reading buddies or tutoring. While this occurs naturally in mixed-age groupings, with ingenuity and creativity it can be fostered in all settings.
- Teacher training: Districts must be mindful that quality teacher training is integral to the effective implementation of any of the curriculum programs used in urban settings across the country. It is imperative that districts fund and provide time for (mandate) teacher training in the implementation process for the new curricula or pedagogy being used. This training should take place over time and in a setting similar to the one in which teachers will work (Danielson & Engstrom, 2002; Silver, Smith, & Stein, 1999).
- Culturally responsive schools: Curriculum and pedagogy can be so static or unbending that it fails to meet the needs of the increasingly diverse population of learners of 21st-century classrooms. Conversely, a culturally responsive curriculum and pedagogy allows for and teaches to these needs instead of minimizing or dismissing them and trying to fit all learners into one mold. To truly be a culturally responsive school, classrooms must be practicing grounds for expected behaviors that groom the children for what is expected throughout life: respect, self-control, independence, responsibility, cooperation, and compassion—that is, they must be focused on teaching the whole student. In conversations with parents who have made the Montessori choice, they note that the Montessori schools have a holistic approach to education; the schools have a heart and soul. These schools develop a larger school community that includes students, staff, parents, and the surrounding community as well.

CONCLUSION

Wood (1992) noted that America's future is held in classrooms in which student work is driven by a purpose and where children's interests help shape conviction. In a global society, our students must be able to function in a world larger than their own community. Montessori education empowers students of any race or socioeconomic background to claim their right to help shape this future. With confidence in one's ability as a learner, motivation, responsibility, independence, and the ability to get along with others, a productive and successful future is within their grasp. With its focus on peace, grace, and courtesy, the Montessori model of education begins providing students with the compassion and empathy to function in this new world. "If education is always to be conceived along the same antiquated lines of a mere transmission of knowledge, there is little to be hoped from it in the bettering of man's future. For what is the use of transmitting knowledge if the individual's total development lags behind?" (Montessori, 1988, p. 4).

REFERENCES

The Annie E. Casey Foundation. (2008). KIDS COUNT Data Center. Retrieved from www.kidscount.org

The Annie E. Casey Foundation. (2010). Kids Count 2010 Special Report: *Early warning! Why reading gaps by the end of third grade matters.* Retrieved from *http://www. aecf.org/~/media/Pubs/Initiatives/KIDS%20COUNT/123/2010KCSpecReport/ AEC_report_color_highres.pdf*

Banchero, S. (2008, February 26). Harder to get into than Harvard. *Chicago Tribune.* Retrieved from www.chicagotribune.com

Borsuk, A. (2007, September 25). Reading gap is nation's worst. *The Milwaukee Journal Sentinel.*

Breitsprecher, W. (2007). *Issues in urban education.* Retrieved October 26, 2010 from http://brietlinks.com/issues

Carlton, M. (2003). *Helping children at home and school.* Bethesda, MD: National Association of School Psychologists.

Chicago Public Schools. (2009). *Stats and facts.* Retrieved from http://cps.edu/ About_CPS/At-a-glance/Pages/Stats_and_facts.aspx

Danielson, L. M., & Engstrom, M. E. (2002). Teachers' perceptions of an on-site staff development model. *Educational Leadership. 79,* 170–173.

Gordon, C. (2001). *Together with Montessori.* Minneapolis, MN: Jola.

Ferguson, R.F., Hackman S., Hanna, R., & Ballantine, A. (2008, June) *Raising achievement and closing gaps in whole school systems: Recent advances in research and practice.* Report on the 2008 Annual Conference of the Achievement Gap Initiative at Harvard University.

Hainstock, E.G. (1997). *The essential Montessori.* New York, NY: Penguin Group.

Henig J., Hula R., Orr M., & Pedescleaux D. (1999). *The color of school reform: Race, politics, and the challenge of urban education.* Princeton, NJ: Princeton University Press.

HighScope. (2004). Long-term study of adults who received high-quality early childhood care and education shows economic and social gains, less crime. Retrieved from http://www.highscope.org/Content.asp?ContentId=282

Jones, A. (2005). *Montessori education in America: An analysis of research conducted from 2000–2005.* California: Plan 4 Preschool Digital Library.

Joyce, B., Weil, M., & Calhoun, E. (2004). *Models of teaching* (7th ed.). Boston, MA: Pearson Education.

Laurens School District 55. (2007). *Percentage of Montessori students meeting/exceeding standards on PACT, 2002–2006.*

Lillard, A. (2005) *Montessori: The science behind the genius.* New York, NY: Oxford University Press.

Lillard, P., & Jessen, L. (2003). *Montessori from the start.* New York, NY: Schocken Books.

Montessori, M. (1946). *Education for a new world.* Oxford, UK: Clio Press.

Montessori, M. (1988). *The absorbent mind.* Oxford, UK: Clio.

Montessori in the United States, 2009. Retrieved January 10, 2010, from www.Wikipedia.org

Montessori Research Summary, 1996–2010. Retrieved from www.montessori-namta.org/NAMTA/geninfo/rschsum.html

Parcel, T., & Dufur, M. (2001). Capital at home and at school: Effects on student achievement. *Social Forces, 79,* 881–912.

Reynolds, A., Temple, J., & Suh-Ruu, O. (2003). School-based early intervention and child well-being in the Chicago longitudinal study. *Child Welfare, 82,* 633–657.

Seldin, T., & Epstein, P. (2003). *The Montessori way.* Sarasota, FL: Montessori Foundation Press.

Silver, E., Smith, M., & Stein, M. (1999). The development of professional developers: Learning to assist teachers in new setting in new ways. *Harvard Educational Review, 69,* 237–269.

South Carolina Department of Education. (2010). Retrieved May 30, 2010, from www.ed.sc.gov

U.S. Census Bureau. (2008). Retrieved August 30, 2011, from http://www.factfinder2.census.gov

Vygotsky, L. (1978). *Mind in society: the development of higher psychological processes.* Cambridge, MA: Harvard University Press.

Walters, B. (2004). *20/20 America's ten most fascinating people 2004.* Retrieved August 30, 2011 from www.montessoricenter.org/2010/companys-founders-talk-about-Montessori-education/

Wood, G. (1992). *Schools that work.* New York, NY: Dutton.

CHAPTER 9

MAKING A CASE TO LEARN

Linking Emphasis on the Achievement and Reporting Needs of African American Females on NAPE Test Results

Patricia J. Larke, Jemimah L. Young, and Jamaal R. Young

ABSTRACT

The ability to access academic achievement information for African American females provides valuable insights to parents and teachers in their quest to teach this population. The following chapter investigates the educational achievement of African American females, using scale scores and achievement levels from the NAEP. Implications for practice are offered.

While there is a plethora of research on African American males as related to academic achievement at all levels from elementary to secondary to higher education, there is very little research on the academic achievement of African American females at these levels (Johnson-Bailey & Cervero, 2008). African American male crisis has caused scholars to "ignore, overlook and minimize" Black females (Fraizer-Kouassi, 2002, p. 15). In fact, issues about African American females have become, as Sue Books (2007) says, "invis-

Yes We Can! Improving Urban Schools Through Innovative Educational Reform, pages 145–165
Copyright © 2011 by Information Age Publishing
All rights of reproduction in any form reserved.

ible" in the discourse about students of color. There have been special journals issues devoted to research regarding African American males (Harper, 2010). More recently, a journal specifically about African American males, entitled *Journal of African American Males in Education* (JAAME), had its inaugural issue in February/March 2010. Moreover, examining one of the most recent handbooks about the education of African Americans, *Handbook of African American Education* (Tillman, 2009), one finds no chapters specifically on African American females, while African American males continued to be addressed.

"Why is the educational achievement of such an important group missing in the literature?" is a resounding question We have posed this question to many scholars and students and the responses are similar: "I know that there is research... let me do a literature search." But to no avail, the same response is: "Why we do not know?" Maybe it is as a 2010 Google search revealed: "Do you mean academic achievement for African American males?" (See Figure 9.1). One response to why the Google search would present that question is that the African American female currently is overshadowed in the research literature and in the educational community. The achievement of African American males seems to be paramount in the minds of many scholars and educational professionals. This attitude is reflected in

Figure 9.1

the enormous amount of literature available about academic achievement of African American males. In Google books there are currently 30 books with a title that explicitly refers to the achievement of African American males, while only eight explicitly refer to African American female achievement. This is more than three times as many published books that are easy accessible, concerning African American males than females.

A search for articles with titles containing the phrase "African American female achievement" yields fewer resources in Eric EBSCO than the same search with the phrase "African American males" as the key phrase. Although this is not an empirical literature study, this suggests that if a scholar or educational professional wanted to better understand the achievement of African American females, this information would be difficult to find and even harder to summarize. The current literature's emphasis on African American male achievement, however, is not without warrant, for on many national and state assessments, their scores are the lowest or near the lowest (Education Trust, 2010; Bandeira de Mello, Blankenship, & McLaughlin, 2009). One of the primary explanations why there is an emphasis on African American male achievement is the marginalization of not just African American women, but women in general (hooks, 1994).

Reporting is also a major factor in the underrepresentation of African American female achievement data in the current research literature. Research reporting practices typically disaggregate data by race or gender, but not by both. This practice, although widely exercised, does not present a complete view of the data set under investigation. This is the practice that is followed mostly in reporting of state standardized testing results, as well as when researchers report the results of such assessment as the National Assessment of Educational Progress (NAEP) (Lomotey, 2009). Furthermore, the connection between race and gender as they relate to student achievement is underdeveloped because these investigations typically focus on one race or gender as the benchmark and exclude all other races or genders from the discussion. The majority of the comparative studies on achievement compare the entire sample of African American students to the entire sample of White students without respect to race or gender. Likewise, when gender achievement disparities are investigated White females are selected as the benchmark and compared to all females. In their investigation of the mathematics achievement and academic progress of students in a Midwestern urban school district Capraro et al. (2009) disaggregated the achievement and academic progress data according to race and gender. This disaggregation of the achievement data lead the researchers to a better understanding of the overall achievement patterns and educational progress attained by the students in the study.

The purpose of this chapter is to (1) briefly discuss three areas that constitute the majority of the studies about African American females; (2)

share the results of academic performance of African American females on the National Assessment of Educational Progress in the subjects of mathematics, reading and science at the 4th, 8th and 12th grade levels; and (3) share the results of the comparison of 2009 data by scale scores of race and ethnicity in subjects areas of mathematics, reading, music, and visual arts.

STUDIES ON AFRICAN AMERICAN FEMALES

Research on African American females can be categorized in three areas. These areas are: (1) higher education achievement and career pathways, (2) social and emotional issues, and (3) health disparities.

Higher Education Studies and Career Pathways

Many studies have tracked the achievement of African American females in higher education from retention to graduation rates (Grant & Simmons, 2008; Sealey-Ruiz, 2007). In fact, one of the most recent studies has shown that there are more African American females going to college than males and, for the first time in history, there are more African American females graduating from college than African American males (Bush, Chambers, & Walpole, 2009). African American females are seeking studies in nontraditional areas such as engineering, medicine, and sciences as well as seeking careers in those areas. Studies also include career development (Hardaway & McLoyd, 2009; McLoyd & Jozefowitz, 2009; Rosenberg-Kima, Plant, Doerr, & Baylor, 2010).

Social/Emotional Issues

Within the literature, there are studies that have examined the social and emotional issues of African American females. These studies range from self-esteem to relationships issues (Rotheram-Borus, Dopkins, Sabate, & Lightfoot, 1996). These studies have discussed hair texture and skin color and their effects on the self-esteem of African American girls and adults (Thompson & Keith, 2001). According to one study, skin-tone variations have an impact on educational attainment, occupation and income as well as skin completion can be a predictor of occupation and income (Keith & Herring, 1991). In another study entitled, "The Blacker the Berry," results show that attractiveness was based on skin color, and skin color was a predictor of self-esteem (Thompson & Keith, 2001). Studies are associated with identity development and family relationships (Grotevant & Cooper, 1985)

Also, studies encounter issues of how African American women deal will issues of racism and sexism in schools, jobs, and life experiences (Cauce, Hiraga, Graves, Gonzales, Ryan-Finn, & Gove, 1996).

Health Disparities

Research on health disparities includes several issues such as obesity, AIDS, and cancer. One study reported that obesity and self-esteem in African American children was related to age, gender, teasing experiences, and parent evaluation of body sizes (Young-Hyman, Schulndt, Herman-Wenderwoth & Bozylinski, 2003). More recently, health professionals have documented the need to address obesity among African American girls (Story et al., 2003). African American women are the fastest growing group with AIDS. In 1991, African Americans were 12% of the population, and 52% of women with AIDS were African Americans (Jemmott, Catan, Nyamathi, & Anastasia, 1995) and in 2004, African American women still accounted for 12 % of the population but now accounted for 67% of women living with AIDS, according to National Alliance for State & Territorial AIDS Directors (NASTAD, 2008). Diabetes, heart attacks, and strokes are prevalent among African American women, and many studies document these health issues (Minority Women's Health, 2010). While all of the aforementioned areas are important and have an impact on school achievement, a critical examination of academic achievement issues is needed to show the performance of African American females. As such, this discussion will follow in the next section.

NATIONAL ASSESSMENT OF EDUCATIONAL PROGRESS (NAEP)

The National Assessment of Educational Progress (NAEP) measures student achievement nationally in grades four, eight and twelve. The most frequent assessments are in the areas of mathematics, reading, science and writing; however, other subjects like visual arts, civics, economics, geography, and U.S. history are also assessed. NAEP administers the same assessment in each of the 50 states and the District of Columbia and also collects such student data as gender, socioeconomic status, and race/ethnicity to examine the results. As such, we selected to examine the NAEP data by gender to see the results for African American students. While NAEP scores are not compared across subjects due to the scale score differences that range from 200 to 500, the scores can be compared across percentiles of how many students made the same scores in the subject matter content. The scores are report-

Level 4–Advanced—superior performance.

Level 3–Proficient—solid academic performance. Students reaching this level have demonstrated competency over challenging subject matter, including subject-matter knowledge, application of such knowledge to real-world situations, and analytical skills appropriate to the subject matter.

Level 2–Basic—partial mastery of prerequisite knowledge and skills that are fundamental for proficient work.

Level 1–Below Basic—scores that fall below the cut off score for basic that demonstrates partial if any mastery of the pre prerequisite knowledge and skills that are fundamental for proficient work. (NAEP does not provide a definition for or description of student performance at the Below Basic achievement level.)

Figure 9.2 NAEP academic levels and definitions.

ed in scale scores, and academic performance levels are calculated based on NAEP's cut-off score for each level. As such, NAEP results are reported as percentages of students performing on three levels, but a fourth level has been added to many states for students scoring below the basic cut-off scores. Therefore the four levels that are reported are: Below Basic, Basic, Proficient, and Advanced. Below basic is for those students who scores fall below the cut-off score for Basic. The definitions for the National Assessment of Educational Progress (NAEP) achievement levels are noted in Figure 9.2.

NAPE ACHIEVEMENT LEVELS FOR AFRICAN AMERICAN FEMALES 4, 8, 12 GRADES

The achievement levels according to academic performance are divided into four levels. These levels are below basic, basic, proficient, and advanced. A critical examination of these levels provides a response to the question, "What are the academic performances of African American females on the NAPE test?" This section begins by sharing NAPE achievement level data by grade and by subject. We used math and reading data from the years 2005, 2007 and 2009 for grades 4 and 8 and science data for the years 1996, 2000, and 2005 for those respective grades. For 12th grade we used math and reading data for the years 1998, 2002, and 2005, and for 12th grade science, we used data from the years 1996, 2000, and 2005.

Fourth Grade

In mathematics for the years 2005, 2007, and 2009, only 13 to 16% of African American females were placed at the proficient and advanced levels. There was a 3% increase in 2007, and it remained in 2009 as noted in Figure 9.3. At the basic level during these same years, the percent increased from 48% to 50%, then decreased in 2009 to 49%, while the group performing below basic decreased from 39% to 35% from 2005 to 2007. The 2009 data show that only 16% were above the basic level.

However, Figure 9.4 poses a similar picture for African American females in reading. Only 16% are above the basic level, with 2007 and 2009 remaining the same. Reading has a larger percent at below basic level than math. Since 2005, more have scored below basic with 53% in 2009, the highest percentage and the latest test result. At every level, except at the advanced level, there has been a decrease in the academic levels in reading. However, there are more achieving at the advanced level in reading than math in 2009.

Science results indicate that 93% were performing at the basic and below level, with none at the advanced level (see Figure 9.5). Yet, there was improvement in the 2000 to 2005 percentages ranging from 31% below basic in 1996 to 37% scoring at basic and above in 2005. There were only 7% who scored at proficient level and none at the advanced level.

Overall at the fourth grade level, African American female students show gains in math and losses in reading and science. More examination of content is needed to understand the losses in reading since in 2009 only 15% of African American students performed at the levels above basic.

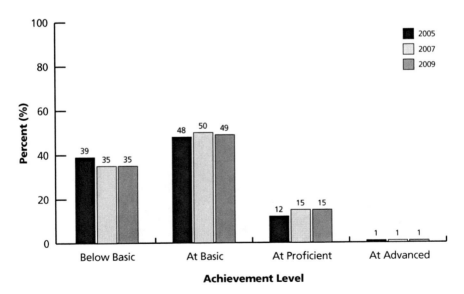

Figure 9.3 African Americn females, Math grade 4. *Source:* U.S. Department of Education, Institute of Education Sciences, National Center for Education Statistics, National Assessment of Educational Progress (NAEP), 2003, 2005 and 2009 Mathematics Assessments.

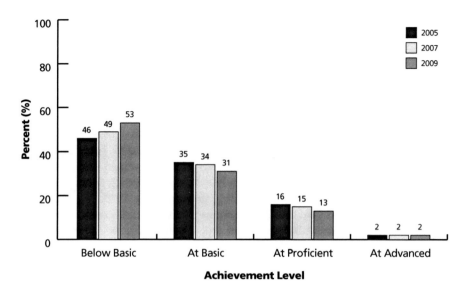

Figure 9.4   African American females, Reading grade 4. *Source*: U.S. Department of Education, Institute of Education Sciences, National Center for Education Statistics, National Assessment of Educational Progress (NAEP), 2003, 2005 and 2009 Reading Assessments.

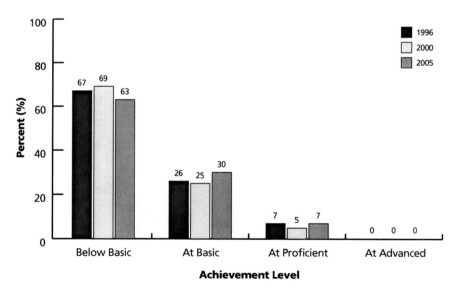

Figure 9.5   African American females, Science grade 4. *Source*: U.S. Department of Education, Institute of Education Sciences, National Center for Education Statistics, National Assessment of Educational Progress (NAEP), 1996, 2000 and 2005 Science Assessments.

Eighth Grade

The 8th grade math achievement for African American female students is shown in Figure 9.6. There was a 4% gain at the basic level and a 3% gain at the proficient level, while the 1% advanced level remained the same for all three years. The only losses that occurred were at the below basic level of 9% since 2005. In 2009, only 12% performed above the basic level.

In reading, according to Figure 9.7, African American females had the same percent at basic and proficient levels. There were no change between the years, 2009 and 2007. However, between 2007 and 2005 there was a difference of 1% at the basic and 2 % at the proficient levels. During these three years, there was a continual decrease in the percent of students scoring below basic. However, in 2009 like 2007, 17% of African American females performed at proficient and advanced levels.

Science had the highest percent of African American females at the below basic level with nearly three-fourth of the students in this category for the years 1996, 2000, 2005 (see Figure 9.8.). At the basic level, years 1996 and 2005 have the same 21% while there was a 3% drop in 2000. Yet in 2000 and 2005, each year reported 6% at the proficient level. Similar to fourth grade science performance, there were none at the advanced level.

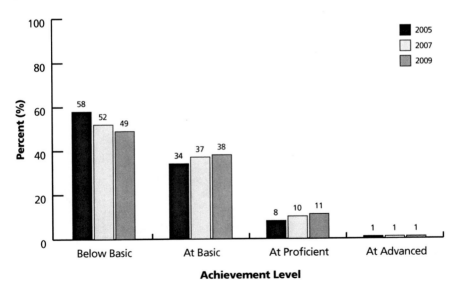

Figure 9.6 African American females, Math grade 8. *Source.* U.S. Department of Education, Institute of Education Sciences, National Center for Education Statistics, National Assessment of Educational Progress (NAEP), 2005, 2007and 2009 Mathematics Assessments.

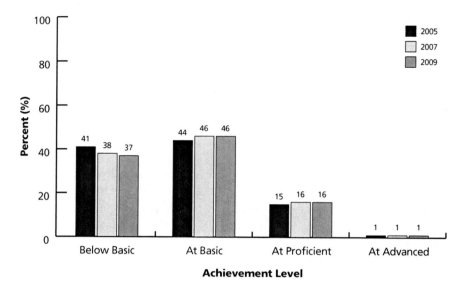

Figure 9.7 African American females, Reading grade 8. *Source:* U.S. Department of Education, Institute of Education Sciences, National Center for Education Statistics, National Assessment of Educational Progress (NAEP), 2005, 2007 and 2009 Reading Assessments.

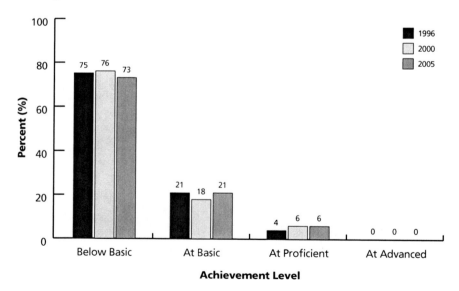

Figure 9.8 African American females, Science grade 8. *Source:* U.S. Department of Education, Institute of Education Sciences, National Center for Education Statistics, National Assessment of Educational Progress (NAEP), 1996, 2000 and 2005 Science Assessments.

Twelfth Grade

Figure 9.9 highlights the mathematics academic levels for 12th grade. At the 12th grade, African American females show an increase at the below basic level. In fact, in 2005, 70% of African American females performed at the below basic level which was an increase from 2000 of 68%. When looking at the proficient level in 2005, there was a slight increase from 2005. In 2005, only 5% performed at the proficient level and none performed at the advanced level in mathematics.

In reading, there were more who performed above basic than for any of grade and subject. The highest was 22% in 1998 to 19% for 2002 and 2005 (see Figure 9.10). In 2005, 61% were at basic and below. The advanced level was the only level that was consistent over three years, at 1%.

Science had the greatest percent of students performing below the basic level according to Figure 9.11. In fact, for each year, there was a one to two percent increase with 2005 showing 82% of the students with a below basic score. Within the three years examined, the number of African American females performing at basic slid from 18% to 16%, while the number performing at proficient moved from 3% to 2%. As in reading, none preformed at the advanced level.

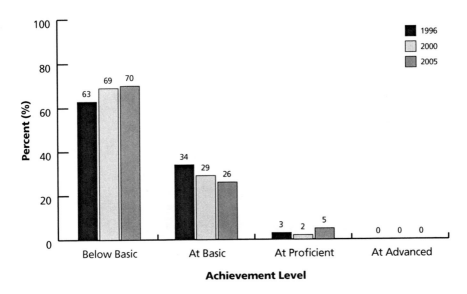

Figure 9.9 African American females, Math grade 12. *Source*: U.S. Department of Education, Institute of Education Sciences, National Center for Education Statistics, National Assessment of Educational Progress (NAEP), 1996, 2000 and 2005 Mathematics Assessments.

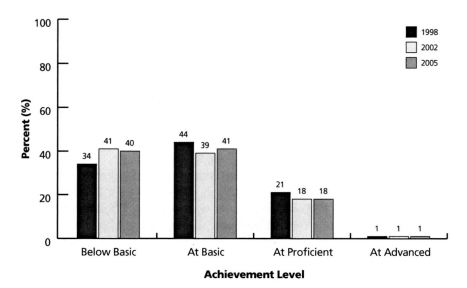

Figure 9.10 African American females, Reading grade 12. *Source:* U.S. Department of Education, Institute of Education Sciences, National Center for Education Statistics, National Assessment of Educational Progress (NAEP), 1996, 2000 and 2005 Reading Assessments.

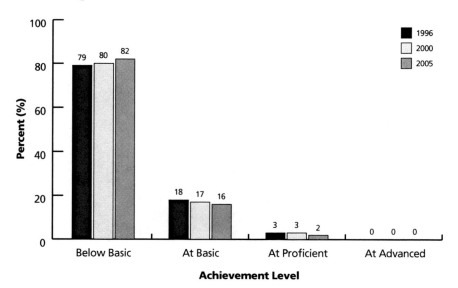

Figure 9.11 African American females, Science grade 12. *Source:* U.S. Department of Education, Institute of Education Sciences, National Center for Education Statistics, National Assessment of Educational Progress (NAEP), 1996, 2000, and 2005 Science Assessments.

An examination of academic levels by subject and grades shows African American females are not performing well on NAEP assessments. In math at the 4th, 8th, and 12th grade levels, African American females had the smallest percent performing above basic at the 4th grade level. As grade levels increase so do the percent of students achieving at basic, proficient, and advanced levels. The only grades where students achieved in math at the advanced level were 4th and 8th grades. Reading paints a different picture. While all grades have African American female students achieving at the advanced level of one or two percent, it seems that the greatest percent of students are scoring at the below basic level is the 4th grade with 2009 having the greatest percent, 53%, and 8th grade showing the least with 37%. A critical examination of the 4th grade content by subject matter is needed. However, science shows the most gains in students at the below basic level. The advanced level was zero for all grades and at the proficient level for grades 4, 8, and 12 ranged from 2 to 7 percentage points. The 2005 data showed the most gains for basic and proficient levels, except for 12th grade, in which there was a loss.

African American females have academic challenges in reading, math, and science, with their greatest challenges in 12th grades math and science. Overall, reading performance has the least percent of students at the below basic level; however, there is concern about the 53% at that level for 2009. African American females have not done well in science at any level with ranges of 63% to 82% at the below basic level, and there were none at the advanced level for grades 4, 8, and 12.

2009 NAPE DATA BY RACE AND GENDER IN MATHEMATICS, READING, MUSIC, AND VISUAL ARTS

There is a need to report on the achievement of African American females, because the achievement of African American students as a whole is not indicative of the achievement of African American females. In the discussion that follows, the most recent results from the NAEP are presented. The data presented are from the 2008–2009 administration of the NAEP. The data were disaggregated by race and gender and compared across several other racial groups. For this purpose, mathematics, reading, music, and visual arts were included to present a more complete view of the national achievement of African American females across the academic spectrum. Further, all data mean scale scores are presented with the 95% confidence interval as well as the standard deviation data. Tables 9.1–9.4 show the mean scale scores in mathematics, reading, music, and visual for all groups.

In the area of mathematics achievement, African American females are the only group of females to outperform their male counterparts. This is

TABLE 9.1 Mean Mathematics Scale Scores on 2008–2009 NAEP across Race and Gender

	M	SD
White Males	294.04	33.55
White Females	291.75	31.87
Black Males	259.85	34.01
Black Females	261.84	32.76
Hispanic Males	267.88	34.81
Hispanic Females	265.01	33.38
Asian Males	301.44	34.81
Asian Females	300.24	35.99

Note: Black includes African American, Hispanic includes Latino. Race categories exclude Hispanic Origin unless specified. The NAEP Mathematics Scale score ranges from 0–500.
Source: US Department of Education, Institute of Educational Sciences, National Center for Educational Statistics, National Assessment of Educational Progress (NAEP), 2009.

TABLE 9.2 Mean Reading Scale Scores on 2008–2009 NAEP across Race and Gender

	M	SD
White Males	268.17	31.04
White Females	277.69	29.61
Black Males	241.13	33.05
Black Females	251.51	31.29
Hispanic Males	244.70	35.65
Hispanic Females	253.41	33.86
Asian Males	269.40	35.05
Asian Females	279.22	35.51

Note: Black includes African American, Hispanic includes Latino. Race categories exclude Hispanic Origin unless specified. The NAEP Reading Scale score ranges from 0–500.
Source: US Department of Education, Institute of Educational Sciences, National Center for Educational Statistics, National Assessment of Educational Progress (NAEP), 2009.

particularly interesting because mathematics traditionally is viewed as a male-dominated discipline. Nonetheless, African American females are the second to last group in rank order of performance in mathematics on the 2009 NAEP. Thus, the only group that did worse on the exam was African American males. A similar trend was present in the Reading Scale scores for African American females; however, one distinct difference was present. African American females were third from the last in reading scale scores, scoring higher than Hispanic males and then African American males. African American female performance in the area of music was their best for this ad-

TABLE 9.3   Mean Music Scale Scores on 2008–2009 NAEP across Race and Gender

	M	SD
White Males	155.33	31.42
White Females	166.49	29.47
Black Males	123.58	32.81
Black Females	135.92	30.30
Hispanic Males	124.43	31.04
Hispanic Females	133.28	30.96
Asian Males	157.45	37.63
Asian Females	159.79	39.65

Note: Black includes African American, Hispanic includes Latino. Race categories exclude Hispanic Origin unless specified. The NAEP Music Scale score ranges from 0–300.
Source: US Department of Education, Institute of Educational Sciences, National Center for Educational Statistics, National Assessment of Educational Progress (NAEP), 2008.

TABLE 9.4   Mean Visual Arts Scale Scores on 2008–2009 NAEP across Race and Gender

	M	SD
White Males	154.64	31.81
White Females	165.38	29.44
Black Males	122.79	31.94
Black Females	134.45	33.70
Hispanic Males	130.17	33.50
Hispanic Females	138.67	34.56
Asian Males	149.89	35.65
Asian Females	162.42	35.16

Note: Black includes African American, Hispanic includes Latino. Race categories exclude Hispanic Origin unless specified. The NAEP Visual Arts Scale score ranges from 0–300.
Source: US Department of Education, Institute of Educational Sciences, National Center for Educational Statistics, National Assessment of Educational Progress (NAEP), 2009.

ministration of the NAEP. African American females scored higher in music than African American males, Hispanic males, and Hispanic females. African American female achievement in visual arts was similar to their achievement in reading, scoring higher than African American males and Hispanic males.

DISCUSSION

Findings from the literature review indicates that studies about African American females can be categorized in three areas: social and emotional issues, health disparities, and higher education achievement and career pathways. While these three areas are important for the overall well-being of African American females, knowing about the academic achievement at elementary and secondary levels is even more critical. African American females cannot enter higher education nor participate in any studies on career pathways if they have deficiencies in reading, math, and science skills. Studies overwhelmingly indicate that reading, math, and science skills are essential for taking and passing the necessary classes for high school graduation and entering higher education. Studies indicated that higher education and career pathways were good indications of post-secondary achievement; however, to better ascertain the pre-collegiate educational trajectories of African American females, it is important to investigate early academic achievement. For example, according to a 2000 U.S. Department of Education report, it was found that taking a greater number of mathematics and science courses positively enhanced achievement, which can lead to more scholarships, higher college acceptance, and access to advanced careers. In order for African American females to enroll in mathematics, English, and science courses, they must have the appropriate skills at the elementary and secondary levels.

In response to the central research question, "What is the academic achievement of African American girls?", we found alarming statistics. When analyzing NAEP data for reading, mathematics, and science for grades 4, 8, and 12 for African American females, there were several trends present in their performance across grade levels and subjects. In mathematics, reading, and science, the percentages of African American females scoring at the advanced and at proficient levels are less than 18%. This means that the majority of African American females have a partial mastery of knowledge and skills. Such inadequate levels of knowledge and skills indicate that they have not mastered competency in mathematics, reading, and science. While much can be debated about testing, the fact remains that African American females have not demonstrated mastery of basic skills in mathematics, reading, and science according to the NAEP results over the past ten years or more. However, there is a glimmer of hope when comparing gender scores across ethnicity, as African American females are the only females who perform better than males in mathematics. The NAEP data show that at 4th, 8th, and 12th grade level, no more than 20% have proficient or advanced level performance in mathematics and reading and in science, fewer than 10% performed at proficient or advanced levels.

Comparing 2009 data by scale scores of race and ethnicity in subject areas of mathematics, reading, music, and visual arts, the performance of African American females yielded some very interesting results. African American females outperformed African American males across all subject areas on the 2009 NAEP. Males in every other racial and ethnic group outperformed the females in their racial and ethnic group. This is worth discussing because much emphasis is placed on the achievement of African American males, but understanding the factors that explain the differences between African American female and male achievement may shed more light on the African American achievement gap. While research on African American males is important, research on African American females is equally important. However, more research is needed to establish and examine all the factors associated with this phenomenon.

IMPLICATIONS

Investigating African American female achievement has valuable implications for parents, educational professionals, and scholars. African American females account for 6% of the U.S. population. African American females comprise the greatest percent in poverty, head of single parent households, and one of the lowest educational levels. Their quality of life is impacted by their educational attainment level. Given these startling statistics, it is imperative to find a response to the question, "What is the academic achievement of African American females?" It is important that educators and parents have a deeper understanding of the factors related to African American female achievement.

As previously mentioned, much of the available literature on African American females focuses on the socio-emotional health of students. These factors influence achievement by means of affecting African American female self-efficacy. According to Gutman and Midgley (2000) academic self-efficacy is important to African American adolescent achievement. Thus, educators and parents must remain vigilant over how their teaching and parenting skills, as well as, the many external factors that may negatively affect female achievement. Research on the gender gap suggests that more attention should be place on African American females during their preteen and teenage years. Greene and Mickelson (2006) found that gender achievement differences did not occur in their sample of elementary students, but in their eighth grade sample the African American females outperformed the African American males. The study concluded that female achievement was highly influenced by their families' socioeconomic status, cultural capital, and school experiences, all of which influence self-efficacy. Educational professionals can also benefit from a better understanding African American female achievement.

The achievement gap is a major educational issue in the United States. African American students in particular fall short in almost every aspect of academic achievement including standardized test scores and grade point averages (Hoffman, Llagas, & Snyder, 2003; Lewis & Kim, 2008). If more classroom attention is placed on examining the educational factors that differentiate African American female achievement from African American male achievement, then educational professionals can maximize on these academic factors. For instance, educational self-efficacy is a major factor in the gender achievement gap between African American females and males that can be addressed in classrooms by educational professionals. Although educational self-efficacy is recognized as a major distinguishing characteristic between African American females' and African American males' achievement, self-efficacy does not account for all of the differences in academic achievement.

Much more research is needed to establish and support new theories to describe the achievement profile of African American females. More studies examining African American female achievement across various grade levels and content areas would help to initiate more discussion among scholars. As the body of knowledge grows, this work should move from the explorations of achievement patterns to the development of sustainable explanations of these patterns. The interdisciplinary nature of these investigations suggests that multiple scholars from many different areas of expertise can add to this discussion. Special attention is needed from multiculturalists, sociologists, psychologists, and many others to create a more representative body of literature supporting African American female achievement.

Lastly, more critical research must examine the subject matter skills content. Conducting a critical analysis of NAEP scores on mathematics, reading, and science assessments by grade levels is needed to assist in the development and teaching of grade level curriculum. Finding out the areas that African American females have the greatest and least challenges is a necessity. For example, do African American females understand reading inferences? do African American females know basic mathematics facts? and do African American females understand critical science issues? A response to these questions will provide accurate and current knowledge about the performance of African American females on subject matter skills in mathematics, reading, and science. Such information will provide all stake holders, African American females, teachers, and parents about their strengths and challenges in these subject areas.

CONCLUSION

No longer can scholars continue to ignore the needs of African American females while focusing on African American males. An examination of scale scores and academic levels on the NAEP assessment indicate that African American females are not doing well academically. While research should continue to focus on the social and health needs of African American females, research must also be done on their achievement. Research should not be done in isolation, but rather with the integration of social, health and educational issues of African American females. To capture a deep understanding of their academic needs, further investigation should include an analysis of the NAEP data by subject matter content by grade level. Such information is paramount to the evaluation of their achievement. In addition, having that accessible achievement information could provide teachers and parents with valuable insights when teaching and working with African American females. There is no doubt that African American females can learn, but their learning cannot be at the expense of competing against the attention being paid to African American males. Data about their learning must be analyzed and shared so that research about the achievement of African American females will not be silenced, which gives a powerful consent that they are "doing well" academically.

REFERENCES

Bandeira de Mello, V., Blankenship, C., and McLaughlin, D.H. (2009). *Mapping state proficiency standards onto NAEP scales: 2005–2007* (NCES 2010-456). National Center for Education Statistics, Institute of Education Sciences, U.S. Department of Education. Washington, DC.

Bush, V. B., Chambers, C. R., & Walpole, M. (2009). *From diplomas to doctorates: The success of Black women in higher education and its implications for equal educational opportunities for all.* Sterling, VA: Stylus Publishing.

Capraro, R. M., Young, J. R., Yetkiner, Z. E., Woods, M. N., & Lewis, C. W. (2009). an examination of mathematics achievement and growth in a midwestern urban school district: Implications for teachers and administrators. *Journal of Urban Mathematics Education, 2*(2), 46–65.

Cauce, A., Hiraga, Y., Graves, D., Gonzales, N., Ryan-Finn, K., & Gove, K. (1996). African American mothers and their adolescent daughters: Closeness, conflict and control. In B. Leadbeater & N. Way (Eds.) *Urban girls: Resisting stereotypes, Creating identities* (pp. 100–109). New York, NY: New York University Press.

The Education Trust. (2010). *Statement of education trust on 12th-grade reading and mathematics results from 2009 national assessment of educational progress.* Retrieved from http://www.edtrust.org/dc/press-room/press-release/statement-of-the-education-trust-on-12th-grade-reading-and-mathematics-r

Frazier-Kouassi, S. (2002). Race and gender at the crossroads: African American Females in school. *African American Research Perspectives, 8*(1), 151–162.

Grant, C., & Simmons, J. (2008). Narratives on experiences of African-American women in the academy: Conceptualizing effective mentoring relationships of doctoral student and faculty. *International Journal of Qualitative Studies in Education (QSE), 21*(5), 501–517.

Greene, A. D., & Mickleson, R. A. (2006). Connecting pieces of the puzzle: Gender differences in black middle school students' achievement. *Journal of Negro Education, 75,* 34–48.

Grotevant, H., & Cooper, C. (1985). Patterns of interaction in family relationships and the development of identity exploration in adolescence. *Child Development, 56,* 415–428.

Gutman, L. M., & Midgley, C. (2000). The role of protective factors in supporting the academic achievement of poor African American students during the middle school transition. *Journal of Youth and Adolescence, 29*(2), 223–248.

Hardaway, C. R., & McLoyd, V. C. (2009). Escaping poverty and securing middle class status: How race and socioeconomic status mobility prospects for African Americans during the transition to adulthood. *Journal of Youth Adolescence, 38*(2), 242–256.

Harper, S. (2010). In his name: Rigor and relevance in research on African American males in education. *Journal of African American Males in Education, 1*(1), 1–6.

Hoffman, K., Llagas, C., & Snyder, T. D. (2003). *Status and trends in the education of blacks.* Washington, DC: National Center for Educational Statistics.

hooks, b. (1994). *Outlaw culture: Resisting representations.* New York, NY: Routlege.

Jemmott, L., Catan, V., Nyamathi, A., & Anastasia, J. (1995). African American women and HIV-risk-reduction issues. In A. O'Learay & L. Jemmott (Eds.), *Women at risk: Issues in the primary preventin of AIDS* (pp. 131–157). New York, NY: Pelnam Press.

Johnson-Bailey, J., & Cervero, R. (2008). Different worlds and divergent paths: Academic careers defined by race and gender. Har*vard Educational Review, 78*(2), 311–332.

Keith, V., & Herring, C. (1991). Skin tone stratification in the black community. *The American Journal of Sociology, 97*(3), 760–778.

Lewis, J. L., & Kim, E. (2008). A desire to learn: African American children's positive attitudes toward learning within school cultures of low expectations. *Teachers College Record, 110*(6), 1304–1329.

Lomotey, K. (2009). *Encyclopedia of African American education.* Thousand Oaks, CA: Sage.

National Association of State and Territorial AIDS Directors (2008). *A call to action: ¡Adelan-te! Strengthening the response to HIV/AIDS and viral hepatitis in Latino communities.* Retrieved from http://www. nastad.org/Docs/highlight/20081013_AD- ELANTE%20-%20Final.pdf.

Rosenberg-Kima, R., Plant, E., Doerr, C., & Baylor, A. (2010). The influence of computer-based model's race and gender on female students' attitudes and beliefs towards engineering. *Journal of Engineering Education, 3*(2), 35–44.

Rotheram-Borus, M., Dopkins, S., Sabate, N., & Lightfoot, M. (1996). Personal and ethnic, identity, and self-esteem among Black and Latino adolescent girls. In B.J. Ross Leadbeater & N. Way (Eds.). *Urban girls: Resisting stereotypes, creating identities* (pp.35–52). New York, NY: New York University Press.

Sealey-Ruiz, Y. (2007). Wrapping the curriculum around their lives: Using a culturally relevant curriculum with African American adult women. *Adult Education Quarterly, 58*(1), 44–60.

Story, M., Sherwood, N., Himes, J. Davis, M., Jacobs, D., Cartwright, Y., Smyth, M., & Rochon, J. (2003). An after-school obesity prevention program for African American girls: The Minnesota GEMS pilot study. *Ethnicity & Disease, 13*(1Suppl1), 54–64.

Thompson, M., & Keith, V. (2001). The blacker the berry: Gender, skin tone, self-esteem and self-efficacy. *Gender & Society. 15*(3), 336–357.

Tillman, L. (Ed). (2009). *The Sage handbook of African American education.* Thousand Oaks, CA: Sage.

U.S. Department of Education, Partnership for Family Involvement in Education. (2000). *Working for children and families: Safe and smart after-school programs.* Washington, DC: Author.

Young-Hyman, D., Schlundt, D. G., Herman-Wenderoth, L., & Bozylinski, K. (2003). Obesity, appearance, and psychological adaptation in young African American children. *Journal of Pediatric Psychology, 28,* 463–472.

PART II

EMPOWERING URBAN STUDENTS AND TRANSFORMING THEIR SCHOOLS

Section 3: Policies, Politics, and Urban School Reform

CHAPTER 10

A CLOSER LOOK AT MEDIA INFLUENCES, IDENTITY FORMATION, AND EDUCATIONAL POLICY

Implications for African American Male Students

Meredith B. Walker and Bettie Ray Butler
Texas A&M University

ABSTRACT

Expanding learning opportunities for African Americans has been an ongoing discussion among policymakers and a persistent theme within education scholarship. However, amid the widespread use of a variety of educational sorting practices (e.g., academic tracking, ability grouping, etc.); access to such opportunities has never been more challenging for this group of students. Yet, beyond school-based sorting explanations, those within both political and academic spaces—with particular reference to policymakers and educators, respectively—have trouble articulating exactly why learning opportunities are

Yes We Can! Improving Urban Schools Through Innovative Educational Reform, pages 169–187

seemingly endless for some, and unavailable to others. Those interested in identifying outside factors that decrease academic self-motivation and inhibit achievement should be cognizant of the profound influence that the media (i.e., television and radio) have in shaping one's identity. Given that African Americans are the most active media consumers (Gandy, 2001), the present chapter takes a closer look at the relationship between media effects and perceptions of education for this subgroup.

The educational success of young African American males is of grave importance as they are often ranked the lowest on a vast number of quality of life indicators (Noguera, 2003). The statistics regarding African American males are staggering. For example, the high school completion rate for African American males in some U.S. states is less than 35% (Schott Foundation, 2008). From an academic perspective, this particular group of students is often overrepresented in lower-track academic courses, has high dropout rates, and is often underrepresented in colleges and universities. At the same time, from a sociological standpoint, this group remains one of the most publically stereotyped and stigmatized populations in America (Swanson, Cunningham, & Spencer, 2003). While the academic perspective has garnered much attention through discussions of sorting practices, such as academic tracking and ability grouping, it is the sociological standpoint that is often tenuously addressed in educational scholarship.

These stereotyped portrayals, to some degree, have damaged how African American males come to view the importance of education. With recent increases in media coverage of young, flashy athletes and blinged-out hip-hop artists, many African American male students find themselves pushing their books aside for a chance to sign a million dollar sports contract or for the opportunity to be discovered by some chart-topping record label. If policymakers and educators are truly interested in expanding opportunities for learning, it is critical that an attempt is made to understand the linkage between African American males' perceptions of education and the influence of media imagery on these perceptions. An examination of this relationship can potentially provide valuable insight into effective strategies that help to alleviate troubling academic standings for this population of students. To be clear, in this chapter *media* refers to broadcast media such as television and radio.

In the interest of clarity, this chapter has been divided into four sections. Section 1 will explain the purpose of the present chapter. Section 2 will provide a more detailed discussion of how opportunities to learn have been minimized through various educational sorting practices. Section 3 will present the theoretical underpinnings that shape the present chapter. Section 4 will discuss and provide practical examples of how the media can potentially have a negative influence on the academic performance of African American males. The final section will not only provide implications for practice, but it will also offer recommendations to policymakers, administrators, teachers, and community leaders on ways to implement practical strategies that ultimately seek to subvert the negative influences that the media can have on African American male students' perceptions of education.

PURPOSE

The present chapter will take a closer look at the external factors (i.e., factors that are not a function of what takes place within the classroom) that shape African American males' values. Going beyond school-based explanations that have been pursued in the extant literature, the purpose, here, is to examine the key role that the media has in shaping African American male students' identity and educational perceptions. Because adolescents are often easily influenced and perceptive (Berry, 2000; Ward, 2004), the salience of media images, sounds, and rhetoric must be taken seriously in understanding how they internalize what is valued and what is not.

Broadly speaking, young African American male students may internalize such values, and this can be a determining factor in how they view education. Accordingly, the primary question guiding this examination asks, *How does the internalization of news media reports and messages shape African American males' identity and their perceptions of education?* We contend the media play a fundamental role in influencing African American male students' perception of education and, consequently, how they perform academically.

Because African American youth are one of the most active groups of media consumers (Gandy, 2001), it is highly probable that they are also the most influenced by media imagery portrayed through specific media. While the media is not the only source of value construction, given its saliency to youth (Bang & Reece, 2003; Rideout, Foehr, & Roberts, 2010), the powerful signals that particular mediums provide into what it is to be valued should not be overlooked. Taken altogether, the present chapter makes use of the modes of television and radio as the primary media under consideration.

OPPORTUNITIES TO LEARN

The conceptual understanding of the phrase *opportunities to learn* has long been muddled. Conventionally, it has served as a potent concept for researchers interested in empirically investigating the varying aspects of teaching and learning (Anderson, 1990). More recently, the phrase has begun to take on a very different purpose—one that seeks to inform policy questions regarding educational equality. Yet, within the context of the present chapter the phrase itself is used in its most elementary form, which is simply to denote one's chances of being taught, or educated, effectively.

While the use of opportunities to learn in this chapter is, in a sense, a rather rudimentary and straightforward approach, the present musings of the concept must still be explored. What follows is a brief review of the two most notorious forms of sorting practices that are commonly used to thwart opportunities to learn for specific groups of students—usually, low-income students of color. Ability grouping and academic tracking will be discussed. Both practices have been known to stratify opportunities to learn by allowing some students, and denying others, access to a more rigorous and enriched curriculum.

Sorting Practices

Ability Grouping

This method of sorting is utilized, in some form, at the secondary level, but it is most common in elementary or primary schooling (Slavin, 1987). Under this practice, students are generally divided into groups in accordance to their measured or perceived intellectual abilities and/or interests (Oakes, 2005). These divisions typically vary by both grade level and academic subject. In theory, the instructional content within each ability group demonstrates some similarities, yet, there is one major difference—the content is taught at a different pace and depth, one that reflects the ability level of students in each group (Lleras & Rangel, 2009).[1]

Due to the notable differences in academic outcomes achieved in the varying ability groups, this sorting practice is often criticized and alleged to be discriminatory in nature. Critics generally argue that those students placed in low ability groupings—namely, low-income students of color—are more susceptible to a slower pace and lower quality of instruction than that which is rendered in higher ability groupings (Slavin, 1987). While this practice has been challenged in several court cases on the count that it violates equal educational opportunities, rulings continue to maintain its legitimacy and fail to declare such methods of grouping unconstitutional.

Academic Tracking[2]

This method of sorting is a common secondary schooling practice that sorts students into a series of courses with differentiated curriculum (Westchester Institute for Human Services Research, 2002). Under this practice, broad, pragmatic divisions are used to separate students into categories with the intent to group them into various types of academic tracks. Students are either placed on a high, middle, or low track, many of which constitute college-bound (i.e., honors/advanced), standard/general, or vocational/remedial course curricula, respectively (Futrell & Gomez, 2008).

Like ability grouping, this sorting practice—allegedly—provides students with different levels of opportunity. According to Archibald and Keleher (2008), academic tracking "exacerbates racial and class segregation and disadvantages those students most in need of exposure to rigorous curriculum and high standards" (p. 27).[3] Those assigned to a high track—usually, middle- to upper-income Caucasian students—are taught more enriched, challenging curriculum by high-quality teachers that focuses on the process of learning and application; whereas those assigned to middle to low tracks—usually low-income African American and Hispanic students—receive a more watered-down curriculum that concentrates on memorization and is generally taught by less qualified teachers (Burris & Welner, 2005; Oakes, 2005). Notwithstanding such criticisms, the debate over tracking—to date—remains unsettled.

THEORETICAL FRAMEWORK

Identity Construction

Recent scholarship has suggested that the identity construction of students should be the foundation to understanding African American male student success (Hopkins, 1997; Majors & Billson, 1992). Recognizing the source of this identity construction can provide beneficial insight into how African American male students view themselves, how they perceive that others view them, and what their future roles should be. All of these factors influence how African American males should perform academically. The argument here is that the media provide a significant outlet in which values are learned and developed, as we shall explain further. In short, understanding the values that the media puts forth regarding African American men can provide insight into their identity formation and academic success.

According to social learning theory, individuals often learn beliefs based on the observation of others (Bandura, 1977). Therefore, observing becomes a way of determining which values are salient. Similarly, cultivation theory suggests that the content of television shapes individuals' perceptions of the world (Gerbner, 1998). Media such as television, radio, and print media have been found to impact a variety of factors, such as perception of risk (Gandy, 2001) and self-efficacy. Because the adolescent years are such an impressionable stage, the effects of media images can have a profound influence. Past research has supported this, suggesting that the media (e.g., television, radio, and newspapers) play a role in socializing African American youth (Berry, 2000; Donohue, Meyer, & Henke, 1978;

Stroman, 1991; Ward, 2004). African American children use the media to learn valuable lessons about future life chances and for guidance (Stroman, 1991). Bang and Reece (2003) also suggest that the advertising in television is a critical avenue where beliefs are conveyed to youth. Bang and Reece (2003) argue that by transferring certain images and values, commercials teach youth not only to buy, but to accept certain values. In other words, the media can shape an individual's value construction.

The media have often depicted certain segments of the population in a very stereotypical manner (Dixon & Linz, 2000; Gandy, 2001; Graber, 2002). For example, in a study of Saturday morning advertising, Greenberg and Brand (1993) found that often when African American males were on television, they were usually portrayed in service occupations and rarely as high-level managers. In other words, it is important to understand what *is* portrayed in the media regarding African American males, as well as what is *not portrayed.* As such, Gaston (1986) suggests that an unproductive lifestyle of young African American men is often due to the impact of the media.

Moreover, the consideration of media consumption by youth is a salient issue as rates of consumption by youth are increasing. According to a recent Kaiser Family Foundation report, over the past five years, media usage by youth ages 8 to 18 has increased by nearly 2.5 hours daily (Rideout et al., 2010). The report indicated that given the use of multitasking (using more than one medium at a time), today's youth pack nearly 11 hours of media content into 7.5 hours. Additionally, television and music are the primary media for youth. In considering media consumption by race among this age group, African Americans and Latinos consume more than 4.5 more hours of media a day compared to Caucasians (see Figure 10.1). For televi-

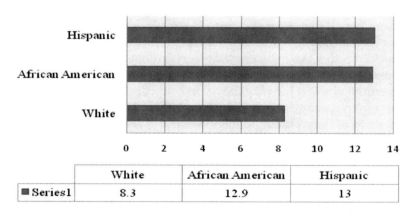

Figure 10.1 Total media exposure, per day, for all Caucasian, African American, and Hispanic youth ages 8–18 years old. Source: Rideout et al. (2010), *Study Generation M²: Media in the Lives of 8–18 Year Olds.*

sion content, African Americans are the largest consumers across all types of TV watching compared to Caucasians and Hispanics. Moreover, boys report higher usage of media than girls per day as well. Taken as a whole, these findings suggest that minority males, particular young African American males, are dominant media consumers.

The Kaiser report also finds that children who are heavy media consumers[4] report getting fair or lower grades than moderate or light media consumers (controlling for other relevant factors such as socioeconomic status, gender and race) (Rideout et al., 2010). Therefore, there is a linkage between media consumption and academic success. Findings such as these may suggest other latent possibilities. Given the media's effect on socialization and value construction (Berry, 2000; Graber, 2002; Ward, 2004), higher consumption can translate into an overexposure to certain values. In other words, higher media usage increases the probability that students are exposed to particular beliefs. For young African American men, the media play a significant role in teaching particular values. As such, the internalization of these viewpoints may translate into patterns and interactions in academic settings; thereby having vast implications for students.

What are the popular images of African American males being represented in these media? While there are various images that could be evaluated, we choose to underscore three prevailing images often portrayed of African American men in the media: the athlete, the entertainer, and the deviant. The subsequent section will underscore such images as well as the impact they have for the educational attainment of African American male youth.

Media Images

The Athlete

One of the most popular images of African American men in the media is that of an athlete. In professional sports of basketball (NBA) and football (NFL), African American males constitute nearly 80% and 65% respectively (Lapchick, 2000). To young African American males, these athletes can represent a type of role model.[5] Because professional athletics is the dominant profession portrayed in the media that represents them, young African American boys may be socialized into believing such a career is what they should pursue as well. The media glamorize the profession, negating the realities regarding the actual pursuit of this type of career. This concern has been explored for decades (Beamon & Bell, 2002; Bush, Martin, & Bush, 2004; Gatson, 1986). Gatson (1986) explains, "A young African American male struggling to develop a positive self-concept in a racist society can turn on the television set and see African American athletes being cheered and sought after by fans and reporters" (p. 376). Generally speaking, the perception is that mainstream society tends to appreciate these athletes—they are respected, well paid, and famous. As a result, young African American men learn early what career paths are valued for people that look like them, and the pursuit of that profession is appealing. Moreover, the underrepresentation of African American male coaches and stakeholders in the sports franchise (Cunningham & Sagas, 2005) can send other signals to these boys as well regarding the nature of African American men's chances in upper level management positions. As such, it is essential to consider holistically what these images portray.

The Entertainer

Another pervasive image in the media is that of an entertainer. A popularized type of entertainer that is most prevalent is that of the African American male rapper or hip-hop artist. Since the 1970s, rap music has been heavily influenced by African American men (Powell, 1991). As such, Elligan (2000) explains that in advertising, marketers use rap music as a way to appeal to young African American males in the media. Young African American men respect the music because the lyrics can portray the very struggles and aspirations that they face in their daily lives as well. To the young African American male, the rapper is "cool"; he is an embodiment of what many of them seek—respect. Majors and Billson (1992) discuss this notion with their development of the theory entitled "cool pose." Cool pose "entails behaviors, scripts, physical posturing, impression management, and carefully crafted performances that deliver a single, critical message: pride, strength and control" (Majors & Billson, 1992, p. 4). Being cool demonstrates to mainstream society that the African American male is strong and should be respected. Majors and Billson (1992) contend that an expressive and creative lifestyle is one way to articulate the cool pose. The authors suggest that this expressive type of lifestyle is entertainment. An African American boy may view the overrepresentation of African American males in the entertainment industry and seek to pursue this type of career. Therefore, the allure of the African American male entertainer stems from this desire for both monetary gains, respect and a "cool" lifestyle.

To be clear, we are not suggesting that entering professional sports or becoming an entertainer is inherently bad—there are many successful African American men in these careers. However, we contend that these professions are often the *dominant* portrayals of these groups, thus African American males are not seeing themselves represented in other fruitful careers. With the limited chances of becoming either a professional athlete or entertainer, it is imperative that African American men are represented in other positive sectors in the media.

The Deviant

One of the grimmest portrayals of African American men in the media is that of a deviant. Media coverage on the news over time has consistently highlighted African American male crime. Dixon and Linz (2006) find that African American and Latinos are more likely to be stereotypically depicted as lawbreakers. Even in popular culture, such as movies and television shows, the image of African American men is often negative. The media celebrate this distortion as well, thereby sending powerful signals to young African American males as to what is acceptable behavior.[6]

Hutchinson (1997) posits that, "If editors constantly feature young African American males as gang members or drug dealers and not as Rhodes, Merit, or National Science Foundation scholars... then the news becomes a grim self-fulfilling prophecy" (p. 47). In other words, the portrayals of African American men as deviants send a powerful message to young African American boys regarding what future life chances are available to them. This deviant representation can also create fear on the part of others. Hutchinson (1997) explains that the media's obsession with "ghetto crimes, gangs"—and the like—scares many Whites. Images of African American males in the media as troublemakers, plays both a role on the African American male psyche, as well as how others might view and relate to this group.

Media Images and Education

How might these media imageries translate into academic performance of young African American male students? These images may shape the value that African American males place on education. If the predominant images for African American males are that of entertainers, athletes, deviants, and "hustlers," then an internal struggle can ensue regarding the purpose of education. The media do not illuminate the educational attainment of African American males to the same extent as the other aforementioned images. As a result, young African American males struggling for both acceptance and significance may become disillusioned with school because it is not perceived as important.

Consider a young African American male student that is already struggling academically. The pursuit of a career in the entertainment industry may be an outlet to express himself in an area where he can be accepted and immediately rewarded, unlike in the education system where acceptance is hard to come by and rewards are delayed. This fantasy, in turn, may dominate his pursuits, allowing school to become more of a distant reality and a place that does not value him. As such, the African American male student may internalize the depictions in the media and attempt to escape the institutional discomfort experienced in schools.

Additionally, if these African American male students actually decide to pursue the media images depicted of an athlete or entertainer, there is rarely a discussion of the process to acquire such positions. Education is often perceived as secondary. Again, the distorted depictions do not underscore the necessity for education, thereby suggesting that education is not valued. This may lead to ambivalence towards academics.

These images are readily accessible to teachers and administrators in schools as well. The teacher may perceive African American male students like the images depicted in the media and treat them differently because of this. For example, if a popular image is that of a deviant, troublemaking African American male, this may cause the teacher to fear him. Similarly, the teacher may not invest ample time with an African American male student who seems more occupied with athletics than education. The teacher may let him "get by" in order to meet requirements to participate in sports. Gaston (1986) suggests that coaches play a role in this process as well, by "running interference" (p. 279) with teachers. African American male students may also respond to how they perceive teachers' views of them. Consequently, if they believe they are viewed in an unpleasant or stereotyped way, they may internalize such views and act accordingly, creating a self-fulfilling prophesy.

Moreover, "the deviant" image and "the entertainer" image may be linked. For example, when a vast amount of the songs by African American male rappers discuss the pursuit of "getting money" and an African American male student finds himself ill prepared to obtain a high-quality job because of an inadequate educational system, then perhaps adhering to deviant activities is an avenue to obtain that career goal. In other words, there can be interplay among these images that the media puts forth.

DISCUSSION

In order to provide a more practical understanding of how the media may influence African American male students, a more elaborate, concrete depiction of what is displayed in the media regarding African American males is warranted. As such, this section will underscore a few different portrayals in the media involving African American males. While this is not meant to be a holistic exposition of African American male imagery in the media, it provides some key occurrences in the past decade.

In this decade, television shows rarely represent African American males in a positive manner, or in upper level professional roles. Ward (2004) explains that African Americans are often depicted in demeaning roles, such as thugs, hustlers, clowns, and lazy individuals. Stereotypical roles are common, with shows such as HBO's "The Wire" and "Oz" often portraying African American men in a negative manner, through crime and drug involvement. Moreover, news media coverage follows this same pattern, with an overrepresentation of negative coverage of African Americans (Graeber, 2002)—especially athletes such as Michael Vick, Plaxico Burress, Packman Jones, Ricky Williams, Allen Iverson, and Ron Artest, just to name a few.

The depiction of African American men in the media is significant because it essentially illuminates different role models for African American boys (King & Multon, 1996). Since the election of President Barack Obama, there has been discussion in the media regarding the role model effect present when African American male students see an African American president represented in the media. In the wake of the election of President Obama, several African American male students expressed that they were inspired and encouraged by the historic election. For instance, ABC News reported that a 17-year-old African American male teen, Aloysius Puff, explained that President Obama is "stepping it up for all of us, especially Blacks... I just hope us African Americans realize he's doing it for us, and we should give back and step up—do what we can do, what we can accomplish" (Gomstyn, 2008, p. 1). Similarly, another student interviewed, David Williams, 17, suggested that "Obama also helps fight negative stereotypes of Black men." Williams also contended that "an African-American like Obama, he shows you can actually obtain an education, you can actually be smart and make a difference. Obama is the perfect role model for all Black men" (Gomstyn, 2008, p. 1).

Moreover, President Obama also underscored the salience of role models and African American males. At the NAACP 100th Anniversary dinner, referring to African American children, President Obama articulated, "They might think they've got a pretty good jump shot or a pretty good flow, but our kids can't all aspire to be the next LeBron or Lil Wayne. I want them aspiring to be scientists and engineers, doctors and teachers, not just ballers and rappers. I want them aspiring to be a Supreme Court justice. I want them aspiring to be president of the United States" (Miller, 2009, p. 2). The grim reality is that there are rarely media portrayals of African American men in the roles that President Obama spoke of. Instead what is prevalent in the media are African American male rappers and athletes. Though, the chances of becoming a professional athlete or rapper are extremely slim.

Furthermore, the language in the hip-hop songs by these rappers is influential and can have an impact on African American male students as well. An assessment of the lyrics of rap songs on *Billboard*'s "Hot 100" Singles Chart indicates that many of the songs have a common theme—money, violence, pursuit of women, and the fame that come along with a hip-hop lifestyle. Three excerpts from popular rap songs by African American male artists that appeared on the *Billboard* "Hot 100" Singles Chart[7] over the past few years illustrates the type of lifestyle that is often showcased and promoted in the media (see below).

"Still Fly" by Big Tymers
(Billboard 2002)
Gator boots with the pimped out Gucci suit
Ain't got no job but I stay sharp
Can't pay my rent 'cause all my money spent
But dat's okay cause I'm still fly
Gotta quarter tank a gas in my new E-class
But dat's alright cuz I'm gon' ride
Got everythang in my momma name
But I'm hoodrich da da da da

"This is How We Do" by The Game (feat 50 Cent)
(Billboard 2005)
Fresh like, unhh; Impala, unnh
Crome hyrdraulics, 808 drums
You don't want, none, n**** betta, run
When beef is on, I'll pop that, drum
Come get, some
Pistol grip, pump
If a n**** step on my white Air Ones
Since red, rum, ready here I, come
Compton, unh, Dre found me inside the, slums
Sellin that skunk, one hand on my gun

"4 My Town (Play Ball)" by Birdman (Feat Lil Wayne and Drake)
(Billboard 2009)
(Chorus) Take yourself a picture when I'm standing at the mound
And I swear it's going down, I'm just repping for my town
Off a cup of CJ Gibson, man I'm faded off the Brown
And I'm easily influenced by the n**** I'm around
See that Aston Martin when I start it hear the sound
I ain't never graduated, I ain't got no cap and gown
But the girls in my class who were smart enough to pass
Be at all my f**** parties, grabbing money off the ground.

Additionally, crime and this hip-hop lifestyle are often intertwined. Since 2000, prominent rappers such as TI (Clifford Joseph Harris), Lil Wayne (Dwayne Carter), and Gucci Mane (Radric Davis), have all faced criminal charges and served jail time.[8] However, once jail time is served, these rappers usually find prosperity again as fans continue to embrace them. As a result, African American boys may not view the consequences of deviant lifestyle as severe. The reality is, however, that if convicted of a crime, obtaining a job in a non-entertainment industry is often extremely difficult (Clark, 2003; Harris & Keller, 2005).

Because of these various media depictions, African American male students are often placed in the position where they have to contend with the negative portrayals and representation. Leroy Hughes of the group Concerned Black Men says that their organization works to mitigate the stereotypes the children see in the media and contends that kids "don't know that they are more than what they see on TV" (Kelley, 2007, p. 2). If African American male students absorb the media images regarding their futures, their educational focus may wane, and their self-efficacy regarding achievement may be hampered. In short, it is evident that the internalization of these images can be deleterious to their educational career.

RECOMMENDATIONS

Armed with information about the potentially devastating influence that the media could have on African American male students, the question now becomes, how might those with a vested interest in the academic success of this group work to mitigate the adverse effects of stereotypical reports and daunting lyrics broadcast through television and radio media. To better answer this question, the following recommendations have been developed specifically for education policymakers, school administrators, educators, and community leaders.

Policymakers (Education)

Generally speaking, the role of a policymaker is to serve as a responsive agent for their constituents, meaning they typically try to address problems presented to them by their voters, and in turn, design solutions for such problems via the implementation of policies. With this in mind, one of the more pressing educational problems for African American constituents is the underperformance of African American male students. Those policymakers whose area of expertise lies in education policy have the challenge of identifying a solution to the dismal test scores and high dropout rates found among this group of students. However, what is more important than finding the solution is identifying the source of the problem.

Textbook Regulation
In this chapter, negative media reports and images have been conceptually linked to the problem of underachievement for African American

males. While education policymakers cannot regulate the press, nor can they censor music, policymakers can, in fact, regulate what type of images are portrayed in school textbooks. As such, policymakers should aim to ensure that the content conveyed in textbooks does not promote racial inferiority nor portray any type of demeaning images. This is especially true of history books that revisit slavery and the Civil Rights Movement.

Administrators

School administrators, otherwise referred to as principals, are often delegated the responsibility of identifying, interviewing, and hiring qualified educators to instruct the students within their school. Yet, despite the fact that schools today are populated with diverse learners; these institutions are perpetually staffed with educators who are overwhelmingly homogeneous. Currently, the majority of the public schools' teaching force is White, middle-class, and female. This mismatch between the average educator (White, middle-class, and female) and the every-day urban African American male student (Black, lower-class, and male) can lead to disciplinary concerns, poor academic performance, and high dropout rates, all of which can be attributed—in some way or another—to the absence of cultural continuity. In this, it becomes important, if not necessary, for administrators to seek out, or aggressively recruit, diverse educators.

Reflective Hiring

In dealing with the effects of imagery on the African American male student, it can be assumed that positive portrayals of African American men can induce empowerment among African American male students that leads to improvements in academic performance (i.e., the adverse effect of negative portrayals). This reflective dynamic can be emulated within schools if administrators seek out qualified, African American male educators who have a willingness to teach, and possibly advise and mentor, African American male students. The ability to not only see, but interact with, educated African American men (i.e., teachers) is potentially a prelude to success among African American male students.

Educators

The impact of an educator often extends beyond the classroom. Because the average public school student typically spends more time at school than at home, it is the teacher who has a significant amount of influence over the student. While many teachers forfeit their ability to influence, those who have embraced it have witnessed its power. Yet, influence is not automatically granted because one is an educator, but rather it is earned by gaining a student's respect. This occurs primarily through communication, one-on-one interaction, and cultural sensitivity/responsiveness.

Cultural Pedagogy

Although an educator may be mismatched with a student, as mentioned earlier, this does not necessarily mean that the educator cannot effectively instruct the student. However, to do so requires additional effort on the part of the teacher to relate to, or connect with, that particular student. It is important to note that while attending culturally responsive professional development is critical in working with diverse learners, that alone cannot be used to acquire the much-needed respect necessary to positively influence African American male students. To build a meaningful relationship, the educator must familiarize herself with the students' culture. For example, she must learn about the students' music, language (both body and verbal), neighborhood, history, and so on. Once she has learned these things, the educator then can use this knowledge in her instruction as a strategic tool to engage the student. As is often thought, learning is not always contingent upon *what* (i.e., content) is being taught, but rather *how* (i.e., teaching methods) it's being taught. The logic stands: Influence is acquired through respect; respect is gained by establishing a meaningful relationship; the presence of a meaningful relationship makes it easier to engage the student in instruction; and when the student is engaged in instruction, learning is more likely to occur.

Community Leaders

The role of a community leader is very different than that of those previously mentioned; they are not elected, appointed, or hired. These individuals are merely volunteers with little to no formal authority. They dedicate their time within communities where they either formerly or presently reside to serve as a spokesperson for the people—that is, one who publicly addresses the needs of the community and occasionally networks with various organizations and corporations to bring the community resources, frequently in the form of financial assistance and/or social capital, that it would otherwise lack.

School Partnerships

For reasons unknown, community leaders seldom interact with school leaders. Yet it is this very relationship that could prove to reverse the influence of the negative news reports and disparaging rap lyrics to which

African American male students are exposed almost every day. "How so?", is the question that school leaders ask. The answer lies with the ability of community leaders to pool their networks together for a good cause. Uniting organizations such as Concerned Black Men, NAACP, Urban League, and Pan Hellenic Council fraternities with schools in an effort to create after-school programs, tutorials, mentoring programs, and so on has the potential to showcase positive examples of African American men—images that work to empower African American male students and counter the damaging stereotypes that are repeatedly broadcast through television and radio media.

After a review of the information above, it is important that we offer this one disclaimer. These recommendations should not be interpreted as complete, all-encompassing solutions designed to combat the effects of negative media influences on the educational aspirations of African American males, but rather they should be used as a very tentative guide for those with a vested interest in promoting the academic success of African American male students. From these recommendations, we hope that policymakers, administrators, educators, and community leaders are able to ascertain a general sense of what is needed to help counter what these young men see in the media, and consequently how they view themselves.

NOTES

1. Epstein (1985) explains that in classes that are sorted by ability, the same material is covered, but at a different pace. At the end of the class one group has covered the material more swiftly than the other. For this very reason, many critics of ability grouping have posed questions of equitability surrounding this sorting practice.
2. Although the terms *ability grouping* and *academic tracking* are used interchangeably, it should be noted that they are inherently distinct, as referenced in the definitions provided. Ability grouping is more an elementary schooling practice, and academic tracking a secondary schooling practice.
3. This is particularly true for African American and Latino students. Asian American students are often stereotyped as model minorities and are intuitively perceived to be intelligent. In general, these students—unlike their ethnic counterparts—are more often assigned to high tracks, discounting racial subgrouping. Tracking can also occur along gender lines. For more on academic tracking and gender see Catsambis, Mulkey, and Crain (1999).
4. Heavy media consumption is defined in this study as children who absorb more than 16 hours of media content in a day. Moderate usage is 3–16 hours per day, and light usage is defined as fewer than three hours of media consumption a day.
5. Role models that are not in direct contact with adolescent are often called "vicarious role models" because they have an indirect effect (Bandura, 1977;

Bush et al., 2004). Bush et al. (2004) suggest that the celebrity athlete represents a vicarious role model.

6. Consider the instance in which noted African American actor Denzel Washington received an Oscar Award for Best Actor, for a depiction as a corrupt, criminally minded cop out of countless other positive roles. While this is an isolated event, it alludes to the *value* placed on the image of the criminalized African American male.

7. *Billboard Hot 100 Chart* is the U.S. music industry's singles popularity chart. This chart is comprised of "the most popular songs across all genres" as ranked by radio airplay and audiences impressions (Billboard.com).

8. It is important to note that there are rappers who at times set positive examples regarding entrepreneurship and philanthropy, such as Shawn Carter (also known as Jay-Z) and Sean Combs (also known as Diddy). However, the representation of the deviant or destructive Black male rapper is often most apparent.

REFERENCES

American Psychiatric Association. (2000). *Practice guidelines for the treatment of patients with eating disorders* (2nd ed.). Washington, DC: Author.

Anderson, L. W. (1990). *Opportunity to learn and the national assessment of educational progress: An analysis with recommendations.* Unpublished manuscript.

Archibald, D., & Keleher, J. (2008). Measuring conditions and consequences of tracking in high school curriculum. *American Secondary Education, 36*(2), 26–42.

Bandura, A. (1997). *Social learning theory.* New York, NY: General Learning Press.

Bang, H. K. & Reece, B. B. (2003). Minorities in children's television commercials: New, improved, and stereotyped. *The Journal of Consumer Affairs, 37*(1), 42–67.

Beamon, K. &Bell, P. (2002). "Going Pro": The deferential effects of high aspirations for a professional sports career on African American student athletes and white student athletes. *Race and Society, 5*(2), 179–191.

Berry, G. (2000). Multicultural media portrayals and the changing demographic landscape: The psychosocial impact of television representations on the adolescent of color. *Journal of Adolescent Health, 27*(2), 57–60.

Burris, C., & Welner, K. (2005). Closing the achievement gap by detracking. *Phi Delta Kappan, 86*(8), 594–598.

Bush, A., Martin, C., & Bush, V. (2004). Sports celebrity influence on the behavioral intentions of generation Y. *Journal of Advertising Research 44*(1), 108–118.

Catsambis, S., Mulkey L., & Crain, R. (1999). To track or not to track? The social effects of gender and middle school tracking. *Research in Sociology of Education and Socialization, 12,* 135–163.

Clark, L. (2003). A civil rights task: Removing barriers to employment of ex-convicts. *University of San Francisco Law Review, 38,* 193–211.

Cunningham, G.B., & Sagas, M. (2005). Access discrimination in intercollegiate athletics. *Journal of Sport and Social Issues, 29*(2), 148–163.

Dixon, T., & Linz, D. (2000). Overrepresentation and underrepresentation of African Americans and Latinos as lawbreakers on television news. *International Communication Association, 50*(2), 131–154.

Donohue, T.R., Meyer, T.P., & Henke, L.L. (1978). Black and white children: Perceptions of TV commercials. *Journal of Marketing, 42*(4), 34–40.

Elligan, D. (2000). Rap therapy: A culturally sensitive approach to psychotherapy with young African American men. *Journal of African American Studies, 5*(3), 27–36.

Epstein, J. L. (1985). After the bus arrives: Resegregation in desegregated schools. *Journal of Social Issues, 41*, 23–43.

Futrell, M., & Gomez, J., (2008). How tracking creates a poverty of learning. *Educational Leadership, 65*(8), 74–78.

Gandy, O.H., Jr. (2001). Racial identity media use, and the social construction of risk among African Americans. *Journal of Black Studies, 31*(5), 600–618.

Gaston, J.C. (1986). The destruction of the young black male: the impact of popular culture and organized sports. *Journal of Black Studies, 16*(4), 369–384.

Gerbner, G. (1998). Cultivation analysis: An overview. *Mass Communication and Society, 3*(4), 175–194.

Gomstyn, A. (2008, November 5). Obama as a role model: Students, educators share excitement. *ABC News.* Retrieved from http://abcnews.go.com/US / story?id=6184328&page=1

Graber, D. (2002). *Mass media and American politics.* Washington, DC: Congressional Quarterly.

Greenberg, B.S. & Brand., J.E. (1993). Learning about minorities from television: A research agenda. In G. L. Berry & M. K. Claudia (Eds.), *Television and the socialization of the minority child* (pp. 37–67). New York, NY: Academic Press.

Harris, P.M., & Keller, K.S. (2005). Ex-offenders need not apply: The criminal background check in hiring decisions. *Journal of Contemporary Criminal Justice, 21*(1), 6–30.

Hopkins, R. (1997). *Educating black males: Critical lessons in schooling, community, and power.* Albany, NY: State University of New York Press.

Hutchinson, E.O. (1997). *The assassination of the black male image.* New York, NY: Simon and Schuster.

Kelley, R. (2007, December 1). The search for thugs. *Newsweek.* Retrieved from http://www.newsweek.com/2007/12/01/the-search-for-thugs.html

King, M., & Multon, K.D. (1996). The effects of television role models on the career aspirations of African-American junior high school students. *Journal of Career Development, 23*(2), 111–125.

Lapchick, R. (2000). Crime and athletes: New racial stereotypes. *Society, 37*(3), 14–20.

Lleras, C. & Rangel, C. (2009). Ability grouping practices in elementary school and African American/Hispanic achievement. *American Journal of Education, 115*(2), 279–304.

Majors, R. & Billson, J.M. (1992). *Cool Pose: The dilemmas of black manhood in America.* New York, NY: Lexington Books.

Miller, S. (2009, July 16). President Obama says pain of discrimination still felt in America. *ABC News.* Retrieved from http://abcnews.go.com/ Politics/ story?id=8104963&page=1

Noguera, P.A. (2003). The trouble with Black boys: The role and influence of environmental and cultural factors on the academic performance of African American males. *Urban Education, 38*(4), 431–459.

Oakes, J. (2005). *Keeping track: How schools structure inequality* (2nd ed.). New Haven, CT: Yale University Press.

Powell, C. (1991). Rap music: An education with a beat from the street. *Journal of Negro Education, 60*(3), 245–259.

Rideout, V.J, Foehr, U.G., & Roberts, D.F. (2010). The Henry J. Kaiser Family Foundation. *Generation M²: Media in the lives of 8- to 18-year-olds.* Retrieved from http://www.kff.org/entmedia/upload/8010.pdf

Schott Foundation for Public Education. (2008). Given half a chance: The Schott 50 state report on public education and Black males. Retrieved from http://blackboysreport.org/node/13

Slavin, R. E. (1987). Ability grouping and student achievement in elementary schools: A best-evidence synthesis. *Review of Educational Research, 57*(3), 293–336.

Stroman, C.A. (1991). Television's role in the socialization of African American children and adolescents. *Journal of Negro Education, 60*(3), 314–327.

Swanson, D.P., Cunningham, M., & Spencer, M.B. (2003). Black males' structural conditions, achievement patterns, normative needs, and opportunities. *Urban Education, 38*(5), 608–633.

Ward, L.M. (2004). Wading through the stereotypes: Positive and negative associations between media use and black adolescents' conceptions of self. *Developmental Psychology, 40*(2), 284–294.

Westchester Institute for Human Services Research. (2002). *Ability grouping. The balanced view: Research-based information on timely topics.* Retrieved from http://www.sharingsuccess.org/code/bv/abilitygrouping.pdf

CHAPTER 11

TWO STEPS FORWARD, ONE STEP BACK

A Brief Fifty-Year Overview of Educational Finance, Politics and Policy Influencing Urban Districts, Schools and Students

Augustina Lozano
Texas A&M University

Anthony Rolle
University of South Florida

ABSTRACT

In the seminal work *Education and the Cult of Efficiency* (1962), Callahan examined the state of public education in the 1960s resulting from business, economic, and political events stemming from the early 1900s. He asserted that district and school leaders of the time incorporated business approaches into public education processes only after decades of political pressure from prominent business leaders. The myriad of debates concerning what consti-

Yes We Can! Improving Urban Schools Through Innovative Educational Reform, pages 189–204
Copyright © 2011 by Information Age Publishing

tutes an excellent education for all students has been roiling for the past 50 years. As such, the purpose of this chapter is to provide a brief overview of the efficiency debate since the 1960s while paying special attention to the issues affecting urban districts, schools, and students.

INTRODUCTION

In the seminal work *Education and the Cult of Efficiency* (1962), Callahan examined the state of public education in the 1960s resulting from business, economic, and political events stemming from the early 1900s. Based on the historical evidence he presents, Callahan asserts that district and school leaders of the time incorporated business approaches into public education processes only after decades of political pressure from prominent business leaders. This quasi-market approach, in Callahan's view, has led to insufficient schooling systems and poor student academic outcomes. Specifically, Callahan states, "Efficiency and economy—as important as they are—must be considered in light of the quality of education that is being provided" (p. 263). This statement—providing an important caveat that extends the concept of efficiency to interactions with community, household, individual, peer, and school characteristics—rings true especially for urban districts and schools that typically utilize relatively inferior human, fiscal, and physical plant resources.

Consequently, Callahan called on educators to end the pursuit of economically efficient schools that he claimed had been strengthen by the cult of the political. An excellent education for all, he claimed, should be the natural pursuit of parents, teachers, schools, and districts. The myriad of debates concerning what constitutes an excellent education for all students has been roiling for the past 50 years. As such, the purpose of this monograph is to provide a brief overview of the efficiency debate since the 1960s while paying special attention to the issues affecting urban districts, schools, and students. For simplicity, significant educational policy – and associated political events – will be presented by decade.

THE 1960S: WILL PURSUING "EXCELLENT" PUBLIC EDUCATION POLICY DISBAND THE CULT OF EFFICIENCY?

In 1961, President John F. Kennedy took office as the second youngest person ever to hold the office of United States president. Issues of equality of opportunity and equitable treatment for all peoples dominated political and public policy discussions at all levels of government. After the assassination of President Kennedy, in a move often characterized as an operationalization of his vision, ascendant President Lyndon Johnson began to incorporate ideas of equality and equity into an education agenda that was part of the Great Society's programs (U.S. Department of State, n.d.). For example, additional instruction, instructional support, and auxiliary services for bilingual, impoverished, and vocational educational programs now were given national attention, and the national media captured these educational policy changes as they unfolded and culminated as part of the Civil Rights Act (Southern Christian Leadership Conference, 2011).

Few not in the education policy arena know that this act released federal funds for public education. The new Civil Rights Act, known to most educators as Title VI, allowed the U.S. Office of Education to release revenues intended to support *compensatory education programs for schools*—particularly urban and rural ones—that served significant numbers of poor students. Later, the Elementary and Secondary Act (ESEA) of 1965, also supported by President Johnson, became one of the most significant contributions to public education in the twentieth century (New York State Archives, n.d.).

Now, the ESEA of 1965 is a significant piece of United States public education history because its purposes were to equalize access to public education, establish high academic standards, and improve accountability among districts and schools (Office of Superintendent and Public Instruction, n.d.). Ironically, as ESEA compensatory education gained attention, especially for educational service improvements to poor urban schools, it re-called attention to the Sputnik-inspired educational objectives of the late 1950s: Additional state and federal revenues were necessary for poor, rural students (New York State Archives, n.d.). In fact, as the political turmoil of the 1960s continued, conservative activists and politicians began to ask: If additional educational funds are being assigned to state educational agencies, how efficiently are these funds were being used? The Equality of Educational Opportunity Report (EEO) attempted to answer this question, and its results highlighted stark differences in access to, fiscal capacity of, and quality of educational services provided to districts, schools, and students (Gamoran & Borman, 2007).

The Equality of Educational Opportunity Report

Also known as the *Coleman report*, the EEO report also was authorized under the Civil Rights Act of 1964. The primary purpose of the report was to conduct a survey that informed the President and Congress on issues "concerning the lack of availability of equal educational opportunities for individuals by reason of race, color, religion, or national origin in public educational institutions at all levels in the United States, its territories and possessions, and the District of Columbia" (Coleman et al., 1966, p.iii).

The Coleman report found two significant results using a technique new to education policy evaluation called production function analysis: "First, the Coleman report found that school resources, including school facilities, curriculum, and teacher quality, do not show statistically significant effects on student achievement. Second, the most significant effect on student achievement was the background characteristics of other students, or peer effects" (Wong & Nicotera, 2004, pp. 129–130).

The reported results were damaging particularly to urban districts and schools that were receiving revenue increases based on their traditionally underrepresented student populations. Also, due to the aforementioned student populations, support for curriculum, teacher, and facility improvements now was in jeopardy. Coleman et al. established that there was little or no significant statistical relationship between human, fiscal, and physical resources with student achievement regardless of district or school size. Wong and Nicotera (2004) discuss the impact of the Coleman Report in educational research:

> It would be an understatement to claim that the research design and findings of Coleman's 1966 report, Equality of Educational Opportunity, have impacted social science research, the field of education, and the policy arena. The Coleman report not only reshaped the ways in which social scientists design and conduct research but it transformed how educators think about the purpose of education and significantly informed the policy arena. Coleman understood that his social science research had a significant impact on education policy and the public. (p. 126)

Nonetheless, traditionally marginalized poor, urban students such as Black, Latino, and limited English proficient students were offered better educational opportunities than they had previously experienced (Gale Research Inc, 1995).

1970s: HIGH PROPERTY TAXES IGNITE RENEWED FOCUS TO REDUCE EDUCATIONAL REVENUES

At this time, there was general support for improvements to basic education in public schools in the United States. However, there also was a backlash among the general population in the United States as standardized test scores, primarily secondary scores, fell dramatically from the previous decade. The primary reason: A new socioeconomic struggle was emerging between designing and implementing a system of schools meeting the academic needs of all students, and the political need for the United States to be competitive internationally (Gale Research Inc., 1995).In response to this new tension, the National Institute of Education (NIE) was initiated by President Nixon in an attempt to connect public policy research with educational practices. President Nixon expressed the urgency for the need of the NIE in a letter to the United States Congress dated March 30, 1970.

> Recent findings on the two largest such programs are particularly disturbing. We now spend more than $1 billion a year for educational programs run under Title I of the Elementary and Secondary Education Act. Most of these have stressed the teaching of reading, but before-and-after tests suggest that only 19% of the children in such programs improve their reading significantly; 13% appear to fall behind more than expected; and more than two-thirds of the children remain unaffected—that is, they continue to fall behind. In our Head start program, where so much hope is invested, we find that youngsters enrolled only for the summer achieve almost no gains, and the gains of those in the program for a full year are soon matched by their non-Head start classmates from similarly poor backgrounds. (The American Presidency Project, n.d.)

As he continued, President Nixon urged Congress not to make decisions regarding programs for poor, urban children based on limited findings. President Nixon also encouraged Congress to ask the pivotal question: "What does good schooling mean?" President Nixon often referred to the Coleman report to discuss how teachers and facilities alone did not make a difference for children, yet he still reiterated that equality in education must be pursued.

Undoubtedly, the federal legislators were feeling pressures as deliberation about changing standards for measuring efficiency facing public education continued to mature. Odden (1979) noted three major sources of educational inefficiency that needed to be addressed in federal legislation:

1. Educational inefficiency included the "proliferation and fragmentation" of federal programs that produced duplication of services and inadvertently created academic gaps, and this "proliferation and fragmentation" resulted in a "piling on" effect of monies for some students while completing ignoring the needs of other students.
2. Educational inefficiency is exacerbated by vague descriptions of district and school services given by the federal guidelines. These amorphous descriptions resulted in differing approaches and levels of services for students with special needs based on circumstance (e.g., bilingual or poor students).
3. Educational inefficiency increases can be attributable to the separation of federal and state dollars at the local level.

Again, this type of action resulted in two separate, often duplicated, and unnecessary service plans for students, while other students were being ignored. As educational services were found to be duplicative in the face of the 1970s stagflation, taxpayers began to question the efficacy of high revenue-generating school property taxes to pay for public education that seemed to be getting more costly but not increasing in quality.

Tax Revolts and Public Education

Leathers, O'Sullivan, Sexton, and Sheffrin (1996) explain two major tax revolts in our nation's history, Proposition 13 in California in 1978 and Proposition 2½ in Massachusetts in 1980 (p. 904).

It is without question Proposition 13 set off a movement across the nation to significantly reduce property taxes for use in public education. The State of California had experienced a series of scandals which resulted in great losses of revenue. Taxes were high, and by the 1970's residents could no longer afford to live in their homes due to taxation. Leathers et al. describe Proposition 13 as having "profound long-term consequences," for education (p. 904). Proposition 13 created a fundamental change of an *ad valorem* property tax to acquisition value tax. California's state constitution was amended when Proposition 13 was brought before the voters.

Ladd (1985) examined Proposition 2½ and voter perspective of how this measure was passed. Ladd concluded Proposition 2½ was an effort on the part of the voters to obtain a more resourceful government and amend the way public services were funded by the state. Massachusetts tax payers were demanding lower taxes as they experienced relatively high taxes compared to the nation. Lowering tax rates would eventually reduce state revenues for public education. California was experiencing a surplus at the time in its economy during the time of Proposition 13, unlike Massachusetts. Nonetheless, economic consequences would later follow not only for both states, but also for the nation as a whole as all states eventually would pass legislation to reduce property taxes, which directly reduced funding not only for public education but for all state-provided public services.

THE 1980s: A NATION AT RISK OF FAILING URBAN DISTRICTS, SCHOOLS, AND STUDENTS

By this time, urban public education was perceived as ineffective: Student academic performance continued to decline while expenditures increased (Hanushek, Rivkin, & Jamison, 1992), and politically, the standards and accountability movement gained force. This movement called for, and established, a system of standardized testing for all public school students. After testing, districts and schools would be measured as effective by student test results (New York State Archives, n.d.). With the revision of the ESEA of 1965 by the 1981 federal Educational Consolidation and Improvement Act (ECIA), the new legislation addressed concerns of economic inefficiency and unwieldy bureaucracies associated with educational organizations (New York State Archives, n.d.). And, importantly, the ECIA was a precursor to the now-famous 1983 report, *A Nation at Risk: The Report of the National Commission of Excellence in Education* (Seeley, 2009).

This now well-known report identified 13 indicators of being at-risk for districts, schools, and students based on mathematics and science test scores, college readiness test scores, literacy levels of adults and minority children, and others that pointed towards failing school systems—characteristics especially important to urban areas. *A Nation at Risk* report stirred the political souls of the United States' population as it reported the United States was no longer the global leader in industries due to mediocrity in society:

> Our once unchallenged preeminence in commerce, industry, science, and technological innovation is being overtaken by competitors throughout the world. This report is concerned with only one of the many causes and dimensions of the problem, but it is the one that undergirds American prosperity, security, and civility. We report to the American people that while we can take justifiable pride in what our schools and colleges have historically accomplished and contributed to the United States and the well-being of its people, the educational foundations of our society are presently being eroded by a rising tide of mediocrity that threatens our very future as a Nation and a people. What was unimaginable a generation ago has begun to occur—others are matching and surpassing our educational attainments. (1983, p. 5)

A Nation at Risk also emphasized how people in urban United States society did not possess the necessary skill levels, literacy, or training crucial to a new era of technology and computers. As such, the message in this report was clear: The citizens of the United States must act immediately in order to save society from educational mediocrity. In response to this news, the choice movement gained momentum. Over the next decade it was undeniable that public schools would face even greater challenges as parents began to make their voices heard.

Education Production Function Research Improves

As the federal government was occupied with distribution of funds for education programs and reform, economists were drawing attention to research in education production function models. Education production function measures inputs to a school compared with some measure of output. This type of analysis can determine which quantities and which qualities of educational dollars are most strongly connected with an established set of measurable student outcomes (Baker & Green, 2008). Education production function models lead to one of two conclusions in research: Money does matter or money does not matter in producing educational outcomes (Houck, Rolle, & He, 2010). Research involving education production functions took fast flight as policymakers, educators, and the public were aligning themselves with either the conclusion money does matter in educational outcomes or money does not matter in producing outcomes.

The demand for education reform was increasing. Why or how individuals were demanding education reform varied among their interests (Hanushek et al, 1992). Quality, costs, and equity were dominating the discussions of education reform. Based on the findings of Hanushek in 1986, increasing public school funding to improve student achievement had little benefit (Card & Krueger, 1992). Research was emerging to counter Hanushek's findings. These conflicting studies were adding momentum to varying views on educational expenditures and investments.

THE 1990s: CREATING LINKAGES BETWEEN ECONOMIC EFFICIENCY AND EDUCATIONAL LIBERTY

President George H.W. Bush campaigned under the phrase "the education President." President Bush put his efforts into America 2000—A National Education Strategy (U.S. Department of Education, 1991), a policy to implement national standards, national standardized testing, and involvement of researchers, business, and labor in curriculum development (New York State Archives, n.d.). President Bush's educational efforts were diminished when America 2000 was not passed in Congress (Stanton & Peeples, 2000). To the contrary, when President William (Bill) Clinton took office in 1993, the Educate America Act—Goals 2000 was implemented along with another reauthorization of the ESEA. These efforts at the national level were not enough to prevent the next era of education: the choice movement.

Choice Movement Gains Momentum across the Nation

In opposition to traditional educational reform efforts, the school choice movement (i.e., school vouchers and charter schools) gained national attention. To better understand the sentiments of the people, a closer look at Cleveland, Ohio offers an example. In 1996 the Cleveland Voucher Program offered nearly 2,000 elementary students scholarship money to attend schools of their choice. Two years later, nearly 4,000 students were participating in this movement. Peterson, Howell, and Greene (1999) conducted an evaluation study of the voucher program. Peterson et al. had three major findings as compared with public schools: higher parent satisfaction, increased academic achievement in both reading and math, and fewer disruptions in student learning. Peterson et al. also noted the vast majority of students participating in Cleveland's scholarship program were African American and mostly from low-income families. Eventually, Ohio's voucher program would be challenged legally.

The U.S. Supreme Court held the state's voucher program to be legal in *Zelman v. Simmons-Harris* (2002) 536 U.S. 639. Walsh (2002) explained the significance of this ruling.

> The U.S. Supreme Court's landmark ruling upholding the Cleveland voucher program has rejuvenated the school choice movement and, to a surprising degree, reinvigorated the debate over how best to improve the education of all the nation's schoolchildren. The decision was perhaps the biggest advance yet for a movement that embraces not only vouchers, but also an assortment of new arrangements in public education, among them charter schools, corporate management of public schools, open enrollment, and other alternatives to traditional schools.

Obviously, the choice movement was not limited to Ohio. In fact, cities across the nation were experiencing the same challenges and legal battles as Cleveland. This movement contributed to the pressed need for research to examine and explain the current state of public education. More than ever before, education production studies were needed on both sides of the debate of the effectiveness of public education.

Education Production Studies Continued

The demand for understanding inputs compared to educational outcomes persisted in research. Federal funds continued to be allocated to states and into school districts. The United States public was growing weary of the federal government's involvement in education (Kazal-Thresher, 1993). The question of whether money did or did not matter was still debated. Hanushek and other researchers maintained expenditure per student and increased teacher salaries were not systematically related to student outcomes (Hanushek et al., 1992). An influential study by Ronald Ferguson (1991) discussing educational expenditures and student achievement provided new evidence of how and when money mattered.

Ferguson's Research (1991)

Distributing resources efficiently and equitably in public education has been an elusive goal prior to this study according to Ferguson. Ferguson concluded enhanced funding can improve the quality of public school education. Ferguson (1991) described his study as "unique" as he included a vast measure of literacy skills of a large group of teachers coupled with a collection of statistics on other school and socioeconomic background measures. Ferguson writes, "Money matters when the real inputs that it purchases matter" (1991, p. 483). Ferguson strongly emphasized in his findings that teacher quality matters. Teacher quality should be at the forefront of any school district's efforts to promote the quality of instruction and enhance learning for students.

Ferguson asserted the findings of his study have three implications for finance reform. First, teachers are attracted to districts with higher socioeconomic status. It is necessary for lower socioeconomic districts increase salaries to attract teachers with more experience in order to draw better teachers. Secondly, class size does matter, especially in lower grades. The student–teacher ratio of 18 students per teacher appears to be the threshold. Third, a consistent set of expenditure rules for school districts to comply with is unrealistic and likely impossible to manage. Ferguson explains how districts have different needs and demands of their financial resources.

Ferguson's research is described as an important contribution to understanding the relationship between school inputs and student outcomes (Kazal-Thresher, 1993). Ferguson was able to present new evidence of how the influence of teacher quality impacts students' assessment performance in both elementary and secondary levels. The results of Ferguson's study also served to revitalize research in school finance (Kazal-Thresher, 1993).

The "Does Money Matter in Education?" Debate

This traditional debate continued to gain attention of researchers and lawmakers through the 1990s. Researchers such as Hedges, Laine, and Greenwald continued to reanalyze Hanushek's analysis of the educational production process in the 1980s (Rolle, 2004). Hedges, Laine, and Greenwald (1994) explain they have serious reservations concerning "the age of some of the data and the measurement and design of some of the studies" (p. 13) as conducted by Hanushek. Hedges et al. also concluded that simply throwing money at schools was not the solution either. Rather, the concerns raised by Hedges et al. are related to whether or not more financial resources are needed to improve student achievement. Hedges et al. concluded money did in fact matter, and this truth could no longer be ignored in the "Does money matter?" debate.

THE 2000S: HERE WE GO AGAIN

President George W. Bush announced his proposal for education reform under the No Child Left Behind (NCLB) Act just three days after taking office in January 2001. Despite a tumultuous year in our nation's history, President Bush was able to pass NCLB the following year with bipartisan support. NCLB gained national attention immediately and is described by the U.S. Department of Education:

> The NCLB Act, which reauthorizes the ESEA, incorporates the principles and strategies proposed by President Bush. These include increased accountability for States, school districts, and schools; greater choice for parents and students, particularly those attending low-performing schools; more flexibility for States and local educational agencies (LEAs) in the use of Federal education dollars; and a stronger emphasis on reading, especially for our youngest children. The new law reflects a remarkable consensus—first articulated in the President's *No Child Left Behind* framework—on how to improve the performance of America's elementary and secondary schools while at the same time ensuring that no child is trapped in a failing school. (U.S. Department of Education, 2004, n.p.)

President Bush emphasized that our nation has already spent over $200 billion since the passing of the ESEA in 1965 with little proof of improved schooling for children. President Bush also highlighted the points of NCLB regarding increased accountability for academic achievement by state and local education boards, better parent and student choice in schooling, and greater flexibility of spending federal funds for state education agencies and local school districts.

> In a fundamental way, NCLB was the next obvious step for a nation already committed to excellence and fairness in education. The legacy of reform preceding NCLB culminated in an opportunity for the country to put real muscle behind what had already been put into place. Funding is now tied directly to accountability expectations. Schools must ensure that all students learn the essential skills and knowledge defined by the state using grade-level standards and benchmarks. All means all, and data reporting required under NCLB must describe the learning journey of each student and the effectiveness of every school in that effort. (Jorgensen & Hoffman, 2003, p. 6)

With this in mind, the nation placed its support behind President Bush and demanded higher academic achievement with higher measures of accountability.

NEW APPROACHES TO EDUCATION
PRODUCTION FUNCTION

There are four values that influence policy development and implementation according to Febey and Louis (2005). These values are efficiency, equity, quality, and choice. Febey and Louis acknowledge how these four values may manifest themselves differently in the type of policy presented, but they are ever present. The issue of efficiency in education has been in the public arena for over a century as presented by Callahan (1962). Monk (1992) and Rolle (2004) each present new methods of analyzing education production function.

Following the study conducted by Hanushek (1981) and several other economic studies, Monk (1992) advocated a new method of research to elicit insight into "more fundamental aspects of education production process" (p. 307). Monk describes how economic studies are often conceptual in nature and points out six reasons why this approach to education production function research is insufficient. Monk writes that (1) economic studies are highly technical; (2) these studies make straightforward assumptions to "make analyses tractable" (p. 315); (3) hypothesis assumed by the models often require data that are not available: (4) there are questions about the relevance of the conclusions made for policy; (5) these studies are buried deep in economic theory that then fails to connect what is occurring in schools and classrooms; and (6) these studies demonstrate "perverse results that work to the disadvantage of sometimes influential stakeholders in the policy debate" (p. 315).

Monk offers a new approach to research that emphasizes the classroom as the unit of analysis. Monk describes this as a "deductive classroom-oriented research program," (p. 326).

> On its face, it appears to be promising. It embraces the idea of an education production function: it takes advantages of reasonably available longitudinal data; it can combine quantitative and qualitative research methodologies; it has more of a dynamic dimension than effective schools research; and it can capitalize on some of the hypotheses being generated by the economically oriented classrooms and school process studies. (Monk, 1992, p. 326)

Monk further explains how this approach, once assessed empirically, can have significant implications for campus administrators and the role states have in advancing education productivity.

Rolle (2004) states traditional economic analyses have not been able to define education production function adequately (p. 42). For this reason, Rolle explains public choice theory should be considered as "an alternative framework to normative educational productivity analyses" (p. 42). Rolle makes his viewpoint clear:

Specifically, researchers investigating measures of economic efficiency for public education need to pursue at least three nontraditional forms of public-choice paradigm: (a) modified quadriform analysis, (b) data envelopment analysis, and (c) stochastic frontier analysis. These methods seem more appropriate to apply to public schools given that a well-defined production function for education has not yet been determined. (p. 48)

These alternative approaches offer new and more concise methods of analyzing data in education production function.

FINAL REMARKS

Does money really matter in education? This question looms from education finance research. While analysts make claims that money has little impact with respect to student achievement, it is time for this issue to be considered for children who are not receiving sufficient funds. Money *does* matter to the thousands of children whose classrooms and school districts go without adequate funds to provide a general disbursement of academic knowledge to their students. Is it merely enough to provide some students with some knowledge while ignoring the thousands of students in urban schools who are objects of discrimination? Public education is deeply associated with the "challenge of income inequality, racial/ethnic disparities, and the urban environment in our society" (Wong, 2008, p. 19). Public education is where decisions are being made about how and which students will receive funding.

Education production function research, in its earlier stages, has provided limited analysis of measuring inputs to outputs (Monk, 1992). Education production research of the past has taken school finance two steps forward in legislation and policy making, yet has taken marginalized students one step back, if not more. The purpose of education production function research "is to improve the quantity and quality of educational opportunities for children" (Rolle, 2004, p. 46). Embedded in this highly contested field are politics, politicians, various ambiguous laws, and sometimes biased funding mechanisms that cannot be easily resolved in a single study such as the Coleman report or *A Nation at Risk*. It is therefore incumbent upon current researchers with more precise methods of analyzing data to conduct studies. Further reasons for precise analyses are clearly stated.

There is well-documented and long standing inequity in the distribution of opportunities for individuals and communities to pursue economic, political, and social self-determination, and one role of educational policy is to intervene in situations where inequities exist and facilitate improvements that better serve the democratic principles of access, participation, and enhanced life chances. (Rodriguez & Rolle, 2007, p. 1)

Educational policy has the potential to impact students and their families in ways far beyond the four walls of a classroom. It is time for new methods of analysis to be utilized. MacPhail-Wilcox (1984) asserts accountability in public education spending is not likely to dissipate, nor should it. It is time for education production function research to take two full steps forward for all children.

REFERENCES

The American Presidency Project. (n.d.). *Special message to the Congress on education reform.* Retrieved from http://www.presidency.ucsb.edu/ws/index.php?pid=2895

Baker, B. B., & Green, P. C. (2008). Politics, empirical evidence, and policy design: The case of school finance and the costs of educational adequacy. In B. S. Cooper, J. G. Cibulka, & L. D. Fusarelli (Ed.), *Handbook of education politics and policy* (pp. 311–334). New York, NY: Routledge.

Callahan, R. E. (1962). *Education and the cult of efficiency.* Chicago, IL: The University of Chicago Press.

Card, D., & Kruger, A. B. (1992). Does school quality matter? Returns to education and the characteristics of public schools in the United States. *The Journal of Political Economy, 100*(1), 1–40.

Coleman, J. S., Campbell, E. Q., Hobson, C. J., McPartland, J., Mood, A. M., Weinfeld, E. D., & York, R. L. (1966). *Equality of educational opportunity.* Washington, DC: U.S. Government Printing Office.

Febey, K., & Louis, K. S. (2008). Political cultures in education at the state and local level: Views from three states. In B. S. Cooper, J. G. Cibulka, & L. D. Fusarelli (Eds.), *Handbook of education politics and policy* (pp. 52–72). New York, NY: Routledge.

Ferguson, R. F. (1991). Paying for public education: New evidence on how and why money matters. *Harvard Journal on Legislation, 28,* 465–498.

Gale Research, Inc. (1995). The 1970s: Education overview. Retrieved from http://www.jiffynotes.com/a_study_guides/book_notes/adec_0001_0008_0/adec_0001_0008_0_02624.html

Gamoran, A., & Borman, G. (2007). *Coleman Report, 40 Years On.* Retrieved from http://www.wcer.wisc.edu/news/coverStories/coleman_report_40_years.php

Hanushek, E. A. (1972). *Education and race: An analysis of the educational production process.* Cambridge, MA: Heath-Lexington.

Hanushek, E. A. (1981). Throwing money at schools. *Journal of Policy Analysis and Management, 1*(1), 19–41.

Hanushek, E. A., Rivkin, S. G., & Jamison, D. T. (1992). Improving educational outcomes while controlling costs. *Carnegie-Rochester Conference Series on Public Policy, 37,* 205–238.

Hedges, L. V., Laine, R. D., & Greenwald, R. (1994). Does money matter? A meta-analysis of studies of the effects of differential school inputs on student outcomes. *Educational Researcher, 23*(3), 5–14.

Houck, E. A., Rolle, R. A., & He, J. (2010). Examining school districts efficiency in Georgia. *Journal of Education Finance, 35*(4), 331–357.

Jorgensen, M., & Hoffman, J. (2003). *History of No Child Left Behind Act 2001 (NCLB).* San Antonio, TX: Pearson.

Kazal-Thresher, D. M. (March 1993). Educational expenditures and school achievement: When and how money can make a difference. *Educational Researcher,* 30–32.

Ladd, H. F. (1985). Proposition 2½: Explaining the vote. *Research in Urban Policy, 1,* 199–243.

Leathers, C. G, O'Sullivan, A., Sexton, T. A., & Sheffrin, S. M. (1996). Property taxes and tax revolt: The legacy of proposition 13 (Book Review). *Journal of Economic Issues, 30*(3), 902–905.

MacPhail-Wilcox, B. (1984). Tax policy analysis and education finance: A conceptual framework for issues and analyses. *Journal of Education Finance, 9*(3), 312–331.

Monk, D. (1992). Education production research: An update and assessment of its role in education finance reform. *Education Evaluation and Policy Analysis, 14*(4), 307–332.

National Commission on Excellence in Education. (1983). A nation at risk: The imperative for educational reform. Washington, DC: U.S. Department of Education.

New York State Archives. (n.d.). *States' impact on federal education policy.* Retrieved from http://www.archives.nysed.gov/edpolicy/research/res_chronology1960.shtml

Odden, A. (1979, April). *State and federal pressures for equity and efficiency in education financing.* Papers in Education Finance, 21. Prepared for the National Symposium on Efficiency and Equity in Educational Finance.

Office of Superintendent and Public Instruction. (n.d.). Retrieved from http://www.k12.wa.us/esea/

Peterson, P.E., Howell, W.G., & Greene, J.P. (1999, June). An evaluation of the Cleveland voucher program after two years. *Program on Education Policy and Governance,* 1–2.

Rodriguez, G. M., & Rolle, R. A. (2007). Why a social justice framing of school finance—And why now? In G.M. Rodriguez & R.A. Rolle (Eds.), *To what ends and by what means? The social justice implications of contemporary school finance theory and policy* (pp. 1–5). New York, NY: Routledge.

Rolle, R. A. (2004). Out with the old-In with the new: Thoughts on the future of educational productivity research. *Peabody Journal of Education, 79*(3), 31–56.

Seeley, D. (2009). A report's forgotten message: Mobilize. *Education Week, 28*(22), 48–35. Retrieved from Professional Development Collection database.

Southern Christian Leadership Conference. (2011). *Rev. Dr. Martin L. King, 1967–1968.* Retrieved from http://www.sclcnational.org/core/item/page.aspx?s=3022.0.12.2607

Stanton, A. Q., & Peeples, J. A. (2000). Educational reform discourse: President George Bush on America 2000. *Communication Education, 49*(4), 303–319.

U.S. Department of Education. (1991). *America 2000: An education strategy source-book*. Washington, DC: Author

U.S. Department of Education. (2004, February). *Executive Summary by President George W. Bush*. Retrieved from http://www2.ed.gov/nclb/overview/intro/execsumm.html

U.S. Department of State. (n.d.). *Lyndon Johnson and the Great Society*. Retrieved from http://countrystudies.us/united-states/history-121.htm

Walsh, M. (2002). Charting the new landscape of school choice. *Education Week, 21*(42), 1–21.

Wong, K. K. (2008). Federalism, equity, and accountability in education. In B. S. Cooper, J. G. Cibulka, & L. D. Fusarelli (Eds.), *Handbook of education politics and policy* (pp. 19–29). New York, NY: Routledge.

Wong, K. K., & Nicotera, A. C. (2004). *Brown v. Brown of Education* and the Coleman Report: Social science research and the debate on educational equality. *Peabody Journal of Education, 79*(2), 122–135.

CAPITALIZING ON OUR INSPIRATION OF HOPE TO MAKE SUSTAINABLE REFORM IN URBAN SCHOOLS

Leanne L. Howell and Chance W. Lewis

As you read this book we hope that you, indeed, have gained insight and will capitalize on the inspiration of hope that successes in urban schools *are* occurring on a regular basis across our great nation. The reality of being associated with urban education is wrought with the realization that it certainly has its fair share of problems, frustrations, and failures. However, we hope that through our valiant efforts of writing this book, we have inspired you to balance those unfortunate issues with visions of endless possibilities and rewards for the sake of all involved in educating urban students—especially for the students themselves. Even though we have some bumps in the road to educate and transform urban education, so must we also realize that each and every one of us has the chance to make a difference in the schools, students' lives, and even the cities in which urban schools are located.

The landscape of urban schools is changing. Data indicate that enrollment of White students is declining in K–12 public school settings, while

Yes We Can! Improving Urban Schools Through Innovative Educational Reform, pages 205–207
Copyright © 2011 by Information Age Publishing

the number of students of color is rising (National Center for Educational Statistics, 2009). As such, this fact must lead us—school boards, administrators, teachers, and other school personnel—to realize that the time is *now* to embrace urban education reform. In this quest, those who teach, as well as those who design curricula and policy, must realize that instructional strategies *alone* will not enable this ever-changing student population to be successful in school. Teaching strategies must be combined with a rigorous effort by all who teach in our cities to embrace students' culture in ways that foster their uniqueness and appreciation rather than their marginalization (Goldstein, 2007). Still further, students' history and culture must be fully investigated and incorporated into pedagogical practices on a daily basis, just as Ryan Varnish shared in Chapter 7. By more fully investigating the aspects of students' culture, teachers are placed at a better advantage to practice pedagogical strategies that reflect the myriad of interrelationships that exist between the walls of all urban classrooms. As a result, urban students themselves will be empowered to embrace their own learning process and inspire hope within *themselves* that academic hope really is alive and life-long success is attainable. Consequently, methods used to evaluate and assess their strengths and weaknesses must also reflect this culturally relevant pedagogy.

Educators cannot make this reform occur alone. It will take a valiant effort from parents and other community stakeholders to stand up and do their part, for education is a business whose problems are a result of many other crises within the city in which they operate—unemployment, poverty, class and racial segregation, equity issues, and so much more. For this very reason, we all have a stake in the success of every student in every urban school in every city across our nation.

Urban schools are at the center of constant crisis and are prone to challenges, simply due to the make-up of their very existence. We hope our book has provided you with practical examples of reform and brought about wonderings within each of you that leave you with the question: How can I do my part in creating sustainable change for urban education? We, the editors, know that hope is alive in the quest to transform urban education. We have seen it in the faces of the thousands of students and teachers who walk the hallways of urban schools on a daily basis.

In closing, we hope you have found our collection of suggestions, remedies, and practical examples ones that leave *you* with hope and ones that seem possible to implement in your own urban schools and communities. The time for urban reform is now. Those who are up to the task must be willing to act with vigilant efforts to ensure that this reform is a non-negotiable element within every urban district in America. What if every student in every urban school had the equitable resources of their more affluent peers in neighboring districts? What if every student in every urban school graduated from high school? We hope you join us in making these hopes a reality for all.

REFERENCES

Goldstein, R. (2007). Who are urban students and what makes them so "different." In S. R. Steinberg & J. L. Kincheloe (Eds.), *19 urban questions: Teaching in the city* (pp. 41–51). New York, NY: Peter Lang.

National Center for Educational Statistics. (2009). *Tables and statistics, 2009.* Retrieved from http://nces.ed.gov/programs/digest/d09/

ABOUT THE EDITORS

Leanne L. Howell, PhD earned her BS and MS degrees in Education from Baylor University. She recently completed her PhD in Curriculum and Instruction, with an emphasis in Urban Education, at Texas A & M University. She can be reached at LeanneLHowell@aol.com

Chance W. Lewis, PhD is the Carolyn Grotnes Belk Distinguished Professor and Endowed Chair of Urban Education at the University of North Carolina at Charlotte. Dr. Lewis is also the Executive Director of the University of North Carolina at Charlotte Urban Education Research and Policy Collaborative that is publishing the next generation of research on what works in urban schools. From 2006–2011, Dr. Lewis served as the Houston Endowment, Inc. Endowed Chair in urban education at Texas A&M University. Dr. Lewis has over 100 publications including 50+ refereed journal articles in some of the leading academic journals in the field of urban education and teacher education. Additionally, he has received over $4 million in external research funds. Also, Dr. Lewis has landed research contracts with government agencies and private corporations as well. To date, Dr. Lewis has authored/co-authored/co-edited 7 books: *White Teachers/Diverse Classrooms: A Guide for Building Inclusive Schools, Eliminating Racism and Promoting High Expectations (Stylus, 2006); The Dilemmas of Being an African American Male in the New Millennium (Infinity, 2008); An Educator's Guide to Working with African American Students: Strategies for Promoting Academic Success (Infinity, 2009); Transforming Teacher Education: What Went Wrong with Teacher Training and How We Can Fix It (Stylus, 2010); White Teachers/Diverse classrooms: Creating Inclusive schools, Building on Students' Diversity and Providing True Educational*

Yes We Can! Improving Urban Schools Through Innovative Educational Reform, pages 209–210
Copyright © 2011 by Information Age Publishing

Equity [2nd ed.] (Stylus, 2011); *African Americans in Urban Schools: Critical Issues and Solutions for Achievement* (Peter Lang, in press) and *Yes We Can!: Improving Urban Schools through Innovative Educational Reform* (Information Age, in press). Dr. Lewis received his B.S. and M.Ed. in business education and education administration/supervision from Southern University and his PhD in Educational Leadership/Teacher Education from Colorado State University. At the University of North Carolina at Charlotte, Dr. Lewis teaches courses in the field of urban education. Dr. Lewis can be reached by e-mail at chance.lewis@gmail.com or on the web at http://www.chance-wlewis.com

Norvella Carter, PhD is Professor of Education and Endowed Chair in Urban Education in the Department of Teaching, Learning and Culture at Texas A&M University, College Station, Texas. She earned a Bachelor of Science degree in Special Education and a Master's degree in Administration and Supervision from Wayne State University in Detroit. She earned a PhD in Curriculum and Human Resource Development from the Graduate School of Arts and Sciences at Loyola University, Chicago. She has been a teacher and principal in urban schools. In addition, she has engaged in the preparation and development of educators for urban and diverse environments at four universities, Loyola University of Chicago, Illinois State University, Texas Southern University (Distinguished Professor and Endowed Chair) and currently, Texas A&M University. Dr. Carter was awarded the Houston, Inc. Endowed Chair in Urban Education based on a proven history and commitment to excellent work in urban education. A career highlight was her invitation to conduct a Congressional Hearing at the Capitol Building in Washington DC on *"Closing the Achievement Gap for Children of Color."* She worked for 2 years with the Black Caucus in Washington DC to develop policies regarding African American children in public schools. Dr. Carter's research focus and expertise are: 1) urban education; 2) African American learners; 3) Professional development for novice and urban teachers in diverse classrooms 4) teacher retention and 5) equity pedagogy as it relates to standards, curriculum and instruction. Dr. Carter is actively involved in the professional development of urban educators through master's and doctoral programs and has received national and international recognition for her work with doctoral students. She has been awarded millions of dollars in external grants and works closely with school districts across the nation. She is a scholar who has served as an editor of national, refereed journals and has a substantial number of publications. She has conducted presentations on her work in many cities nationally and internationally (including Study Abroad Programs) in countries such as Canada, England, France, Mexico, Niger, South Africa, Zambia and Botswana. She can be reached by e-mail at norvella@comcast.net.

ABOUT THE AUTHORS

Jamilia J. Blake is an assistant professor of school psychology in the Department of Educational Psychology at Texas A&M University. Dr. Blake earned her doctoral degree in School Psychology at The University of Georgia. She is a Licensed Specialist in School Psychology (LSSP) and is certified in School Crisis Response. Her research interests surround peer-directed aggression in ethnic minority populations and females and familial risk and protective factors that either promote or discourage children's engagement in aggression. Dr. Blake's teaching interests include emotional and behavioral assessment, cultural competence in the delivery of psychological services, and school-based crisis intervention. She can reached at jjblake@tamu.edu

Bettie Ray Butler is an assistant professor of urban education in the Department of Middle, Secondary, and K–12 Education at the University of North Carolina Charlotte. Dr. Butler earned her doctoral degree in Curriculum and Instruction and her masters in Political Science at Texas A&M University. Her research interest focuses on education policy with specific attention to issues of equity, represetation, and academic achievement among underrepresented populations in urban settings. She can be reached via email at Bettie.Butler@uncc.edu

Robert D. Carpenter is an associate professor at Eastern Michigan University. Dr. Carpenter is the director of the PhD program in Educational Studies in the Teacher Education Department. He can be reached at rcarpen1@emich.edu

Yes We Can! Improving Urban Schools Through Innovative Educational Reform, pages 211–216
Copyright © 2011 by Information Age Publishing

Lamont A. Flowers is the Distinguished Professor of Educational Leadership and the Executive Director of the Charles H. Houston Center for the Study of Black Experience in Education in the Eugene T. Moore School of Education at Clemson University. He can be reached at Lflower@clemson.edu

Tiffany A. Flowers is an Instructor of Education at Georgia Perimeter College. She can be reached at tflowers@gpc.edu

Stephen D. Hancock is an Associate Professor of Multicultural Education in the Department of Reading and Elementary Education at UNC–Charlotte. Dr. Hancock serves as an instructor, researcher, and leader. He is currently the MEd Program Coordinator, Chair of the Internationalization Committee, Vice Chair of Faculty Council, and Coordinator of the Teacher Education Study Abroad Collaboration. His primary research interest is sociocultural perspectives in urban elementary school context, which include foci on the development of healthy academic relationships as they relate to the perceptions and psychology of self and others. In addition, his research interest focuses on intercultural identity in domestic and foreign spaces. He primarily employs research practices in qualitative design, which include auto ethnography, action research, and narrative; however, he is also interested in mixed method analysis. He can be reached at sdhancoc@uncc.edu

DeMarquis M. Hayes is an assistant professor in the Department of Educational Psychology at the University of North Texas. He completed his graduate training at Tulane University in School Psychology. Prior to joining the faculty at the University of North Texas, Dr. Hayes worked as a Licensed Specialist in School Psychology for the Dallas Independent School District. His research examines issues of resilience and vulnerability in children and adolescents, especially those from racial minority and low socioeconomic backgrounds. Along these lines, he has specific interest in examining how home and school environments influence student achievement and normative development and how context variables contribute to success in higher education for students of color. He can be reached at DeMarquis.Hayes@unt.edu

Julie Landsman is a retired Minneapolis public school teacher and administrator of 25 years. She has been a writer in the schools, consultant, college professor and diversity trainer. She is the author of three memoirs: *Growing Up White: A Veteran Teacher Reflects on Racism; A White Teacher Talks About Race;* and *Basic Needs: A Year With Street Kids in a City School.* She co-edited the book *White Teachers/Diverse Classrooms* with Chance W. Lewis as well as consulted on the DVD that accompanies this book. This book will be coming out in a new edition with extended chapters and a new DVD in April 2011. She is also co-editing a new book called *Going Deeper,* which is about having honest and open discussions about race and how to close the opportunity gap. Her articles frequently appear in *Educational Leadership* magazine. Julie conducts training and workshops both nationally and internationally on inclusive, anti-racism education and social justice education. In her spare time, she enjoys painting and is currently writing a novel. She can be reached at jlandsman@goldengate.net

Patricia J. Larke is a Professor in the Department of Teaching, Learning, and Culture at Texas A&M University in College Station, Texas. Dr. Larke's research interests include multicultural education, mentoring programs, culturally responsive teaching, and academic achievement of African American females. She can be reached at plarke@tamu.edu

Augustina Lozano is currently a PhD student in the Department of Educational Administration and Human Resource Development at Texas A & M University. Ms. Lozano conducts research that investigates conceptions and applications of economic efficiency for public school finance systems. She has 10 years of experience working in public education, serving as both a bilingual educator and a school administrator. Ms. Lozano earned her bachelor's degree in Communications at Angelo State University and her master's degree in Public School Administration from Concordia University. She can be reached at aclozano@tamu.edu

Michelle J. Moody has worked in public education for over 27 years in the Chicago public school system. Dr. Moody earned her bachelor's degree from Northwestern University Evanston, master's degrees in Curriculum and Instruction and Educational Leadership from National Louis University and Chicago State University, respectively and her doctorate degree in Curriculum and Instruction from Loyola University, Chicago. Dr. Moody spent 20 years as a classroom teacher at the elementary school level, teaching grades K–8. Since 2003, she has served in an administrative capacity managing federally funded grants. Dr. Moody currently serves as Grants Manager and oversees the expansion of magnet programs throughout the district, which has included the development of three public Montessori magnet programs. She received her Montessori training at the Early Childhood (EC) level. Dr. Moody currently serves as President-Elect of Magnet School of America and is a member of the research committee of the American Montessori Society. She can be reached at moodyfrazier@sbcglobal.net

Collette Nero currently serves as the Coordinator of Psychological Services for the Omaha Public Schools. She completed her Bachelor's degree at the University of North Texas and her PhD in School Psychology from Texas A & M University. Dr. Nero is a licensed psychologist and serves as the training director for the Omaha Public Schools site within the Nebraska Internship

Consortium in Professional Psychology. She continues to provide direct services to students in one of the district's alternative programs, as well as an intensive program for English Language Learners. She can be reached at Collette.nero@ops.org

Ginny Riga earned a masters degree in Special Education from Hofstra University in New York and a doctorate in Curriculum and Instruction from the University of South Carolina. She has held numerous teaching and leadership positions in public education for the last 30 years. The majority of her work has been in Columbia, South Carolina, where she was principal of the first total Montessori public school in the state in the early 2000s. She now coordinates the Montessori public school program at the State Department of Education in South Carolina, conducts numerous workshops, and consults in several states. Dr. Riga currently serves on the board of directors of the American Montessori Society (AMS) and is a member of the AMS research committee. She is a past board member of Montessori Educational Programs International (MEPI) and a founding member and officer of the South Carolina Montessori Alliance, partnership between public and private school Montessori educators, which began in 2001. She can be reached at griga@ed.sc.gov

Concepcion M. Rodriguez currently serves as a Licensed Specialist in School Psychology for the Dallas Independent School District (DISD) in the department of Psychological & Social Services. She earned her Bachelor's degree at the University of Miami and her Master's degree from The University of North Texas. In her current position, she provides direct psychological services to elementary and secondary students on five different campuses. She also coordinates the crisis response teams for the department and provides training on suicide and violence risk assessments to the district's school counselors. Her research interests include the use of mindfulness meditation practice with school age children, the use of risk assessments in schools, as well as cultural diversity. She can be reached at crodriguez1@dallasisd.org

R. Anthony Rolle is Professor and Chair of the Department of Educational Leadership and Policy Studies at the University of South Florida. He conducts research that explores and improves relative measures of economic efficiency for public schools. Concomitantly, his research explores and applies measures of vertical equity to analyses of state education finance mechanisms. Utilizing these techniques, he recognizes that demographic differences among communities affect organizational processes and does not assume that all public schools have the same expenditure priorities. Dr. Rolle's work is published in books, journals, and monographs such as *To What Ends and By What Means? The Social Justice Implications of Contempo-*

rary School Finance Theory and Policy (2007), *Modern Education Finance and Policy* (2007), *Measuring School Performance and Efficiency* (2005), *Journal of Education Finance, Peabody Journal of Education, School Business Affairs, School Administrator,* and *Developments in School Finance.*

In addition to his academic work, Dr. Rolle has conducted K–12 education finance and policy research for such organizations as the University of Washington's Institute for Public Policy & Management, the Washington State Legislature and Democratic House Majority Whip, the Indiana Education Policy Center, the National Education Association, the Texas House of Representatives' Office of the Speaker, the Office of U.S. Representative Jim Cooper (5th District–Nashville, TN) as well as agencies and commissions in Arkansas, Colorado, Missouri, North Carolina, South Carolina, and Tennessee. Formerly a member of the Board of Directors for the American Educational Finance Association (AEFA), and the 2002 AEFA Jean Flanigan Dissertation Award winner, he also serves as the Executive Vice President of R. C. Wood & Associates. Dr. Rolle received a Bachelor of Science in Political Science from Santa Clara University; a Master's Degree in Public Administration from the University of Washington's Graduate School of Public Affairs; and, a PhD in Educational Policy Analysis from the School of Education at Indiana University. He can be reached at arolle@usf.edu

Robert W. Simmons III is an assistant professor in the Teacher Education Department at Loyola University in Maryland. Dr. Simmons is a former middle school science teacher in the Detroit Public Schools. He can be reached at rwsimmons@loyola.edu

Tehia V. Starker is an assistant professor in Educational Psychology and Elementary Education in the department of Reading and Elementary Education at the University of North Carolina at Charlotte. Dr. Starker earned her Bachelor's degree in Elementary Education from Bethune-Cookman college; her Master's in Educational Technology from the University of Northern Iowa; and PhD in Educational Psychology from the University of Nebraska–Lincoln. Dr. Starker's research interests include culturally responsive teaching, motivational factors in teaching and learning, and parental involvement in schools. She can be reached at tstarker@uncc.edu

Molly S. Taylor received her Bachelor's degree in Communication Sciences and Disorders from Baylor University. She received her Master's degree, as well as her PhD, in Child Development from Texas Women's University. Dr. Taylor spent nine years working at The Rise School of Dallas as a classroom teacher as well as the educational coordinator. She recently served as a consultant for Texarkana Independent School District (TISD) in the role of Parent Liaison and Early Childhood Specialist. She can be reached at mollystaylor@sbcglobal.net

Ryan M. Vernosh teaches 6th grade at Maxfield Magnet Elementary School in Saint Paul, Minnesota. In addition to teaching, Ryan facilitates national workshops focusing on sharing strategies and the effectiveness of culturally relevant pedagogy. Recently he was selected as the 2010 Minnesota State Teacher of the Year and is currently Minnesota's candidate for the 2011 National Teacher of the Year. He lives with his wife Sara and two daughters, Miah and Raeanna. He can be reached at ryan.vernosh@spps.org

Meredith B. L. Walker is a post-doctoral fellow in the Department of Public Administration and Policy at American University. She received her doctoral degree in Political Science from Texas A&M University. Dr. Walker's research interests include education and health policy, representation in bureaucratic organizations, intersectionality, and the academic achievement of disadvantaged students, with a focus on African American males. She can be reached at meredith.b.walker@gmail.com

Jamaal R. Young is a graduate student in the Department of Teaching, Learning, and Culture at Texas A & M University in College Station, Texas. His research interests are technology integration and utilization in mathematics classrooms, technological pedagogical content knowledge (TPCK) for mathematics teachers, as well as culturally responsive pedagogy for STEM education. He can be reached at Jamaal-rashad-young@tamu.edu

Jemimah L. Young is a graduate student in the Department of Teaching, Learning, and Culture at Texas A & M University in College Station, Texas. Her research interests include non-traditional students of color, the achievement gap, culturally relevant teaching pedagogy, and the sociology of education. She can be reached at jlea0002@tamu.edu

CPSIA information can be obtained at www.ICGtesting.com
Printed in the USA
LVOW071919020212

266790LV00003B/22/P

9 781617 356353